GREAT WOMEN OF INDIA

GREAT WOMEN of INDIA

Leaders-Saints-Warriors-Artistes-Writers

K. S. Bhalla

Publications

KALPAZ PUBLICATIONS

DELHI-110052

Great Women of India

Rs. 490

ISBN: 81-7835-470-5

Published in 2015 in India by
Kalpaz Publications
C-30, Satyawati Nagar, Delhi-110052
E-mail : kalpaz@hotmail.com

Laser Typesetting at : Master Computers, Delhi
Printed at : Salasar Imaging System, Delhi

To
My Mother
Smt. Asa Devi

Contents

Foreword

Women have been occupying a high place of pride and honour in India since Aryan times. They have performed difficult roles in trying times, in the public domain as well as at home. Their contribution to society has been no less than that of men, though one has to search a little harder to discover it. They have accomplished far more in many fields than men give them credit for. Their achievements deserve special praise, especially considering that they often worked without societal support and in spite of family restrictions. Such women have become role models for the future generations.

In his address at the 11th anniversary celebrations of the Indian Women's Press Corps in New Delhi in October 2005, President APJ Abdul Kalam referred to Mahakavi Subramaniya Bharatiar poem, composed in 1910, in which the poet described his vision of Indian women:

> *She walks with raised head, with her eyes looking straight,*
>
> *She has her principles, unafraid of anybody!*
>
> *She has a lofty and knowledge based pride,*
>
> *Women of excellence, don't falter from the chosen path.*
>
> *She drives ignorance away. She welcomes the bliss of life.*
>
> *With learned mind, this is the Dharma of emerging woman.*

Women's roles are no different from men. They are equal partners in nation's development. Like men they have excelled in every walk of life. There have been great women rulers, warriors, leaders, freedom fighters, saints, scholars, writers, social workers, sports persons, doctors, engineers, advocates, teachers, administrators, professionals, business persons, mediapersons and pilots. They have now also Joined the Police and Defence Forces. There is Kanchan Choudhry Bhattacharya, the first woman to become the director general of police of Uttaranchal. There are two very senior Air Force and Naval Officers, Air Marshal (Mrs) P Bandopadhyay, director general, Medical Services (Air) and Surg Vice Admiral (Mrs) Punita Arora, director general, Medical Services (Navy). Capt (Ms) Sipra Majumdar and Capt (Ms) Ashwini AS Pawar have climbed Mt Everest.

In the struggle for India's freedom, Wives, mothers, and daughters fought heroically shoulder to shoulder with men. Gandhiji believed that the difference between men and women was only physical but in many matters especially those of tolerance, patience, and sacrifice, the Indian woman was superior to the male. He held that "Womanhood is not restricted to the kitchen". He wanted women to outgrow the traditional responsibilities and participate in the affairs of nation.

The "Great Women of India" written by K S Bhalla gives sketches of 108 great women leaders in the social, political, spiritual and cultural life of this sub-continent from medieval times till date. This book is a tribute to women and should be an inspiration to the younger generation of today and tomorrow, as it has been to me.

"Great Women of India" is a seminal work which I have enjoyed reading. I commend it for reading by all-men as well as women.

Director General, Home Guards and
Commandant, Civil Defence,
New Delhi

Dr. Kiran Bedi
IPS

Preface

The worth of a civilization can be judged by the place given to women in the society. In India, they occupied a high place in the social life of the early Aryans. The milder and more beneficent forces of nature were addressed as female deities and invoked with prayers. Women in medieval and modern India have distinguished themselves in various spheres of life as rulers, leaders, freedom fighters, saints, scholars, writers, social workers, artistes, warriors, politicians, administrators and diplomats.

The role played by women in the struggle for India's freedom was no less decisive than that of men. The rigours of struggle were borne by wives, mothers, and daughters determinedly, heroically and stoically. In a Resolution passed by Indian National Congress on January 26, 1931, the women's role in freedom struggle was befittingly recognised: "We record our homage and deep admiration for the Womanhood of India who in the hour of peril for the motherland forsook the shelter of their homes and with unfailing courage and endurance stood shoulder to shoulder with their menfolk, in the frontline of India's national army to share with them the sacrifices and triumphs of the struggle".

This book sketches out the life and role of great women of India–past and present-who have made and are making history. Only 108 women figure in the book. The list is obviously not exhaustive. There are many more great women than those included in this book. The sketches are brief and informative, not critical.

S-327, Greater Kailash-I,
New Delhi-110048 (India)

K. S. Bhalla

Introduction

Every nation has individuals who they define as great. Great men have created major social transformation and contributed significantly to society. Their views and actions have served and lifted others. Their influences have lasted for generations. They have stirred people's souls and lifted their vision. They had deep convictions, religious or moral, and lived their lives according to them. They had a cause for which they devoted their lives and some of them even sacrificed them. It is not that they were perfect. But their greatness came from their striving for perfection. They worked at it. They encouraged others to do the same. They taught by the example of their lives. They were persons of character, compassion and kindness. They possessed a great ability to communicate, to influence and to mobilize. They brought humility to their work, and learnt from the people and places around them. They had a vision with creativity and insight.

These qualities show that greatness is not one act or moment; it is a way of life. It is an attitude, a re-dedication every day not to do what's easiest, but to do what's right.

According to Thomas Carlyle "No great man lives in vain. The history of the world is but the biography of great men." Henry Eyring said they are the people who "can catch hold of men's minds and feelings and inspire them to do things bigger than themselves, are the people who are remembered in history... those who stir feelings and imagination and make men struggle toward perfection."

No right thinking person would say that greatness is the monopoly of 'men' only though a general perception is that women did not contribute much of significance to our civilization other than as caretakers of families. A little search would bring out that the number of accomplished women is endless. Their contribution to society has been no less than that of men, though one has to search a little harder to discover it. Women have accomplished far more than we officially give them credit for. Their contributions are quite impressive, especially considering that they worked without societal support and often in spite of family restrictions. It is time to give women their due. They deserve credit according to their contribution, not according to their sex. We need to know what they did and how they did it so that we may learn from them and be inspired by them. We need this to be common knowledge.

God made men and women to be different, but equal nonetheless. Through women, God brought forth kings, leaders, prophets, pastors, and even the Son of God. The founder of Sikhism, Guru Nanak, said: "So kyon manda aakhiye, jit jamme rajaan"–How can you call women inferior? They gave birth to kings. Guru Hargobind, the sixth Sikh Guru, called women "the conscience of man". According to Islam, women are not inferior to men. Allah creates both of them and both of them are equal in the sight of Allah. If they are equal in the sight of Allah, then how can they be inferior in the society or in the sight of men. Gandhiji said: "Intellectually, mentally, and spiritually, woman is equivalent to a male and she can participate in every activity."

In the field of managing the affairs of the State alone, women have held every office that men have held and with distinction. There have always been female rulers. Some Egyptian Queens are believed to have governed from around 3000 BCE, and the first to be named by the sources without any doubt is Ku-baba, who ruled the Mesopotamian City-State of Ur round 2500 BCE.

In recent times, three women held their countries' highest elective offices by 1970. Sirimavo Bandaranaike was Prime Minister of Ceylon (now Sri Lanka) from 1960 to 1965 and from 1970 to 1977). Indira Gandhi was Prime Minister of India from 1966 to 1977 and from 1980 to 1984. Golda Meir was Prime Minister of Israel from 1969 to 1974.

Women held the highest office of President in Argentina (1974), Iceland (1980), Philippines (1986), Ireland (1990) and Nicaragua (1990). They occupied the office of Prime Minister (Premier) in Central African Republic (1975), U K (1979), Norway (1980), Yugoslavia (1980), Pakistan (1988), West Australia (1990), British Columbia–Canada-(1991), Bangladesh (1991) France (1991), Poland (1992). There have also been women Prime Ministers in New Zealand, Mozambique, São Tomé e Princípe and Ukraine. Of the monarchies, there are Queens in Denmark, The Netherlands and the United Kingdom. In 1999, Sweden became the first country to have more female ministers than male-11 women and 9 men.

Women's role in other spheres–cultural, religious, literary, artistic, business, industry, sports–has been as impressive as in the sphere of statecraft. It is seen that higher standards are often imposed on women to attain leadership roles and to retain them. Women have to be more skillful leaders than men because they have to meet higher standards. Despite these handicaps, women have been nation builders and path-breakers though their contributions have not received as much recognition as was and is due. But they are no longer victims of society's prejudices. Today they are victors and compel society's respect and attention. They are the bedrock of society. They are vital part of society.

This book is confined to the great women of India only.

One of several factors that justify the greatness of India's ancient culture is the honourable place granted to women in society. Like men, they have excelled in every walk of life. If we turn the pages of History we come across Indian women who have been rulers, queens, warriors, leaders, freedom fighters, saints, scholars, writers, social workers. The country remembers them and honours them.

In 2000, the UN Day theme in India was "women hold up half the sky"–the words of Mao Zedong. India's then First Lady, Usha Narayanan, said: "and women hold up more than half the earth!".

The important place assigned to women in India is as old as history. It dates back to the time of the *Vedas* and the *Smritis*. Manu declared that where women were adored, gods frequented that place, During the Vedic age the women were regarded as equal partners with men in all respects. In recent times, Indian women-wives, mothers and daughters-stood shoulder to shoulder with men in the freedom struggle and bore the burden of tears and toils of long years of struggle patiently, heroically and cheerfully.

In India who has not heard of Maitri, Gargi, Sati Annusuya and Sita? In medieval age, in managing the affairs of the State, Ahilyabai Holkar, Chand Bibi, Jijabai, Maharani Jindan, Rani Durgawati, Rani Lakshmibai of Jhansi, Raziya Sultana and numerous others left an indelible imprint on the sands of time and played historic roles no less momentous than men. In the modern era, achievements of Indian women in every sphere of life are countless and epoch-making.

This book is a tribute to Indian women–past and present-and is intended to be an inspiration to the women of today and tomorrow. It covers 108 outstanding women from medieval period onwards till date from all corners of

India. They are from all religions and all political hues. The criterion of selection has been their contribution in the political, cultural, social, literary, and religious fields and their impact on national scene. Mythological figures have not been included in the book. The narrations are based on published data.

The number of great women of India is much more than those covered in this book. Selection of only 108 such women has been with trepidation and under compulsion of space.

1

Ahilyabai Holker (1725-1795)

A magnificent ruler and saintly administrator, Ahilyabai was born in 1725 in the village of Chondi, in Bhid district, Maharashtra. Her father, Mankoji Shinde, was the *patil* of the village, a member of the proud Dhangar community. Malhar Rao Holkar, a commander in the service of the Peshwa Bajirao and lord of the Malwa territory had seen the eight-year-old Ahilyabai at the temple service in her village Chondi and was struck by her piety and character. He immediately sought the hand of Ahilyabai as bride for his son, Khande Rao. Ahilyabai's husband was killed in a battle in 1754. Ahilyabai was barely twenty then. She wanted to commit 'sati', as was the custom, but her father-in-law, Malhar Rao persuaded her not to do so. Twelve years later, her father-in-law, Malhar Rao also died.

After the death of Malhar Rao Holkar, Ahilyabai's son Malerao was nominally made the 'Subedar' but Ahilyabai, who had been trained in administrative and military matters by her father-in-law, was the ruler *de facto* and she was permitted by the Peshwa to take over the administration of Malwa. The army of Holkar, which had witnessed her leadership in military matters, supported her. She had an inborn religious bent. She rose early, said prayers, listened to recitations from scriptures, distributed alms and gave food to a number of Brahmins. Throughout the day she held court and attended to affairs of the State. She was an excellent administrator and an impartial judge. She was very brave and won many battles to uphold the honor of the state.

After the death of her father-in-law Malharrao, Chandravats, a Rajput clan, rose in revolt against Ahilyabai. Ahilyabai accepted the challenge. She led her troops personally and put down the revolt with a heavy hand. Sometime later, Bhil tribes in Satpura grew troublesome. She arrested their leader and put him to death. When Raghoba, the uncle of ruling Peshwa, was planning to invade Ahilyabai's territory, she sent a message which was strong enough to discourage himfrom embarking upon the invasion.

Ahilyabai was an ideal daughter, daughter-in-law, mother and stateswoman. The death of her daughter, Muktabai, who had burnt herself on the pyre of her husband was too severe a shock for her. Grief-stricken, Ahilyabai withdrew from worldly and State affairs and lived a rigid life of austerity till she died on 13 August 1795.

The administrator and historian, Sir John Malcolm wrote about her abilities some 40 years after her death:

"Her first principle of government appears to have been moderate assessment, and an almost sacred respect for the native rights of village officers and proprietors of land. She heard every complaint in person; and although she continually referred cases to courts of equity and arbitration, and to her ministers for settlement, she was always accessible. So strong was her sense of duty on all points connected with the distribution of justice, that she is represented as not only patient but unwearied in the investigation of the most insignificant cases, when appeals were made to her decision."

American historian, Stewart Gordon, adds that a definite proof of her ability as a ruler was that her territories in Malwa were not attacked or disrupted by local battles during her reign, in spite of wars all around. According to Gordon, "Ahilyabai had one of the most stable reigns of the 18th century." And Malcolm adds that she kept, almost to the man, the same set of ministers and administrators throughout her reign.

Among Ahilyabai's accomplishments was the development of Indore from a small village to a prosperous and beautiful city. The many good things that Ahilyabai did remain as monuments to her piety She built forts and roads in Malwa, sponsored festivals and gave donations for regular worship in many Hindu temples. Outside Malwa, She initiated many public welfare programmes including construction of highways, wells, ghats, resthouses and temples. The most noteworthy among these are the road from Calcutta to Banaras, and the temples of Somanatha in Saurashtra, of Vishnu at Gaya and of Vishweshwara at Varanasi. Her unique pan-Indian look is reflected in the fact that she built Dharmashalas at Badrinath and Rameshwaram, established Anna Chhatras at Dwarka, Jagannathpuri, Omkareshwar and Ujjain. She also established charitable institutions at Gaya, Varanasi, Ayodhya, Prayag, Haridwar and Pandharpur. She helped widows retain their husbands' wealth. She supported widows' right to adopt a son.

Ahilyabai's capital at Maheshwar was the scene of literary, musical, artistic and industrial activities. Craftsmen, sculptors and artists received salaries and honours, and she established a textile industry in the city of Maheshwar.

Ahilyabai was a magnificent woman, an able ruler and a great queen. She was noted for her piety. To honour the memory of Ahilyabai Holkar, in 1996, leading citizens of Indore instituted an award in her name to be bestowed annually on an outstanding public figure. The first award was given to Nanaji Deshmukh.

2

Aishwarya Rai (1973-)

The green eyed Miss world 1994, Aishwarya Rai, popularly known as Ash, was born on 1st November 1973 at Mangalore into a traditional south Indian family of Merchant Navy officer Krishna Raj and Vrinda Rai. She learnt classical dance and music for five years while in her teens. She was inclined towards fine arts right from the beginning. Aishwarya did her schooling at Arya Vidya Mandir, Santacruz. Academically, she did very well and earned her position as the head girl of her school. Ash chose the science stream while at DG Ruparel College, her favourite subject being Zoology. Aishwarya wanted to do medicine, but circumstances didn't let her. Instead she chose Architecture and passed the interview at Raheja College with flying colors. By this time, Aishwarya had started getting modelling assignments. She then decided to take a break from architecture and concentrate on modelling. From that stage there was no looking back. The ad campaigns which brought her into the limelight were the Garden sari and the Pepsi ad. She also modelled for Pamolive, Lakme,Casio pager, Philips, Sheetal diva, Pamoliveand Prudent.

Aishwarya Rai was the runner-up in the 1994 Miss Femina India competition. At that time, she was 19, just past her Class XII. Later that year, She burst upon the world stage, winning the Miss World crown in 1994. She also won the title of "Miss Photogenic" in the 1994 Miss World Pageant.

The Miss World title opened for her the doors to acting in films. Rai made her film debut in Mani Rathnam's "Iruvar" (1997). Her performance in Rahul Rawail's "...Aur Paar Ho Gaya" (1997) garnered her the Best Female Debutante Award. In 2000 she was awarded Best Actress by FilmFare and Zee Cine for her work in Sanjay Leela Bhansali's "Hum Dil De Chuke Sanam". In 2001 Ash was nominated for Film Fare's Best Supporting Actress Award for Satish Kaushik's "Hamara Dil Aapke Paas Hai". Aishwarya Rai re-teamed with Sajay Leela Bhansali in "Devdas," a highly successful film in Bollywood history. It became the first Bollywood picture to ever receive a special screening at that year's Cannes Film Festival and turned out to be a big hit in India and the United States.

Julia Roberts calls her "the world's most beautiful woman". In South Indian films, she was best known for her role as Madhumita/Veishnavi in Jeans (1998) and Kandukondain Kandukondain (2000). She acquired international fame in acting and was invited to sit on the jury of the 2003 Cannes Film Festival, the first Indian actress to be so honoured. Aishwarya Rai made her English-speaking debut in "BRIDE and PREJUDICE." and has acted in "Chaos" opposite Meryl Streep, Roland Joffe's "Singularity" with Brendan Fraser, and in the lead role of "Mistress of Spices" which Gurinder Chadha has produced with Paul Mayeda Berges as director.

Aishwarya has the honour of her wax figure installed in Madame Tussaud's museum in London. She was judged by the Time magazine as one of the world's 100 most influential people. She was voted as the world's most attractive woman of 2003 by Hellow Magazine. She has been Ambassador for Longines watches since 1999. She was the Coca Cola Girl for the Middle Eastern countries. She has won over 50 awards since 1994. British Government has honoured her with the Next Step World Diversity Champion Award which has been instituted to honour individual who have encouraged pride in being a member of the ethnic minority community as well as stronger sense of personal fulfillment. Aishwarya Rai has joined Catherine Deneuve and Andie MacDowell as a member of the elite L'Oreal Dream Team. She has graced the covers of India Today, TIME Magazine and was listed on Rolling Stone Magazine's annual "Hot List."

According to Aishwarya, she is in quest of excellence and to this end her philosophy is: "I want to compete with myself; test myself; stretching my talents in this exciting voyage of self-discovery that is cinema." She is determined to prove herself not only as a personification of excellence but also as a total professional.

3

Amrita Pritam (1919-2005)

Amrita Pritam, born on 31 August 1919 in Gujranwala (now in Pakistan), is a household name in the Punjab, being the first most prominent woman Punjabi poet and fiction writer. She was the only child of a school teacher and a poet. Her mother died when she was eleven and she grew up with adult responsibilities. She underwent turbulent childhood days. She began to write in Panjabi at an early age and her first collection was published when she was only 16 years old, the year she married an editor to whom she was engaged in early childhood. When her first collection of verse was published in 1936 it was greeted with shock and outrage in the Punjabi literary society. Her poetry was something which her father thoroughly despised because of its unconventional tone. What he anticipated from his exceptionally talented daughter was religious verse and not the sensuous and spontaneous outpourings of love. In fact, she often provoked the whole community when she essayed to transcend her intense sexual impulse into poetic images of rare beauty.

Her writings were an expression of women's pain and a lifelong outcry against male oppression. They betrayed the women's lyric cry against existential fate and suicietal abuse. In her later day poetry, Amrita Pritam dexterously employed the snatches of verse from Farid and Guru Nanak, from Waris, Bullehshah and Shah Hussain. In course of time Marxian thought and idiom affected the tenor of her verse and altered her sensibility in a radical manner but Marxism as a complete and unified philosophy of life did not quite possess her poetic imagination. With the publication of "Patthar Gitte" (Gravel Stones–1946) one started sensing those sharp accents of self-pity and protest which were to give Amrita's poetry her distinctive voice, her 'signature tune', so to say.

In 1947 at the time of the Partition she moved to New Delhi, where she began to write in Hindi also. She worked for All India Radio until 1961. She was divorced in 1960. After that, several of her stories and poems reflected her unhappiness in marriage. She has to her credit twenty-eight novels, 18 volumes of verse, five short stories and 16 miscellaneous prose fifteen collections of short stories and twenty-three volumes of prose including two volumes of autobiography, Kaala Gulab and Rasidi ticket (1970). Her immortal poem on the tragedy of the Partition, *Ajj Akhan Waris Shah Noo* became a legend, sung with great pathos allover the Punjabi-speaking areas on both sides of the border. Two of her novels ***Dharti Sagar te Sippiyan*** (1965) and Unah Di Kahani (1976) have been made into films entitled *"Kadambari"* and *"Daaku"* for which she even composed songs. Her works have been defined as a 'woman's lyric cry against existential fate and societal abuse', and have been widely translated.

In 1953 Amrita Pritam became the first woman to win the coveted Sahita Akademi award with her epic poem, Sunehre. She was also the first Punjabi writer to receive the Padma Shri in 1969. Her works have been translated in English, Albanian, Bulgarian, French, Polish, Russian, Spanish, Danish and Japanese and in 21 Indian languages. *Mehfil*, a quarterly from Michigan State University published an issue on her works. She received the

Vaptarow Award from Bulgaria in 1980 She got Jnanpeeth Award in 1982 for her lifetime contribution to Punjabi literature. She has received five D Litt degrees including three from Delhi, Jabalpur, Vishva Bharti Universities in 1973 and 1983. Amrita Pritam made her mark on the international scene, because of her lyrical sensibility and projected sensitivity. In 2005, she was awarded a prestigious literary honour of France–La Route des Indes Literary Prize–for the French translation of her famous novel "Pinjar". Inspite of her poor health, she was till recently active writing and editing a monthly magazine in Punjabi *Nagmani*. Amrita Pritam was accorded Padma Vibhushan, second highest civilian award, in 2004.

Amrita Pritam passed away on 31st October 2005.

4

Amrita Shergil (1913-1941)

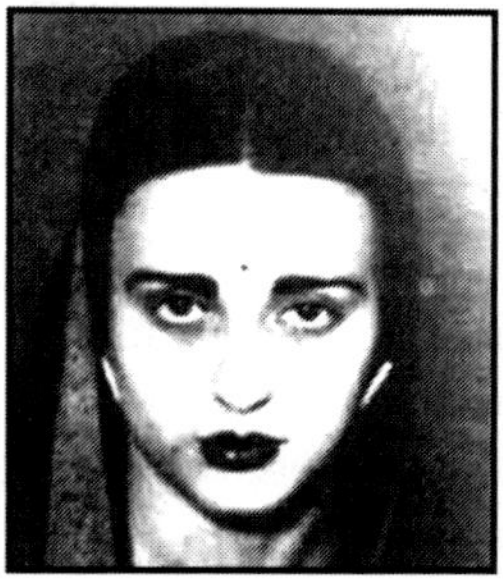

The beautiful Amrita Shergil, daughter of a Sikh aristocrat Umrao Singh and Hungarian mother Marie Antoinette Gottesman, endowed with considerable artistic talent, was born on January 30, 1913 in Budapest. The outbreak of the World War kept the family in Hungary for six years. Amrita, alongwith her family, returned to India in 1920. The family made their home in Summer Hill, Shimla, for the next nine years. In Simla, despite Amrita's own opposition, she was put into a convent school. She disapproved of the compulsory church attendance and told her father that she was an atheist. From the convent she wrote a letter denouncing all religious practices, laying a special emphasis on the Roman Catholics whom she considered bigoted and ostentatious in their rituals. The letter got into the hands of the mother superior who forthwith expelled Amrita from the school. It was in Simla that Amrita started painting

In 1929, when Amrita was only sixteen year old, she went to Paris to study art. She learnt first at the Grande Chaumiere under Pierre Vaillant and subsequently at the Ecole des Beaux-Arts, where she was taught by Lucien Simon. Amrita showed her talent early. From 1930 to

1932, Amrita did hundreds of sketches and studies of male and female nudes, mainly in charcoal. Her painting 'Young Girls' won the Gold Medal in 1933, leading to her election as an associate of the Grand Salon. Towards the end of 1933, she began to be haunted by an intense longing to return to India, feeling in some strange inexplicable way that there lay her destiny as a painter.

Shergil returned to India at the end of 1934, not yet twenty-two, but already a technically accomplished painter, equipped with some of the most essential ingredients that make an artist great–an unquenchable thirst to *know*, a virile tenacity of purpose and a single-mindednesss about her role in life. On return to India, Amrita spent some months in the palatial Majitha house, her ancestral home in Amritsar, and at her uncle's enormous estate in Saraya and then she came to Simla where her liberated lifestyle caused a stir.

Overnight Amrita became the focus of attention among the elite of Indian society who had moved to Simla for the summer. Her name was included in invitations to all the parties thrown by the complacent Rajas and bureaucrats who desired her company for titillation and amusement.

After settling down in Simla in early 1935, she took an important decision of interpreting "the life of Indians, particularly the poor, pictorially." This, she said, she would do "with a new technique, my own technique" and "this technique though not technically Indian, in the traditional sense of the word, will yet be fundamentally Indian in spirit." These words suggest that she had a clear idea of what she was to accomplish in the near future. By 1937, she had achieved that perfect blending of western techniques and Indian spirit, which no Indian painter had been able to achieve till then. She had laid the foundation of modern Indian art. For purely financial reasons she did a large number of commissioned portraits between 1935-1938 which she disliked intensely. In search for inspiration, she visited Bombay, Cochin, Trivandrum, Cape Comorin, Madurai and Ajanta and many temples in the south.

The artist's mother disapproved of her daughter's Bohemian life style. She was keen that Amrita should settle down with some well-to-do respectable husband, and had in mind a particular young Indian whom she had recently met. Amrita was persuaded to become involved with him and they were engaged for a few months-until the girl broke it off, realising that she had nothing in common with him. Almost in the way of avenging herself upon her mother's idea of an arranged marriage, she tended towards promiscuity and did not want to be committed to a single man. She declared in a letter: 'I am always in love, but unfortunately for the party concerned, I fall out of love or rather fall in love with someone else before any damage can be done'.

In June 1938 much against her parent's wishes, Amrita left for Hungary to marry her cousin Dr. Victor Egan who was a doctor of medicine. There were lots of well to do Indians who were keen to marry her, but she was apprehensive of being an 'ideal' wife, and held the view that she could not be a mother as well as a painter. She felt that Victor was the only person who not only understood her, but accepted her as she was. After marriage, Amrita and her husband fled from Fascist dominated Hungary and the impending threat of war. The couple reached India via Ceylon and on their way to Shimla they visited Mahabalipuram and Mathura.

Amrita's life at Saraya (Amritsar) where she started living, had two facets. Saraya was a haven where she and her husband could set up a home in the comfortable lap of the Majithia house-hold, relax; and she could go for long horse rides, take part in elaborately organised tiger hunts on the back of elephants, and, indulge herself in a life of feudal extravagance. But there was no stimulating company, no one with whom she could hold an intelligent conversation and no opportunity to expand her ideas. She felt trapped and suffocated there.

In September 1941 Amrita and her husband managed to get away from the claustrophobic Saraya estate and went to settle in Lahore. Although Lahore had a number of conservative people, there were numerous students, writers and artists who held progressive views and were sympathetic to the nationalist struggle. They created an intellectually lively atmosphere and brought out a number of magazines and journals. Amrita enthusiastically participated in the cultural life of the city, gave talks on the radio and met a number of interesting people.

While in Lahore, Amrita died suddenly on the 5th of December 1941 before she had even reached the age of twenty-nine.

Amrita's work done during her stay in Europe till 1934 was largely academic, consisting of still-life, nude studies, portraits and the like. Her genius was to flower only after her return to her fatherland, India. Despite her training in western art, she had complete awareness of and deep respect for India's artistic traditions. She was haunted by the faces of the unhappy and dejected, poor and starving Indians whom she saw first around Shimla, then in the South and finally in Punjab, where she was to spend the last days of her life. She began painting poor hill people who, to her romantic and naïve mind, embodied the spirit of India. She gave them large doleful eyes and vacant stares, exuding an expression of utter hopelessness. Her lanky and angular figures shrouded in homespun materials looked fragile and melancholic, reflecting, perhaps, an inner melancholy of her own. She became acquainted with Indian miniatures and fell in love with the intense Basohli school. She even attempted to include certain elements of Rajput painting in her later work, doing so with feeling and flair and avoiding Abanindranath's sentimentality. Amrita Shergil ushered in a strong current of modernity and cosmopolitanism with her portraits of ordinary people and prepared the ground for others.

Amrita Shergil was certainly many years ahead of her time in India in the mid-1930s as only in the 1960s did Indian artists begin to display her kind of self-assurance and purpose. Emancipated, yet responsible, fun-loving but serious, assertive yet fragile, she provided a role model for women artists of future generations.

5

Anandamayee Ma (1896-1982)

One of India's greatest women saints, Anandmayee Ma was born on the 30th of April 1896 in a small village of Kheora in Tripura(now in Bangladesh) to Bengali parents, Sri Bipin Bihari Bhattacharya and Srimati Mokshda Sundari Devi. Her father, Bipin Behari Bhattacarya, sang Vaisnava songs often appearing to be intoxicated. He would rise at 3 AM and sing songs, and was given to wandering for long periods. His wife would go searching for him and bring him back home. On one occasion, during a storm, the roof blew off the house and he continued singing in the rain. Anandamayi's mother, Moksada Sundari Devi, was also known for her states of *bhava* or religious emotion. She was visited by avatars and deities who shown with light as she performed her household duties. While pregnant with Nirmala (Anandamayee's given name), she would see visions of sages and statues of deities which would appear, and then suddenly disappear. She later took vows and became a female renunciant.

Anandmayee Ma was originally named Nirmala Sundari. Anandamayee Ma was very sensitive to religious ritual as a child, and the sound of religious chanting would bring about ecstatic feelings in her. At temples, she would also see religious figures emerging from religious statues and reentering them. She was often distracted and would be seen gazing into space, her eyes not focused on outer objects. Her education was very limited and her writing skills were minimal.

She was married at the age of thirteen to Sri Ramana Mohan Chakravarty, from the village of Atpara (now Bangladesh), who later came to be known as Baba Bholanath. It was an unusual marriage. It was a celibate marriage though not by her husband's choice. When thoughts of sexuality occurred to Bholanath, Anandamayee's body would take on the qualities of death and she would grow faint. He had to repeat mantras to bring her back to normal consciousness. Sometimes in such situations, her body would become distorted in various ways or it would stiffen. Bholanath thought the situation was temporary but it proved to be permanent. His relatives said he should remarry but he did not follow their advice. Her husband realised very soon that his spouse was not an ordinary being, and his rapport with her was one of veneration mixed with fear. Later she gave him initiation and he became a *sannyasi* under the name of Tibhatananda.

While living in Dacca, people came to recognize her spiritual qualities. At the sound of religious chanting, she would become stiff and even fall to the ground in a faint. Her body would occasionally become deformed during these events. Sometimes it would lengthen. At others, it would shrink or its limbs would seemingly go into impossible positions as if the skeletal structure had changed shape beneath her skin. She would hold difficult yogic positions (*asanas*) for long periods and spontaneously form complex tantric hand positions (*mudras*) and gestures. Her husband thought she might be possessed, and took her to exorcists. One physician suggested she was not mad in the conventional sense but instead had a kind of god intoxication-a divine madness for which there was no secular cure.

In 1916, she became ill and moved back to her parent's home in Vadyakuta. In 1918 she and her husband moved to Bajitpur where she began to do Shaivite and Vaisnavite spiritual practices. Inner voices would tell her what actions to perform and which images to visualize. Anandamayee would shed profuse tears, laugh for hours, and talk at tremendous speed in a Sanskrit-like language. Other unusual actions included rolling in the dust and dancing for long periods whirling like a leaf in the wind. She would also fast for long periods and at other times consume large quantity of food.

Ma, as she was lovingly called, developed intense devotion to Lord Krishna and underwent gradual inner transformation, which led to her self realization at the age of 26. A divine power is believd to have taken possession of her body, making it move with a supernatural grace. She danced, ran towards the place where the *kirtan* was being held, sometimes animated by an undulating movement, at other times with a speed almost impossible to follow with the eyes. She often used to become unconscious of the external world and remained immersed in the happiness of *samadhi* for hours. Ma was a counsellor, educator in the spiritual realm, healer and loving mother, all at the same time She travelled extensively preaching love, compassion and self discipline. She established Ashrams charitable institutions and hospitals everywhere. She had a temple built for her by disciples in Dacca but left the day it was completed. She traveled to Dehradun where she lived in an abandoned Shiva temple for almost a year without money and often in freezing temperatures without blankets. As time went by, her popularity grew and people from far and wide started visiting her to seek her blessings. Her message to her devotees was: "To know *Bhagavan* (God) is to know oneself, and to know oneself is to know God." "Everybody is your friend, a well-wisher. Everybody possesses the same soul-the Supreme Soul. All are linked with one another; the One manifests itself in all forms". "In whatever state He keeps anyone at any time it is all for the good, for verily everything is ordained by Him, is of Him." "Try always to bear in mind that God sends all the worries of life for purifying yourself." "Remember always repetition of His name has enough power to wash away all sins if there be any whether of this life or of the past ones."

Anandamayi was a holy woman without formal religious training or initiation whose status was based entirely on her ecstatic states. She did not have an outer guru, though she did hear voices that told her what religious and meditative practices to perform. She emphasized the importance of detachment from the world and religious devotion. She also encouraged her devotees to serve others. An ecstatic child of ecstatic parents, she became a famous saint who like many other female Indian saints stood on the edge of several religious traditions, and in the midst of none. She influenced the spirituality of thousands of people who came to see her throughout her long life.

Ma passed away in August 1982.

6

Anjolie Ela Menon (1940-)

Anjolie Ela Menon was born of American parentage in 1940 in West Bengal. She went to school in Lovedale in the Nilgiri Hills, Tamil Nadu and thereafter had a brief spell at the J.J. School of art in Bombay. Subsequently she earned a degree of English Literature from Delhi University. Her mother, a naval gynaecologist, died when Anjolie was 14. This led to anguish and loneliness and these traits remained conspicuous in her works for the next forty years. At 18 she was drawn towards the romantic elongated forms of Modigliani and lyricism of Amrita Sher Gill. What fascinated her was Sher Gills' sense of aesthetics and all that was beautiful in rural India. She was also deeply influenced by M.F. Hussain, Van Gogh and Munch.

After holding solo exhibitions in Bombay and Delhi in the late 1950s as a teenager, Anjolie Ela Menon worked and studied in Paris at the Ecole des Beaux Arts in 1961-1962 on a French Government scholarship. There, she was influenced by her exposure to the techniques of the medieval Christian artists. While in Paris, she began to experiment with a muted palette of translucent colors, which she created by the repeated application of oil paint in thin glazes. Painting on hardboard, Menon enhanced the finely textured surface of her paintings by burnishing the finished work with a soft dry brush, creating a glow reminiscent of medieval icons. As her style continued to evolve, Menon utilized the characteristics of early Christian art-including the frontal perspective, the averted head, and the slight body elongation-but took the female nude as a frequent subject. The result is a dynamic relationship of eroticism and melancholy. As can be seen in these two works, Menon developed her iconography of distance and loss in her later works through her thematic depiction of black crows, empty chairs, windows, and hidden figures. With paintings like these, she has established herself internationally as an artist of note.

Before returning home, she travelled extensively in Europe and West Asia studying Romanesque and Byzantine art. Since then she has lived and worked in England, the U.S.A., Germany and the erstwhile USSR. One of the most creative women artists of South Asia, Anjolie Ela Menon has held over 30 solo shows and several group shows including those at Black heath Gallery-London, Gallery Radicke-Bonn, Winston Gallery-Washington, Doma Khudozhinkov-USSR, Rabindra Bhavanand Shridharani Gallery-New Delhi, Academy of Fine Arts-Calcutta, the Gallery-Madras, Jehangir Gallery, Chemould Gallery, Taj Gallery, Bombay and Maya Gallery at the Museum Annexe, Hong Kong. Her works were exhibited in the fifty years celebration of Indian art at the National Gallery of Modern Art in New Delhi. A retrospective exhibition was held in 1988 in Bombay and Menon participated in it.

In addition to paintings in private and corporate collections, her works have been acquired by museums in India and abroad. She is also a well-known muralist and has represented India at he Algiers Biennale, the Sao Paulo Biennale, Brazil and three triennials in New Delhi. She has been invited by the British Council, the U.S. State

Department and the French Ministry of Culture to confer with leading artists in those countries. Menon has served on the advisory committee and the art purchase committee of the National Gallery of Modem Art, New Delhi, where she was co-curator with Henri Claude Cousseau for an exhibition of French Contemporary Art in 1996. A book titled "Anjolie Ela Menon: Paintings in Private Collections" has been published on her life and work.

Anjolie Ela Menon is the recipient of several awards including the Padma Shri Award conferred on her by Government of India in 2000 in recognition of her contribution to Indian art. Anjolie Ela Menon, who now lives and works in Delhi, is married to Raja Menon, a retired Indian Navy officer and strategist, and has two sons.

7

Anju Bobby George (1980-)

A sportsperson of renown, Anju was born on 19 April, 1980, in Cheeranchira Kochuparambil family in Changanasseri, Kerala to K.T. Markos and Gracy. She was initiated into athletics by her father and her interest was further kindled by her trainer Mr. Thomas in Koruthode school. She did her schooling in St. Ann's High School and CKM Koruthode School and graduated from Vimala College. In the School Athletic meet in 1991-92, she came first in 100 m hurdles and relay and second in long jump and high jump events. In the National Schools Games she won third place in 100 m hurdles and 4 × 100 m relay. She was the Calicut University Champion during her college days.

Although she started with Heptathlon, she later began to concentrate on her jump events and went on to win long jump medal in the 1996 Delhi junior Asian championship. In 1999 she set the national record for triple jump in the Bangalore Federation Cup and won Silver medal at the South Asian Federation Games in Nepal. In 2001 she bettered her own record in long jump in the National Circuit Meet at Thiruvananthapuram. In the same year she also won gold for triple jump and long jump in the Ludhiana National games.

Anju became the first Indian woman to win a Bronze medal clearing 6.49 m at the Commonwealth Games at Manchester 2002. She won the Bronze medal in Long Jump at the World Athletics Championships 2003 in Paris clearing 6.70 m, the first Indian athlete ever to win a medal in a World Athletics Championship.

Anju has won *Gold Medals* in Srilanka Open Meet (2000), Asian Games Busan, South Korea (2002), International Circuit Meet, Bhopal (2000) and Afro-Asian Games in Hyderabad (2003). She was the Best Performer in the World Indoor Athletic Championship, Birmingham. Anju won *Silver Medals* in SAF Games in Kathmandu (1999), Asian Grand Prix Hyderabad (2002), Asian Grand Prix Thailand (2002), Asian Grand Prix Manila (2002), and IAAF Super Grand Prix Tournament, Stockholm (2003). She won *Bronze Medal* in International Meet Balaton, Hungary (2001).

In the year 2004, Anju ranked First in Doha Qatar Athletic Super Grand Prix, clearing 6.82 metres (Long Jump) ; Second in Madrid meeting (6.62 metres), Third in Eugene Prefontaine Classic (6.83 metres). In Athens Olympic Games (2004), she ranked Sixth with 6.83 metres clearance in Long Jump event. In 2005, she won Gold in Asian Athletics Championship in Incheon (South Korea) and Silver in the World Athletics at Monaco.

Anju now ranks 6th in the world. Anju's journey to success from rank 61 in 2001 to rank 6 in 2003 within a short span of two years, was one of sheer hard work and intensive planning. The credit for her success goes to her husband and coach Bobby George who according to her was the biggest influence who helped her in realising her potential and achieving the goal. Bobby who is a Mechanical Engineer and a former National Champion in Triple jump himself, gave up his career to become a full time coach to Anju in 1998. He belongs to a prestigious sports family and is the younger brother of the famous Volley ball player Jimmy George. Anju and Bobby, realising that international exposure is essential for competing in World class events made necessary arrangements and trained with Mike Powell, a world record holder before the World Athletics meet which gave her valuable exposure in technique.

Anju received the prestigious Arjuna ward (2003) for eminent sports persons from the Government of India after her success in the World Athletic meet. In 2004, she was honoured with Padma Shri award. Both Anju and Bobby George work in the customs department and are settled in Chennai.

8

Annie Besant (1847-1933)

Annie Besant, the daughter of Irish couple William Wood and Emily Morris, was born in London on 1 October 1847. She had an unhappy childhood, partly due to her father's death when she was five. Without any savings, Annie's mother found work looking after boarders at Harrow School. Mrs. Wood was unable to care for Annie and she persuaded a friend, Ellen Marryat, to take responsibility for her upbringing. In 1866 Annie met the Rev. Frank Besant. Although only nineteen, Annie agreed to marry the young clergyman. By the time she was twenty-three Annie had two children. However, Annie was deeply unhappy because her independent sprit clashed with the traditional views of her husband. Annie also began to question her religious beliefs. When Annie refused to attend communion, Frank Besant ordered her to leave the family home. A legal separation was arranged and Digby, the son, stayed with his father, and Mabel went to live with Annie in London.

After leaving her husband Annie Besant completely rejected Christianity. In 1874 She became a member of the National Secular Society, which preached 'free thought'. Annie soon developed a close relationship with

Charles Bradlaugh, editor of the radical *National Reformer* and leader of the secular movement in Britain. Bradlaugh gave Annie a job working for the *National Reformer*. In 1877 Annie Besant and Charles Bradlaugh decided to publish *The Fruits of Philosophy*, Charles Knowlton's book advocating birth control. Besant and Bradlaugh were charged with publishing material that was "likely to deprave or corrupt those whose minds are open to immoral influences". Besant and Bradlaugh were both found guilty of publishing an "obscene libel" and sentenced to six months in prison. At the Court of Appeal the sentence was quashed. After the court-case Besant wrote and published her own book advocating birth control entitled *The Laws of Population*. The idea of a woman advocating birth-control received wide-publicity.

Besant joined the socialist group, the Fabian Society, the noted socialist organisation whose members included George Bernard Shaw and Sidney and Beatrice Webb and in 1889 contributed to the influencial book, *Fabian Essays*. In 1889 Annie Besant was elected to the London School Board. Some of her many achievements included a programme of free meals for undernourished children and free medical examinations for all those in elementary schools.

Annie Besant became a leading labour organizer, strike leader and reformer but her political wheel took another turn in 1889 when she read madame Blavatsky's "The Secret Doctrine" and, like many leading artists of the day, she became interested in Theosophy, a religious movement founded by Madame Blavatsky, as a way of knowing God. Theosophy was based on Hindu ideas of *karma* and reincarnation with *nirvana* as the eventual aim By the time of Madame Blavatsky's death in 1891, Annie Besant was theosophy's most famous and prominent member and in 1907 she was elected President of the

Theosophical Society, a position she held for the remainder of her life.

Annie Basant came to India in 1893 and lived at Adyar in Madras, which became the headquarters of the Theosophical Society. She supported Sanatan Dharam movement advocating that Hindu children be taught Sanskrit and Aryan 'simplicity and spirituality'. She believed in equal rights of men and women. Initially she felt that India needed to educate herself before she was capable of self-government, but by the outbreak of the First World War she was campaigning for self-government. In 1914 she joined Congress and in 1916 was one of the founders of Home Rule League. In June 1917 she was arrested under Defense of India Act. Her arrest was followed by a series of protest meetings all over the country and abroad. Consequently she was released. In the same year she was elected president of Indian National Congress at the Calcutta session. In December 1917, she along with Margaret Cousins, Sarojini Naidu and eight other Indian women, went to meet Mr. Montague to demand voting right for Indian women. Her appreciation of the strength of women was similar to Gandhiji's. But in regard to Gandhiji's 'Satyagrah' movement to achieve Independence, she had her differences with him.

In the late 1920s Annie Besant travelled to the United States with her protégé and adopted son Jiddu Krishnamurti, whom she claimed was the new Messiah and incarnation of Buddha. Krishnamurti rejected these claims in 1929 and broke away from Annie Besant.

In 1924 she led a deputation to England to demand Dominion Home Rule for India. In 1925 she drafted a Bill on the constitution for self-government which was approved by Gandhiji and supported by the Labor Party but did not go through. With the active support of Sir Tej Bahadur Sapru and Rt. Honourable V.S. Srinivasa

Shastry, Annie Besant worked whole heartedly towards fulfilment of Indian political aspirations. From the time she landed in India in 1893 and till her death, she worked whole heartedly for the advancement of India in every field-educational, social, religious and political.

Of Annie Besant, Sarojini Naidu had said: "Mrs Annie Besant was a great woman, a warrior, a patriot and a priestess......Her essential qualities were her unquenchable thirst for freedom."

Annie Besant died in 1933 in Adyar.

9

Aruna Asaf Ali (1909-1996)

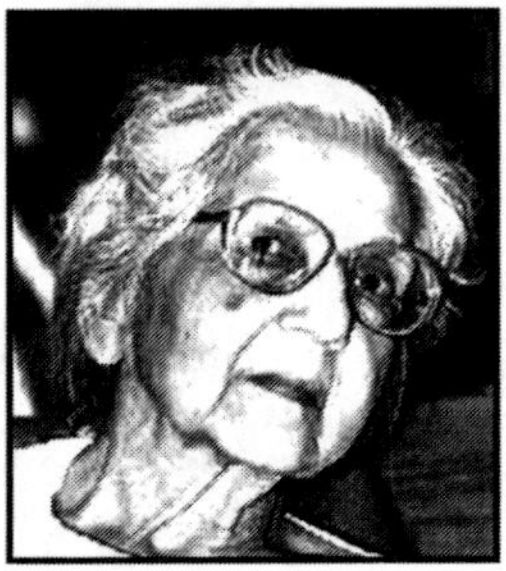

Aruna Asaf Ali (nee Ganguli) belonged to Hindu Bengali family which had come from East Bengal and settled in Calcutta. Aruna Ganguli was born in Kalka (Haryana) and lived with her father who ran a hotel in Nainital (UP). She was educated at Sacred Heart Convent in Lahore, and then in Nainital. After finishing her school education, she taught at the Gokhale Memorial School in Calcutta.

At the age of 19, she became engaged to Asaf Ali, a prominent Congress leader of Delhi over twenty years older than herself, and married him in 1928, despite her father's vehement opposition on the ground of age and religion.

Her marriage bought her face to face with the freedom struggle and social service, which she pursued as a part of Gandhi's Satyagraha movement. Her first major political action was during the Salt Satyagraha in 1930, when she was thrown into jail by the British, for being a 'vagrant', and sentenced to one year's imprisonment. A few months later, most political prisoners were released on the signing of the Gandhi-Irwin pact, but since she was not a political prisoner, she was not released. After a public agitation, she was released from prison. She was arrested again in

1932 and put in Tihar Jail, where she went on a hunger strike against the treatment of political prisoners.

In 1942 she went to the Bombay Congress Session with her husband, and was present at the passing of the Quit India resolution on 9th August. The Quit India Movement, 1942, was a turning point in her life. Following the arrest of all prominent Congress leaders, Aruna went underground, built up an underground center and directed the movement in Delhi and North India. She toured Calcutta, Bombay and Delhi evading police and made heroic efforts to regroup the forces after the collapse of the movement in 1943. Her property was seized by the Government and sold. She became the symbol of the spirit of youth in this country guiding and leading the National Movement from underground. She became editor of 'Inquilab', the monthly magazine of the Congress, along with Ram Manohar Lohia and fought the British through the paper. The Government meanwhile announced a Rs. 5000 reward for her capture. She remained underground till 1946 when the warrant of arrest was withdrawn by the Government of free India.

Emerging from underground in 1946, Aruna, with the halo of a National leader, was elected President of Delhi Pradesh Congress Committee in 1947. But her radical views came into conflict with Congress politics. Her views on political issues were at variance with those of her husband. In 1948, she was elected Delhi's first Mayor and held the office for the second term until 1959, when she resigned.

In 1948 she joined the Socialist Party. Two years later, she broke with it and formed Left Socialist Group and took an active part in the trade union movement. In 1955 this group merged with Communist Party of India and she became a member of its Central committee and a Vice President of the

All India Trade Union Congress. In 1958 she left the Communist Party of India and remained unattached to any political party. On the morrow of Jawaharlal Nehru's death, she came back to Congress Party but ceased to play any active part in politics.

Aruna Asaf Ali worked in the women's league which was affiliated to the All India Women's Conference. In 1954 she helped to establish the National Federation of Indian Women (NFIW), the women's wing of the Communist Party of India. The NFIW was meant to be a radical alternative to existing women's organizations, and one that would reach beyond a middle class membership. She had been a leading member of the Indo-Soviet Cultural Society and All India Peace Council.

Aruna Asaf Ali came to be known as the 'Grand old Lady of the Independence Movement' and the Heroine of the 1942 Movement.' She was a fiery leader who plunged headlong into politics at a time when the freedom struggle was raging and the youth were laying down their lives for the country's Independence. After Independence, Aruna Asaf Ali could not adjust herself with political realities.

Aruna Asaf Ali was awarded the Lenin Prize for peace in 1975 and the Jawahar Lal Nehru award for International understanding for 1991.

She passed away on 29th July 1996 at the ripe age of 87. The country honoured her with its highest civilian award, the Bharat Ratna, posthumously. She is the third woman after Indira Gandhi and Mother Teresa to be conferred with the Bharat Ratna.

10

Arundhati Roy (1961-)

Modern India's emerging human rights activist and multi-causal writer, Susanna Arundhati Roy was born on 24th November 1961, in Bengal to Christian mother, Mary Roy, and a Bengali Hindu father. Her mother was herself a social activist and a crusader for human rights.

Arundhati spent her crucial childhood years in Aymanam village, Kottayam (Kerala). There, her mother Mary Roy ran an informal school named Corpus Christi where Arundhati developed her literary and intellectual abilities unconstrained by the set rules of formal education. When she was just 16, she left her home and settled in Delhi in a squatters' camp, in a small hut with a tin roof, within the walls of Delhi's Ferozshah Kotla. She did her degree in Architecture at the Delhi School of Architecture. During this period she met Gerard Da Cunha a fellow architecture student and married him but their marriage lasted only four years.

After a brief stint in the field of architecture, Arundhati took a job at the National Institute of Urban Affairs, where she met Pradeep Krishen, a film director, now her husband, who offered her a small role in 'Massey Saab'. They had barely got to know each other when she got a scholarship to go to Italy for eight months to study the restoration of monuments. During that period in Italy she discovered the writer in her. On return from Italy, she did a couple of writings and acting assignments for TV and films and came to be known as a screen writer. In 1988 she scripted and acted in cult classic, *In Which Annie Gives it Those Ones*. Her other film assignment was a role in the screen play of *Electric Moon* (1991).

Arundhati received media attention when she wrote a series of essays in support of Phoolan Devi, who she felt had been exploited by Shekhar Kapur's film Bandit Queen. She wrote her first book, *The God of Small Things*, which was published in 1997. This won the prestigious British Booker prize in London and £20,000 as prize that went with it. It became an international best sellerselling nearly 400,000 copies globally by October that year. Roy is the first non-expatriate Indian author and the first Indian woman to have won this prize. The book, which took Roy five years towrite, is not strictly autobiographical, but she said "the sadness of the book" * has stayed with her, and that she may never write another novel.

In the years following her success, Arundhati has turned to activism and political journalism. She has agitated against nuclear proliferation, participated in the Narmada Bachao Andolan and passionately opposed the Iraq War. In July 1998, Arundhati Roy published an article in India called 'the End of Imagination' in opposition to the nuclear chic engulfing her country. She has written against Indian Government' s massive dam projects which displaced millions of poor people. In May 1999, Arundhati Roy published in the 'Outlook' and 'Frontline' a lengthy political commentary on the Narmada dam project, its history and context, and its impact on the people it is displacing. An abridged version of the same article entitled *'Lies, Dam Lies and Statistics'* was published in the

Guardian newspaper in the UK two weeks later. The full article, entitled 'The Greater Common Good' makes the point that India has 3,600 big dams and they have devoured 50 million people already, but the promised gains from the dams have never arrived, and no-one in the Indian Government has been willing to own up to the vast cost in human misery.

In April 1999, Arundhati Roy donated 1.5 million rupees, equivalent to her Booker Prize money, to the Narmada Bachao Andolan (NBA-Struggle to Save the Narmada) campaign. While holding a protest rally, she was arrested on 11 January 2000 along with an estimated 300-400 villagers in Mandleshwar whilst protesting the construction of the dam. Those arrested were released on 13 January. In 2001, for her writings against the Supreme Court of India's judgement in favour of construction of dams, Arundhati found herself held in contempt of court and faced the threat of imprisonment. In March 2002, Arundhati Roy was eventually sentenced to a single day's 'symbolic' imprisonment and fined for contempt of court. Her account of the submerging of 700-year old town of Harsud by Sardar Sarovar Dam, *The Road to Harsud*, was intensely touching and received country-wide attention.'The End of Imagination' and 'The Greater Common Good' have been published in a new single volume, entitled 'The Cost of Living". She has also written for equal rights for lower castes and against the Iraq war.

Arundhati Roy has been honoured with Sydney Peace Prize at the Sydney University.

Arundhati Roy has won the 2005 Sahitya Akademi Award for her book "*The Algebra of Infinite Justice*"—a collection of essays on the hubris of the rich and the plight of the poor.

11

Asha Bhonsle (1933-)

The famous playback singer Asha Bhonsle, one of the Mangeshkar sisters, was born on 8th September, 1933 to the renowed Maharashtrian parent, actor and singer Dinanath Mangeshkar in 'Goar' in Maharastra. Having been trained in classical music by her father Dinanath Mangeshkar, it was natural for her to turn to playback singing like her elder sister Lata Mangeshkar. She started her career in her elder sister Lata Mangeshkar's shadow. She also initially did small stints as a child artist. She was extremely shy as a child. In April 1942 her father Dinath Mangeshkar died and Asha, alongwith her family, moved from Pune to Kolhapur and then to Bombay. Around the age of ten she sang her first film song in the Marathi film Majha Bal. Asha made her playback debut in 1948 in the film Chunariya. She sang her first solo for the movie *'Raat Ki Raani'* (1949). Asha went through years of toil before she achieved recognition. Her life has been difficult one. An ill-advised marriage alienated her from Mangeshkars while her career took a long time to bring success.

When her talent was not recognized by anybody in Bollywood, O P Nayyar recognized her potential and gave her a big break in *CID* (1956). Her break-through came in

1957 when her close relationship with O P Nayyar fructified in successful songs for *Naya Daur* and *Tumsa Nahin Dekha*. In 60's her amazing tonal control was made full use of by O P Nayyar in songs like *'Jaiye aap kahan jayega'* and *'yeh hai reshmi zulphon ka andhera'*. Her penchant for experiencing the emotions exposed in her songs was seen in the '*Bandini*' melody '*Ab ke baras bhej bhaiyya ko babul'*. O P Nayyar and Asha Bhonsle are remembered for the breezy songs with galloping beats. Some of their famous songs include *Aaiye meherbaan* from *Howrah Bridge* picturized on sensuous Madhubala, *Yeh Hai Reshmi Zulfon ka Andhera* from *Mere Sanam* and *Aao huzur tumko* from *Kismat, Main pyaar ka rahi hoon* from *Ek Musafir Ek Haseena*. Asha recorded her last song for O P Nayyar in the movie *Pran Jaye Par Vachan Na Jaye* (1974).

Another music director who recognized Asha's talent was Khayyam who recorded his most memorable songs with Asha in the superhit movie *Umrao Jaan*, picturized on Rekha. They recorded four ghazals: *Dil cheez kya hai, In aankhon ki masti ke, Ye kya jagah hai doston* and *Justju jiski thi*. The film won her the first National Award in 1981. The songs in Umrao Jaan proved her versatility and established her talent.

Sachin Dev Burman, one of the most famous Bollywood composers, used Asha as his lead female voice in a number of unforgettable films. Most famous of these songs were Asha's duets with Mohammed Rafi and Kishore Kumar.

Asha also sang for Sachin Dev Burman's assistant, Jaidev in *Hum Dono, Mujhe Jeene Do* and other movies. It is said that C Ramachandra had offered '*Aye mere watan ke logon'*-the ever green patriotic song in the context of Indo-China war in 1962-to Asha first, but he gave it to Lata at the last moment under pressure.

A new era dawned in Bollywood music history when S D Burman's son, Rahul Dev Burman (aka Pancham) made his entry in films. Rahul Burman and Asha Bhosle created more than just music together. Asha married Rahul Dev Burman. Asha rendered hit songs for Rahul's first successful movie-*Teesri Manzil.* In the 1970s, Asha and Rahul Burman's youthful, Western songs took Bollywood music by storm-the raunchy cabret *Piya tu* from *Caravan* (1971), the rebellious *Dum Maro Dum* from *Hare Krishna Hare Rama* (1972), the sexy *Duniya mein* from *Apna Desh* (1972) the romantic *Chura liya hai* from *Yaadon Ki Baarat.* About *Dum Maro Dum,* Kishore Kumar said "the song is powerful enough to bring a dead person to life".

Young music director A R Rahman got Asha to sing *Tanha tanha* for *Rangeela.* Rahman went on to record many more hits with Asha including *Rang de (Thakshak), Radha kaise na jale* with Udit Narayan (*Lagaan*) and *Kahin aag lage (Taal), O Bhanware* with K J Yesudas (*Daud*).

In 1980s, Asha went on world tour, staging concerts in the USA, Canada and the UK. In the mid-1980s, she sang with Boy George and Stephen Lauscombe. In 1997, she sang a love song with Code Red, a boy band. She also recorded the song "The Way you Dream" (One Great Leap) with Michael Stipe that was used in the English movie, The Bullet Proof Monk.

In 1997 Asha did a private album with Leslie Lewis-*Janam Samjha Karo* that won her 1997 MTV Award. Asha Bhosle also worked with the Indo-Pakistani singer Adnan Sami for *Kabhi to Nazar Milao,* which went on to became the best-selling album.

Asha is one of the the most versatile singers Hindi film industry has produced. She has sung all kinds of songs, experimented with all kinds of styles, Hindi rock-n-roll, pop, cabaret, qawwalis, bhajans, ghazals–she has done them all. Asha has also sung for private albums. Asha has sung in almost every Indian language, in English, Russian and Malay, and Rabindra Sangeet. In the 1990s Asha further widened her horizon by succesfully coming out with albums in Indipop giving her singing a western touch. Asha Bhosle has been a name to contend with in the Hindi film industry for the last four decades during which she has sung over 20,000 songs and given playback songs in over 722 films.

Asha Bhonsle won Filmfare Awards in 1968, 1969, 1972, 1973, 1974, 1975, 1978,1996 and National Awards twice in 1981 for 'Dil Cheez Kya Hai' (Umrao Jaan) and in 1986 for 'Mera Kuch Samaan' (Ijazat). She was the first Indian singer to be nominated for the Grammy Award in 1997. In 2001 she won the Dada Phalke Award and Dayawati Modi Award. The other Awards won by her are: Nightingale of Asia Award–1987; Lata Mangeshkar Award by Government of Madhya Pradesh–1989; MTV Award Janam Samjha Karo–1997 and Screen Video Cone Award Janam Samjha Karo–1997

12

Begum Akhtar (1914-1974)

One of the most popular musicians in the Indian subcontinent, Akhtaribai Faizabadi, or Begum Akhtar as she was more popularly known, daughter of Asghar Hasan and Mushtar Jahan, was born on 7th October, 1914 in the small town of Faizabad, Uttar Pradesh (India). She was born in a high class family that was not musically inclined. Young Akhtari took to music instinctively. As the family opposed it, she had to pursue it clandestinely in the initial years. Later, as her mother and uncle began to support her, she was sent to train under Ustad Imdad Khan, the great sarangi exponent, and later under Ata Mohammed Khan. Later she travelled to Calcutta with her mother and started learning music from classical stalwarts like Mohammad Khan, Abdul Waheed Khan and finally she became the disciple of Ustad Jhande Khan Saheb. She gave her first performance at a charity show in aid of Bihar flood victims in 1921. Though only seven years old at that time, she sang continuously for six hours. The famous poetess Sarojini Naidu appreciated her singing. After that, she sponsored and took part in many fund-raising programmes. She took the music world by storm. Her interpretation of the Ghazals of Ghalib had no equals. As an exponent of *thumri*, she was not a traditionalist and experimented with it and created her own style. She cut her first disc for the Megaphone Record Company at that time. A number of gramophone records were released carrying her ghazals, *dadras, thumris,* etc.

Begum Akhtar made her debut on the screen in 1937 and acted in a few Hindi movies including *Ek Din Ka Badshah, Nal Damyanti, Ameena, Mumtaz Begum, Jawaani Ka Nasha, Naseeb Ka Chakkar, Roti*. Like others of that era, she sang her songs herself in all her films. In the fifties, Music Director Madan Mohan persuaded her to sing in two Hindi movies viz. *Daana Paani* (1953) and *Ehsaan* (1954). Satyajit Ray's Bengali film '*Jalsa Ghar*' (1958) was her last film where she played the role of a classical singer

In 1945, Begum AKhtar was married to barrister Ishtiaq Ahmed Abbasi, a connoisseur of Urdu poetry and music and became known as Begum Akhtar. Her husband helped her acquire literary appreciation of the great ghazals of Ghalib, Faiz Ahmed Faiz and Jigar Muradabadi. Due to family restrictions, she did not sing for about 5 years. In 1949, she returned to the recording studios. She sang three *ghazals* and a *dadra* at Lucknow Radio Station. She wept aferwards and returned to singing in concerts, a practice which lasted until her death.

She acted on stage as well. However, the theatre required her to raise her voice so that she could be heard everywhere in the hall. Her voice was adversely affected by it. So, she gave it up.

Begum Akhtar had immortalised her definitive style of ghazal gayaki-a style that few have been able to match.

Her voice matured with time, adding richness and depth. She was gifted with sonorous and melodious voice and her singing was characterized by effortless ease The notes which she produced were so limpid, so hauntingly sweet, that the audience was immediately captivated. She would render it so endearingly that her every note would grip the hearts of the audience. During her recitals, whenever she reached a high note her voice would crack, considered by connoisseurs the highlight of her recital. The audience would wait eagerly for that pleasing crack in her voice!

She possessed all the qualities that are so vital for a good ghazal singer. She had the uncanny ability of choosing the right kind of ghazal and adorning it with a befitting tune. The expression, naturalness, spontaneity in her unconventionally gifted voice (which was not the typical sugar-syrup kind, but rather 'angular' and bore a classic crack in the higher scale) had left her audiences completely charmed. Mohan Nadkarni has described her singing as "an uncanny amalgam of the singing idioms in vogue not only in Lucknow and Varanasi but also in Punjab", in his book called *'The Great Masters'*. According to Sutapa Mukherjee, "Her voice had the seductiveness of mellow wine. When Begum Akhtar sang, she could make her audience sway to every emotion in the lyrics of a ghazal."

Begum Akhtar is popularly known as Mallika-e-Ghazal. She enthralled the audiences by her singing for nearly three decades from 1940. She has nearly four hundred songs to her credit. She was a regular performer on All India Radio. She usually composed her own ghazals and most of her compositions were *raag* based.

She trained many disciples including Hiranand and Rita Kothari. Over 250 of her songs have been recorded by various gramophone companies. She was associated with the reputed *tabla* player M A Khan for 38 years. She was deeply religious, offered *namaz* and recited Koran daily and performed Haj twice.

She travelled widely both in the country and abroad. In 1963, she was a member of the Government of India's cultural delegation to Afghanistan, where she gave several recitals which were greatly appreciated. She also went to the Soviet Union in 1967 and sang ghazals at Moscow, Tashkent, Samarkand, Al-Malik and Bukhara, receiving tremendous applause.

During her last concert which was held in Ahmedabad, she had raised the pitch of her voice as she felt that her singing that day had not been as good as she had wanted it to be. She had not been feeling well that day to begin with. The additional demand and stress she put herself under resulted in her falling ill and being rushed to the hospital. She passed away on 30th of October, 1974 leaving a big void in ghazal lovers' hearts.

Begum Akhtar is a legend who lives on. She is the greatest ghazal and thumri maestro to have been born and she has remained an icon till date. She was honoured with the Sangeet Natak Academy Award in 1972. She was posthumously honoured with the Padma Bhushan.

13

Begum Hazrat Mahal (1820-79)

One of the most stirring women leaders of India's first war of independence in 1857-58, Hazrat Mahal, born in 1820, was wife of Nawab Wajid Ali Shah of Lucknow (Uttar Pradesh). The King gave her the title of Iftikhar-un-Nisa (the Pride of all Women) at the time of marriage. After her only child Birjis Quder was born, her husband gave her the title of Hazra Mahal. Hazrat Mahal was also known as the Begum of Oudh.

Hazrat Mahal was born into a poor family in the city of Faizabad, located in the state of Oudh with the family name of Iftikarun-nisa. The name indicated that she was of Iranian descent. She was educated as a dancing-girl and attracted the attention of the king of Oudh, Wajid Ali Shah who admitted her into his harem and raised her to the rank of his wife. In addition to being gifted with irresistible physical charm, she had an inborn genius for organization and command.

The British had annexed Oudh in 1856 and Wajid Ali Shah was exiled to Calcutta with most of his family. Begum Hazrat Mahal, whom he had divorced about six years ago, chose to stay in Lucknow with her minor son Birjis Qadr.

She threw in her lot with the freedom fighters and when the revolutionary forces succeeded in wresting the city from the British, they chose the mother and son as the royal symbol of their leadership. The Begum proved to be lion-hearted as well as an adroit strategist. After the under-age Birjis was crowned Nawab in July 1857, the Begum acted as Regent. The Begam headed a Government, with top revolutionary leaders in key positions, under whose banner the different sections of the soldiery assembled to form a united front.

For about six months the revolutionary Government kept the British troops at bay and held the city of Lucknow under its control. During all these operations the Begam was the supreme commander. Under the seal of King Birjis Qadar she issued proclamations to the people in general, and to the zamindars and taluqdars of Oudh in particular, to unite under the banner of the new Government to fight the English. It is understood she even toured the province to stir up feeling against foreign rule. Among her important associates were Rana Beni Madho Baksh of Baiswara, Raja Drig Bijai Singh of Mahona, Khan Ali Khan of Shahjehanpur, Maulvi Ahmad Ullah Shah of Faizabad, Raja Man Singh and Raja Jayelal Singh, to name only a few.

To fortify the city of Lucknow against advancing forces of the English she sanctioned five lakhs of rupees to "have a wall built round the city." Then, when she was informed that the English had purchased the friendship of Rana Jang Bahadur of Nepal with the promise of Gorakhpur and a share of Oudh, she immediately made the Rana a counter-offer of "Gorakhpur, Azimgurh, Arrah, Chupra and the provinces of Benaras, if he would unite with her." Her battle tactics too bear the stamp of an expert schemer. Through efficient agents she contacted the officers of the

Indian regiments serving the English at Cawnpore and settled with them that when they were to face the the Begam's forces "the regiments should fire blank ammunition" and afterwards "turn upon the Europeans." She even personally appeared in the field (on February 25, 1858) on elephant back, along with other officers to supervise defence operations. In the battle of Musabagh, Hazrat Mahal personally led 9,000 troops against the English invaders. When her palace at Kaiserbagh was being stormed and five thousand faithfuls turned traitors, she struck to her guns like a man. Hazrat Mahal was the last leader to retreat when the Indian forces were finally defeated in Lucknow on March 18, 1858.

When Lucknow fell to the British forces, the Begum fled to Bundi to avoid capture. While the English were busy in re-establishing their authority in Lucknow, the Begam once again succeeded in stirring the rest of Oudh to rebellion. In fact, 1858 saw a series of sporadic outbursts in different areas of Oudh, and the English experienced some of the toughest encounters of the whole history of the rebellion. The heroes were, mainly and obviously the taluqdars and zamindars of Oudh, and there is enough evidence on record to show their attachment to the Begam.

At one time, the British offered her clemency and an irresistible pension of 12 lakh. The Begum rejected all temptations. To avoid the ignominy of capture by the British, she fled to the forests of Terai, from where she negotiated with Jung Bahadur of Nepal for asylum. Though the Rana agreed, once the Begum went to Nepal, she was treated as a prisoner, stripped of the wealth and jewels of the House of Oudh. Begum Hazrat Mahal died in Kathmandu in 1879. She had built, with her own money, an Imambara in Kathmandu where she was buried after her death.

Thus ended the life of a dancing girl who rose to eminence and who commanded the respect of all. Begum Hazrat Mahal behaved like a queen to the end. She was a brave woman and a daring leader who had resisted British troops with all her might. Lord Russel called her "a better man than her husband and lord (Wajid Ali Shah, Nawab of Oudh)".

14

Bhikaji Cama (1861-1936)

Madame Bikaji Rustom Cama was born on 24th September, 1861 of rich Parsi parents. Her father, Sorabji Framji Patel, a famous merchant and man of means, had a large family. Young Bhikhaiji received good English education, but from the beginning she was a rebel, and a nationalist. She was married to Rustom K.R. Cama, a rich handsome social worker and lawyer who was manager of *Bombay Chronicle*, from 1915-18. But ideologically they were poles apart. Mr. Cama adored British, loved their culture and thought they had done a lot of good to India. Madame Bhikaji, now a full fledged nationalist, believed that British had fleeced India, and practised worst form of imperialism. Their marriage proved to incompatible. Madam Cama meanwhile plunged in several social activities. She left in 1902 for London which was to become her home for the rest of life.

Madam Cama served as private secretary to Dadabhai Navaroji, a great Indian leader in the forefront of national movement. In 1907 she attended the second International Socialist Congress at Stutgart, Germany where she presented India's case for Independence most forcefully and at the end of her speech she unfurled the Indian Tricolour with Vande Mataram insignia thereon for the first time on foreign soil and made history by asking the congregation to stand up and salute the flag with the following words:-

"This flag is of Indian Independence! Behold, it is born! It has been made sacred by the blood of young Indians who sacrificed their lives. I call upon you, gentlemen, to rise and salute this flag of Indian Independence. In the name of this flag, I appeal to lovers of freedom all over the world to support this flag."

B. Cama, Stuttgart, Germany, 1907

At this Conference she declared that India would be a Republic and Hindi would be the national language.

Among other activities, she smuggled revolvers concealed in toys (sent as Christmas presents) and revolutionary literature into India. She financed revolutionaries in and out of India. In 1909, her group started B*ande Mataram,* a monthly organ for Indian independence, and published it from Geneva. Another magazine "Madan's Talwar" was also started in memory of Madanlal Dhingra who had laid down his life for the country. Both the magazines were outlawed in India and England. Bhikaji Cama regularly addressed meetings in Hyde Park explaining her mission of freeing India. She fought for unity of Hindus and Muslims. She also fought for the cause of women. British were not happy with her activities and there was a plot to finish her off. Getting the wind of the plot, she moved to France in 1909.

Her Paris-home became a shelter for world revolutionaries. Her activities for freedom of the motherland continued unabated in France. She established contact with Russian revolutionaries and corresponded with Lenin. It is believed that Lenin met her in Paris and exchanged views. Savarkar got all encouragement in writing the history of 1st Indian War of Independence from

Bhikaji Cama. She helped its printing in Holland as no English publisher came forward to publish it. It was a banned book but found its way to India. She made efforts to save Savarkar who jumped into the ocean from the ship "Morena" near Marseilles but a few minutes delay saw the famous revolutionary back into chains, a fact which Madam Cama regretted in life. The British had banned her entry in India being afraid of her revolutionary past and confirmed nationalistic outlook. Under pressure from British Government, she was arrested and spent 3 years in jail. Bhikaji Cama lived in Paris for 30 years. Madam Cama was getting old and 35 years fighting on foreign land had taken its toll. In 1935 at the age of 74, when her health was failing, she was allowed by the British Government to return to India. After reaching Bombay, she was hospitalized and she died on the 13th of August 1936 un-noticed, un-honoured.

A fearless woman, Madame Bhikaji Cama brought in awareness of Indian struggle forIndependence in Europe and America and was instrumental in helping several revolutionaries. She is remembered as the mother of Indian revolution. Her role in the Independence struggle was recognized much later. A street in Mumbai was named after her and a birth centenary stamp in her honour was issued on 26 January 1962.

15

Brinda Karat (1947-)

One of the most vocal voices of women's rights in India Brinda Karat was born of mixed parentage on October 19, 1947 in Kolkata. Perhaps she inherited her spirit of rebellion from her mother Asrukawna who defied tradition by marrying a Punjabi, Suraj Lall Dass at a time when self-choice marriages, more so those outside the accepted norms of caste and nationality were frowned upon. Brinda was the third of four children, Surajit, Shukanta, and Radhika the youngest.

Brinda lived in Kolkata studying at Loreto House, a well known convent school. At the age of 13 she joined Dehradun's famous Welham Girls' School. Here she excelled in sports and won the best athlete trophy in the district sports competition for two years running. At 15 she was probably among the youngest athletes selected to participate in the national athletic meet representing Uttar Pradesh! After school she went to Delhi to graduate from Miranda House. While studying in the college, she was elected Miss Miranda House. In college she participated in several plays as one of the most active members of the college dramatic society.

After graduation she got a job with Air-India as an employee in its London office. While working for Air-India she refused to accept what was then a mandatory skirt uniform on the grounds that as employees of a national airline women should be allowed to wear the national dress if they so wanted! The Air India management ultimately accepted the point after which even non-Indian employees could wear the saree! During her four year stay in the UK, Brinda became greatly influenced by the huge anti-war upsurge among the youth all over Europe and England against the US war against Vietnam. Joining the anti-war mobilizations Brinda was drawn to Marxism and started studying Marxist texts which opened up a new world to this 23 year old. She decided to leave her job in London and return to India to join the communist movement. She returned in 1970 to join the CPI(M). She became a full time worker of the party in Kolkata. During the Emergency the party asked her to shift to Delhi. Here she started working among textile workers. She became a secretary of the textile workers union and also joined organizations of industrial workers. Her trade union activities also led to many cases against her and she was arrested several times. During the emergency she was known as Comrade Rita and even today many old textile workers refer to her by that name!

During her political and trade union work she was deeply affected by the plight of working women. She was the founding convener of the Working Women's Coordination Committee affiliated to CITU. Later she was elected the founding secretary of the Delhi committee of the Janwadi Mahila Samity a branch of the All India democratic Women's Association. This was among the first women's organizations in Delhi which concentrated its work among the urban poor women. Along with her colleagues Brinda led numerous struggles of poor women in Delhi. The organisation quickly became known as one of the most militant women's movements in the Capital.

Brinda started taking more responsibilities at the national level working with legendary communist women leaders like Suseela Gopalan, Vimal Ranadive, Ahilya Rangnekar as a Secretary in the All India Democratic Women's Association. Combining political work in the party organization with her trade union and women's struggles, she was elected the national General Secretary of the All India Democratic Women's Association in 1993 and continued in that post till 2004. She is now the Vice-President of AIDWA. She has been an impassioned and articulate campaigner for the rights of women and has emerged as a highly popular Communist leader. Recently she made her debut in an award winning film "Amu" on the anti-Sikh riots.

Brinda is the first woman to be elected to the CPI(M) Politburo, the highest policy making organ of the party. Her election to the Politburo is a recognition of her work and standing in the party. Her rise from trade unionism to the highest decision-making body of the party has been on her own strength. She was elected to Rajya Sabha from West Bengal in 2005.

Brinda is married to Prakash Karat-two individuals-bound by the same ideology-married in an underground ceremony during the Emergency year in 1975. They decided not to have children for the sake of the cause to which both were committed. They make a formidable partnership. Her husband is the General Secretary of CPI(M) and an enigmatic hardliner and she the dedicated fighter for the poor and the downtrodden.

16

Chand Bibi (1547-1599)

Chand Bibi, daughter of Hussain Nizam Shah, king of of Ahamadnagar, was a Moslem Princess who lived from 1547 until 1599 AD. At a very young age, she was married to Ali Adal, Sultan of Bijapur. Ali Adal Shah consulted her in all administrative matters and reviewed parades with her. She took keen interest in military campaigns. On the Sultan's death (he was murdered) in 1580, his young nephew Ibrahim Adil Shah II was raised to the throne under the guardianship of Chand Bibi. She gave him sound training. She ruled with great prudence and intelligence till the young king came of age. She attended the court in white muslin robes. Her figure was very small and light, like a girl. She rode with fashion of a man on a milky-white Arab. With the exception of high yellow leather Persian boots which reached above her knees, she wore only white and no colour at all.

The State was entrusted to the care of Kamil Khan. He was not a good person. When he tried to seduce Chand Bibi, he was thrown out. Kamil Khan's successor, Kishwar Khan, was no better. He confined her in the fortress of Satara. Her people came ouit in her support, freed her and restored her to the former position. The third person appointed in place of Kishwar Khan had also to be removed by Chand Bibi. Disgusted with the state of affairs, Chand Bibi left for her parental place, Ahmadnagar, in 1584, and lived there for 12 years. She returned ti Bijapur when the people of Bijapur invited her to defend them from the attack of Moghul army under Prince Murad (son of Emperor Akbar). She declared her nephew, Bahadur Khan, as king and assumed the reins of government on his behalf.

Chand Bibi brought order. With veil on her face and with sword in her hand, she directed the army, exhorted her troops and compelled the Moghul army to raise the siege of Bijapur. When Prince Murad sought to mine the walls of the fort, with her own hands, she removed the powder from two mines and showed her troops how counter-mine. When the army succeeded in exploding the third mine, her officers fled away. She shamed them by taking their place. The Moghuls found her troops invincible and suffered heavy losses of men and material. The Moghul army returned the next morning and found a new wall which Chand Bibi had erected overnight. It was in appreciation of this that Prince Murad namd her "Chand Sultana". She was quite aware of the enemy's strength and when Prince Murad offered to withdraw his troops in return for the cession of Berar, she accepted the offer and the moghul army returned.

But there was treachery for her in Ahmednagar. One Mohammad Khan, whom she had appointed Peshwa, tried to usurp the throne. He sought the help of Moghul Governor of Berar, promising to hold Ahmednagar as a vassal state to the Delhi empire. When the Mughal army marched towards the city, the people of Ahmednagar came to know of Mohammad Khan's treachery and rose against him. The people restored the government to Chand Bibi.

The dissensions among the people of Ahmednagar gave the Moghuls another oppostunity soon to attack the town. The imperial troops reached Ahmadnagar and laid siege of the fort. Chand Bibi organised the fight against the Mughal army and repulsed the attack.

She thought of an honourable peace with the Moghuls but a enuch, Hamid Khan, betrayed her. He ran through the strets shouting that Chand Bibi had betrayed the people to the Moghuls. Chand Bibi's own troops were taken in, rushed to the fort, seized her and executed her. After her death, the city was stormed by Moghul troops who put the defenders to the sword and the kingdom of Ahmednagar became a part of the Moghul empire.

Chand Bibi's courage and fighting spirit in the face of overwhelming odds were legendary and, no wonder, she came to be known as Chand Sultana. She was not only a military genius and an able administrator, but also a good scholar of Arabic and Persian and a patron of scholars.

17

Dalip Kaur Tiwana, Dr (1935-)

A leading Punjabi novelist and short story writer, Dr Dalip Kaur Tiwana was born on May 4, 1935 in Village Rabbon of Ludhiana district in a well-to-do land-owing family. She was adopted by her uncle (father's sister's husband) who was an Inspector-General of Prisons in the princely state of Patiala. At the age of thirteen, her engagement was broken. In disgust, she became an introvert and a skeptic questioning each and everything. She wanted to assert herself and felt compelled to excel in everything she did–studies, sports, knitting, and embroidery–to prove her worth. This was and is true of her writing.

She was educated at Patiala. She had a distinguished academic career, getting a first class first in M.A., and the first woman in the region to get the Ph.D. degree from Punjab University in 1963. Dalip Kaur Tiwana joined the Punjabi University at Patiala, as a Lecturer and then went on to become Professor and Head of the Department of Punjabi and Dean, Faculty of Languages. She was a brilliant teacher and researcher and made a significant contributions to literary and critical studies in Punjabi. She was a UGC National Lecturer for a year. Her husband, too, occasionally publishes poetry under his pen name Sarvan Minhas.

Dalip Kaur Tiwana is fond of reading literature, listening to music, watering plants and doing other related things. In deep down she always remembered ancient Rishis, who wrote the Vedas but never put their names to anything they composed.

Dalip Kaur's literary career as a creative writer commenced with the publication of her first book of short stories.Sadhna' in 1961, which was declared the best book in its genre by the Department of Languages, Government of Punjab. She produced seven collections of short stories before switching over to novel-writing. Her second novel 'Eho Hamara ZeeUna' won her the Sahitya Akademy Award in 1972. Thereafter, virtually every one of her works won her an award. The Ministry of Education and Social Welfare honoured her book of stories for children called 'pal1jan IJiCh Parmeshwar' in 1975, while the Department of Languages, Government of Punjab, conferred the "Nanak Singh Puruskar" on her novel 'Peele Patian di Dastan' in 1980 and "Gurmukh Singh Musafir Puruskar" on her autobiography 'Nange parion da Safar' in 1 982. Awards and honours have flowed from outside the Punjab as well. In 1985, the International Association of Punjabi Artists and Authors (IAAPA) based in Canada honoured her with an award in 1985. "Nanjanagudu Thirumalamba" award for her novel 'Katha Kuknoos Di' came from Shashwathi, Karnataka and "Vagdevi" award for 'Duni Suhava Bagh' was given by Bhartiya Bhasha Parishad, Calcutta, in 1998.

For her outstanding contribution to Punjabi literature, Dalip Kaur received the "Shiromani Sahityakar" award from the Punajb Government in 1987, the "Best Novelist of the Decade" award from Punjabi Academy, Delhi, in 1994 and the "Kartar Singh Dhaliwal" award from Punjabi

Sahit Academy, Ludhiana. She was among the distinguished Sikh personalities who were honoured on the occasion of the Tricentenary Celebrations of the Birth of the Khalsa at Anandpur Sahib in 1999. She won 'Saraswati Samman' for the Year 2001 from KK Birla Foundation. In 2004, she was awarded "Padma Shri" for her contribution to literature.

Dalip Kauru's works have been translated in English, French, Russian, Urdu, Hindi, Bengali, Gujarati and other Indian languages. Three novels have been telecast from doordarshan. She is associated with the Sahitya Academy (Delhi), Punjab Arts Council (Chandigarh), Punjab Sahit Academy (Chandigarh), Punjabi Sahit Academy (Ludhiana), National Book Trust of India, Bhartiya Janapith, K.K. Birla Foundation, Kendn Punjabi Lekhak Sabha in various capacities. She is President of the Punjabi Sahit Academy, Chandigarh and Life-Fellow auld nominated Senator of the Punjab University.

Dalip Kaur chaired sessions at the International Punjabi Conference held in U.K. in 1980 and international literary meet organised by California Sahit Sabha in the U.S.A. in 2000.

18

Devika Rani Roerich (1914-1994)

The icon of the Thirties and Forties, Devika Rani was the first Dream Girl and the first First Lady of Indian Screen. Daughter of Col. M.N. Choudheri, I.M.S., and Mrs.Leela Choudheri, and grand niece of Rabindranath Tagore, Devika Rani was born in Waltair in 1914. Her father had a distinguished medical career and was the first Indian Surgeon General of Madras. Devika Rani studied at Shanti Niketan. In 1920, Devika Rani went to England for education. While studying in England, she received a scholarship from the Royal Academy of Dramatic Arts and the Royal Academy of Music in London to study acting and music. She took up the study of applied arts in London, specialising in textile designing and decor, and also studied architecture. At an early age, she was earning her living as a textile designer at a leading art studio in London.

While in London, she met the well-known Indian producer Himansu Rai who produced famous Indian films like "The Light of Asia", "Shiraz" and "A Throw of Dice" for Indian and international markets. She designed the sets of his first production *Light of Asia (1925)*. In 1929, they got married and after marriage they left for Germany where Himansu Rai made *A Throw of Dice (1929)* in collaboration with Germany's famous UFA Studio. Himansu Rai made a bilingual *Karma (1933)* with Devika Rani in the lead.

In Germany she learnt costumes designing, make-up, decor and other different branches of film production with special training in acting. At the time, Devika Rani also acted with Himansu Rai in a play which took them to Switzerland and the Scandinavian countries, where they were received with the highest honours.

On return to India, Devika Rani and Himansu Rai produced their first international talking picture "KARMA" in which Devika Rani and Himansu Rai acted. "KARMA" was produced both in English and Hindusthani. It was the first Indian talking picture in English and Hindusthani to be released in England and on the Continent as well as in India. "KARMA" was received with the highest approbation everywhere. The premier in England was inaugurated by Lord Irwin.

During the screening of "KARMA", Devika Rani was honoured by an invitation of the B.B.C. at London to act in the first television broadcast in Britain which was relayed throughout the country. She was also chosen to inaugurate the first B.B.C. broadcast on the short wave length to India.

Himansu Rai and Devika Rani st up the Bombay Talkies Ltd. in 1934 in Malad, Bombay. Devika Rani played the lead in most of the early productions of Bombay Talkies. Her outstanding portrayals, her style of acting and new approach created a distinct form and tradition. She acted in numerous films, many of which have become classics of the Indian screen. Among her most famous pictures were "Jawani-Ki-Hawa", "Jeevan Nayya", "Achoot Kanya", "Savitri", "Jeevan Prabhat", "Durga", "Vachan", "Nirmala" and "Izzat". Going with the trend she even sang her own songs in films with *Main Ban ki Chidiya* with

Ashok Kumar in *Achut Kanya.* She was acclaimed as India's greatest film actress, and was popularly known as the "First Lady of the Indian screen".

After the death of the great founder of the Bombay Talkies Mr. Himansu Rai in 1940, Devika Rani assumed the control of the Bombay Talkies which kept on producing outstanding pictures as "Punarmilan", "Kangan", "Bandhan", "Basant", "Kismat", "Hamari Baat", etc.

In 1945 at the height of her film career, Devika Rani decided to retire from the Bombay Talkies Ltd. She came into contact with Dr. Svetoslav Roerich, a Russian artist settled in India and married him. They stayed at their huge estate near Bangalore in South India. After her second marriage, Devika Rani did not appear on screen.

Devika Rani was a member of the Central Government Audio Visual Education Board, National Academy of Dance, Drama, Music and Films, Sangeet Natak Akademi, Lalit Kala Akademi, National Handicrafts Board and Indian Council for Cultural Relations.

On Republic Day, 1958, the President of India conferred the award of "PADMA SHRI" on Devika Rani for her valuable contribution to Indian motion pictures. On November 21, 1970, the Government of India conferred on her the first Dadasaheb Phalke Award for her outstanding services to the film industry. In 1978, she was honoured with the Bulgarian Medal of Honour and, in 1981, with a special award from the Indian Academy of Motion Pictures, Arts and Sciences. She was the recepient of the prestigious Soviet Land Nehru award conferred on her in 1989.

Devika Rani Roerich passed away in Bangalore in 1994.

17

Durgabai Deshmukh Dr. (1909-1981)

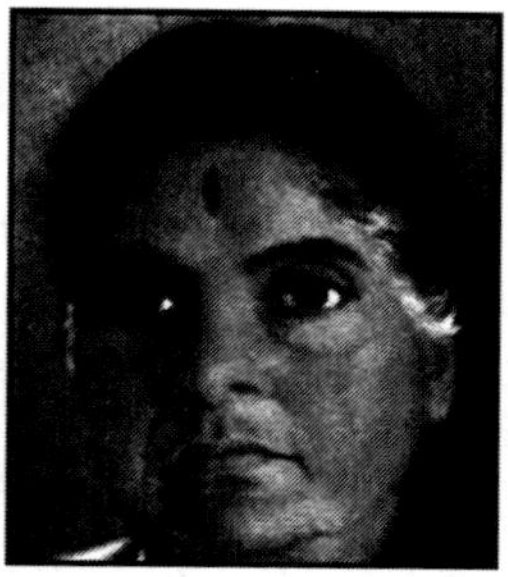

A 'Mother of Social Work in India' and a "Legend among women in her lifetime", Dr. Durgabai Desmukh was at once a freedom fighter, planner, administrator, educationist, social reformer and parliamentarian. She was born on 15 July 1909 to Rama Rao and Krishnavenamma in a middle class Andhra family in Rajahmundry (Andhra Pradesh). Her father died when she was very young and she had to start supporting her family from an early age. Durgabai was not able to pursue higher education when she was young because of the prevailing social conditions. She could learn only Telugu and Hindi. While she herself was a learner, she began teaching some girls what she was learning.

In the early 1920s, Mahatma Gandhi addressed a public meeting in Kakinada. Durgabai, then 12, was a volunteer at that meeting. She requested him to address women separately because some women, including Muslims, could not attend. He obliged her. Her interest in the freedom movement began with that. At that tender age, she came under the magic spell of Mahatma Gandhi, boycotted English-teaching school, made a bon-fire of her foreign clothings, took to *charkha* and joined Hindi Rashtra

Bhasha Prachar Movement. She started Balika Hindi Pathshala in 1922. As a volunteer she joined Mahatma Gandhi, Rajendra Prasad, Madan Mohan Malaviya, Motilal Nehru, Sardar Patel and other stalwarts travelling all over the country to raise popular consciousness about the freedom movement.

Moved by the plight of devdasis and burqa-clad women of Kakinada, she led hundreds of them to Bapuji. Her capacity to lead and an indomitable spirit to fight oppression was once again tested during the Salt Satyagraha in Madras in 1930's, when she succeeded Shri T. Prakasham as its 'dictator'. Durgabai led the salt satyagraha. She organised processions, was lathi-charged and thrice jailed. On her release in 1933, she resumed her education and obtained B.A. (Hons) and M.A. (Pol. Sc.) and B.L. degrees. A brilliant student, she secured five medals for distinction in Political Science and Constitutional History in the M A examination. She practiced at the Madras bar for a few years. In 1937, she founded Andhra Mahila Sabha, which today runs two hospitals, an orthopaedic centre, two colleges, three High Schools and functional literacy projects. As President of Blind Relief Association, Delhi, she set up a school-hostel and a light engineering workshop for them.

Durgabai was a member of Constitution Assembly of India and Provisional Parliament of India. She carried her fight for the poor and weak by getting enacted a number of social laws and mustered support for a national policy on social welfare in the Planning Commission of which she was a member (1952-1953). The result was the setting up of the Central Social Welfare Board on 13th August 1953. She became its founder Chairman (1953-1962) and mobilised thousands of voluntary organisations and workers to carry out the programmes of the Board, aiming at education, training and rehabilitation of the needy women, children and the handicapped. Another feather in her cap was the founding of Council for Social Development at New Delhi.

On 22nd January, 1953 she married Dr. C.D. Deshmukh, the then Finance Minister, Government of India. She was honoured for her outstanding contribution to the cause of Peace, Social Welfare, Literacy and work among the downtrodden by national and international agencies. She won Nehru Literacy Award, UNESCO Award for outstanding work in the field of Literacy and was decorated with PADMA VIBHUSHAN.

Durgabai Deshmukh was Member of UN Social Defence Committee; Member of UNESCO's International Liaison Committee for Eradication of Illiteracy 1966-69; Executive Chairman of Population Council of India; Member of All India Nurses Council and Red Cross Society; Chairman of Editorial Committee of Social Welfare in India and Social Legislation; Chairman of Editorial Board of the Encyclopaedia of Social Work in India.

She was a powerful orator in Telegu and English.Her services for women's welfare were truly invaluable

Dr Durgabai Deshmukh died on 9 May, 1981.

20

Durga Khote (1905-1991)

Durga Khote has been one of the most outstanding personalities of Indian cinema, her glorious career covering acting, production and direction. Durga Khote came from an enlightened family of lawyers, shattering the myth that acting was a profession only for women of shady backgrounds. She had enlightened children who married beyond their caste—also remarkable, considering that most married in 1940s/1950s. Her daughter-in-law is the renowned stage director, Vijaya Mehta, whose credits include reviving great Sanskrit plays like *Mrichhakatika* and *Hayavadana* (reinterpreted by Girish Karnad into Hindi and Marathi); performing Brecht's *Caucasian Chalk Circle* in Marathi (as *Ajab Nyay Vartulacha*); and getting a German team to perform Kalidasa's *Shakuntala* in Germany. She is at present the director of the National Center for the Performing Arts at Nariman Point in Bombay. One of the grand-daughters, Tina Khote, made a film on Durga Khote's life.

Her illustrious career in films commenced with the silent movies, Farebi Jaal, in 1931, just before the talkie was emerging. Her first talkie was the bi-lingual (Hindi and Marathi) Ayodhyecha Raja which was produced in

1932. Her career covers a broad spectrum of film making as she moved up from her first silent film to be recognised as one of the greatest actresses of her time. With the studio system in vogue, she worked with Prabhat Film Co. Poona, New theatres and East India (both at Calcutta), Prakash Pictures and was one of the first women, froma respectable middle class family, to break through social barriers by entering films.

As early as 1937, she produced and directed the feature film Saathi, one of the first women to do so. She acted in over 200 films in her career of over 50 years. She diversified into short films, Ad films and documentaries, running her own company, with a great deal of success, for over 25 years.

Though she hit the spot lights with Prabhat Film Co.'s Amar Jyoti, one of her most powerful characterisation was in the title role in Sita which was produced by East India Film Co. at Calcutta. The film was directed by the renowned Debaki Kumar Bose, and she had Prithviraj Kapoor as her co-star. In later life, she moved to character roles and remained active till the age of 80.

Durga Khote was an active participant of the Indian People's Theater Association (IPTA), a progressive, left-leaning movement of artists, writers and playwrights with links with the Communist Party and the Progressive Writers' Association (PWA), and which was incorporated as an all-Indian movement in 1943. She was committed to "democracy" as she understood it. Her family opposed and campaigned against emergency (1975-1977). Durga Khote's grandson, Ravi, makes movies; another grandson, Deven, works with TV, and another relation formed a company called Durga Khote Productions, which produced *Wagle Ki Duniya,* a TV program created by the noted cartoonist, R.K. Laxman.

Durga Khote was the chairperson of the 30th National Film Festival, a member of Jury for short films in 1993. She received National Sangeet Academy Award, State Award for Dhartichi Lekre (1970). BFJA Award for best performance in Charnon Ki Dasi (1941) and Bharat Milap (1942), and Filmfare Award for best supporting actress in Bedai (1974). She was the recipient of the Dadasaheb Phalke award for 1983 and was honoured with Padma Shri award by the President of India.

21

Gangubhai Hangal (1913-)

The renowned Hindustani vocalist, Gangubhai Hangal was born in 1913 to a family of hereditary courtesan musicians from Hangal, a small village near Dharvad in North Karnataka. She was married at the early age of sixteen. As a young girl of eight, she used to stand for hours outside gramophone shop listening to music of the 'magic box' was making. Seeing her daughter's inclination towards Hindustani music, which was somnthing exotic and attractive in the 20's, Ambabai decided to let Gangubai pursue her newly found love. Her mother taught the young Gangubai Carnatic music with a variety of Tyagaraja's compositions. Gangubai learnt Kathak from Shamlal and Prataplal, the Jaipur brothers who were then in Hubli. Sensing her interest, her mother put her under a Hindustani music guru Krishnacharya Hulgur. Gangubhai also learnt Hindustani music from the Kirana Gharana master Sawai Gandharva. She was 16 when put under Sawai Gandharva who lived in the village of Kundgol near Hubli. She used to travel daily from Hubli to Kundgol, where Sawai Gandharva lived, by train to undergo training in the Kirana style of Khayal singing and through sincere efforts, strict discipline and ceaseless practice, perfected the vocal art. This was in the 1930s, when Gangubai—a young mother herself—struggled to do her *sadhana*. She also trained under the great Abdul Karim Khan and made her stage debut at the age of twenty, in Mumbai, where she rendered raga Miya Malhar.

Belonging to the *Kirana Gharana*, Gangubai's music was filled with *bhakti*. She has a very powerful voice, almost masculine, very suitable for traditional classical music. It is husky and robust and has a timbre that leaves a deep impression on the listeners. She sticks to authentic traditional music and does not dabble in the light *bhajans*. Gangubhai's daughter Krishna Hangal has been singing with her and giving much needed support for last 3 decades.

Gangubai's broadcasts from All India Radio made ger name a household word in Maharashtra and Karnataka; and her gramophone records made her known all over India. Gangubhai has been giving concerts for more than 5 decades. In the shadow of this wave of appreciation, she remains a simple woman, wearing a nine-yard Poona cotton sari at home, doing her *riaz* (practice) and treating us to several impromptu sessions of soulful music.

A woman of extraordinary talent and courage, Gangubai Hangal has kept her place in the male-dominated world of Hindustani music for almost a century. She has an air of authority and an almost masculine majesty and she matches sonorous strains of her guru Sawai Gandharwa's style of singing.

Gangubai is one of the four Kannadiga celebrities of Hindustani music, the others being Mallikarjun Mansur, Kumar Gandharva and Bhimsen Joshi. She may not have a high profile like the men in this pantheon. Nevertheless she has held her own and has dedicated her life to the arduous cultivation of her style of expression. Her followers know her emotional involvement with music and appreciate her personal commitment to creative endeavour. These qualities have earned her a pride of place among the great musicians of our time. She always did justice to the *Khayal* in all its intricacy, taking her time over the *alaap* in slow tempo, and thundering her way through the fast *swaras*. She gave new dimensions to *raga Khamaj. Durbari Kanada,* which Gangubai usually began in the lower octaves, was also a *raga* suited to her majestic style. She knew the power of each note and filled the air with the right *rasa* that the raga represented. Perhaps because of her South Indian leanings, Gangubai, like Kishori Amonkar after her, reserved devotional songs for the latter half of a concert. The *Thumri* was not part of her repertoire.

She is counted among the world's oldest performing artists today and among the world's most renowned as well. Gangubai Hangal is the doyen of the Kirana gharana that flourished under the baton of the highly revered Sawai Gandharva.

Gangubai received several honours in recognition of her music. Padma Bhushan, Sangeet Natak Akademi award, Tansen Samman, Dinanath Pratishthan Award are just a few top accolades. In 2002, she was honoured with Padma Vibhushan, the second highest civilian award. Gangubai has toured abroad, notably France, the U.S., Canada and Germany. Gangubai has become a legend in her lifetime.

22

Girija Vyas Dr. (1946-)

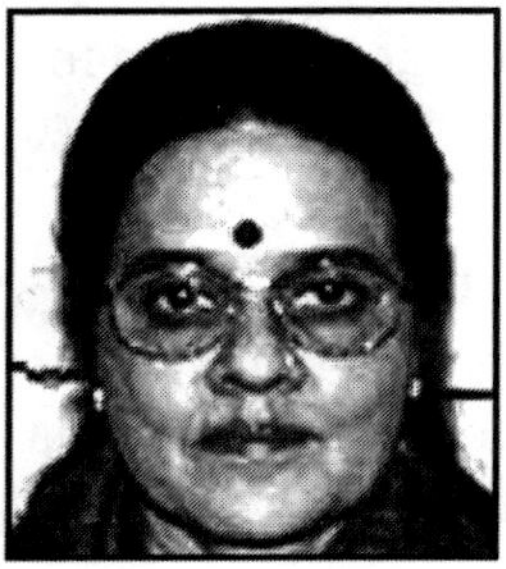

Born on 8 July 1946, Dr. Girija Vyas did her Masters in Philosophy, 1967, and doctrate (Ph D), 1973, from the University of Udaipur and post Doctoral Fellowship at the University of Deleware (USA) in 1979-80. She was awarded Gold medal for securing 1st position in M.Phil in the University in 1967. She worked as Associate Professor, Professor and Head of Department of Philosphy, University of Udaipur. She also taught at University of Deleware, USA, in 1979-80.

In 1985, she was elected member of Rajasthan Legislative Assembly from Udaipur and was Minister of the Rajasthan Government till 1990. In 1991, she contested Lok Sabha election and won and was appointed Deputy Minister in the Central Government. She was re-elected to Lok Sabha in 1996 and 1999 and has been Member of Lok Sabha till 2004. Dr Vyas was appointed Chairperson of the National Commission for Women in February 2005.

Dr Girija Vyas was President, All India Mahila Congress and Spokesperson of All India congress Committee, 1996-2000, and President, Pradesh Congress Committee, 2001.

Dr Vyas visited Chicago, Ohio, Pennsylvania to deliver lectures at various universities and academic institutions on the 'role of Indian Women', The Song of Mahandura, Hindu Philosophy, Love and Sex, respectively. She organized 29th 04. Currently, she is Chairperson, Media Department, All India Congress Committee and Member, Indo-EU Civil Society. session of All India Philosophical Congress at Udaipur, 1982; chaired World Urdu Conference in Mauritius, 1992; attended World Conference on women issues in Berlin, 1993 and chaired Women Conference in Sri Lanka, 1995; was a member of Indian delegation to UNO, 1997; attended UN summit on women in Beijing, 1997, World Spiritual Conference in Taiwan, 1997; represented India on the occasion of Queen Elizabeth Golden Jubilee function in London, 2002.

She has written several books including 'Ethical Teaching of Gita and Bible', 'Philosophy of Shuddhavaita', 'Seep, Samandar, Moti', 'Nostalgia and other poems', 'Philosophy of Democracy'.

23

Hema Malini (1948-)

Born in a remote village of Tamil Nadu on Oct 16, 1948, Hema Malini rocked the Hindi filmdom for nearly two decades and is still going on well. Having faced rejection, at the hands of a little known Tamilan director early in her life when she was barely 15, Hema Malini turned her attention to Bollywood and became one of the most popular and probably the single most admired female stars of 70s Hindi cinema. Hema Malini was the second South Indian actress after Vyjayantimala to be a major Hindi film star. Her beauty was considered beyond comparison and her screen presence simply excellent. She was popularly called the evergreen Dream girl and that perception still lingers on in peoples' minds.

A trained Bharat Natyam dancer, she made her debut in films with Raj Kapoor's 'Sapnon Ka Saudagar' in 1968. After a few moderate films she got break with 'Johnny Mera Naam', which turned out to be a golden jubilee hit, co-starring with the evergreen Dev Anand. But it was with 'Seeta Aur Geeta' in 1972, that she established herself as queen of box-office. The double role in this film as twin sisters won her the Best Actress Award. Following a series of hits like 'Raja Jani' (1972), 'Jugnu' (1973), 'Sholay'

(1975), 'Dream Girl' (1977) and many more with Dharmendra and also starring opposite Amitabh Bachchan, in series of hit films like 'Naseeb' (1981), 'Desh Premee' (1982), 'Satte Pe Satta' (1982) 'she strengthened her position further. With a glamour girl image attached to her, she proved her acting abilities with sensitive performance in 'Laal Patthar' (1971), 'Khushboo' (1975), 'Kinara' (1977), 'Meera' (1979). Some of her other films which became popular were : Kasauty,Sharaafat, Razia Sultan (as director), Jwaar Bhaata, Raja Jani, Mehbooba. The late seventies and early eighties was the golden era of her career when she held the number one slot for excellent roles and song-dance sequences. Along with Rekha and Vijayanthimala, Hema Malini possessed a style and grace in her dance that was transcendent. In the late 70s she concentrated on 'character' roles as in *Rihaee,* often with feminist undertones. She also put her creative instincts to good use by producing films like Swami (1977), Sharara (1984), Aawargi (1987. Her latest picture *Baghban* (2003) in which she played a charater role was a hit. Hema Malini is expected to figure in Telugu remake of *Baghban.*

At a time when she was riding the crest of popularity, certain famed actors proposed her for marriage. But Hema Malini married Dharmendra in 1980. The marriage not only prospered, but also made Dharmendra-Hema one of the most sought after Bollywood couples.

Hema Malini has played romantic heroine in over 100 Hindi films. She directed TV serials Noopur (1990) and Women of India (1996). Hema Malini was and still remains one of the most popular and most loved female stars of Hindi cinema.

Apart from being one of the best loved actresses of Hindi cinema, Hema is also a superb dancer. She has performed over 1000 shows in India and abroad and runs a popular school for classical dance and music in Chennai, known as Natya Vichar Kalakendram.

Lately Hema is busy casting the careers of her daughters Esha and Ahna. She edits two women's magazines, namely, "Meri Saheli" (Hindi) and "New Woman" (English). In the latest scramble of stars joining political parties, Hema too has joined BJP. Hema got the Filmfare award in 1972. In 1992, Hema Malini was awarded the Padma Bhushan for her contribution to Indian films and the society. In August 2003, the President of India nominated her to the Rajya Sabha.

24

Indira Gandhi (1917–1984)

Prime minister of India from 1966-77 and 1980-84 and one of the most famous women in 20th century politics, Indira Gandhi was the only child of Kamla Nehru and Jawaharlal Nehru Independent India's first prime minister (1947-64). She was born on November 19, 1917 in Allahabad and named Indira Priyadarshni. She had education in Switzerland, Oxford, Bombay, Pune and at Shantiniketan. In early teens, Indira became the leader of Monkey Brigade, a children's group set up by Congress Party to keep a watch on the police movements and be a medium of communication between freedom fighters. In 1938, Indira Gandhi formally joined the Indian National Congress Party. In 1942, she married journalist Feroze Gandhi to whom she bore two sons, Rajiv (who went on to become Prime Minister after her death) and Sanjay. Soon after their marriage, she joined the 'Quit India' Movement (1942) along with her husband and was arrested and jailed. The imprisonment lasted from September 11, 1942 until May 13, 1943 at the Naini Central Jail in Allahabad. Feroze Gandhi died in 1960

After attainment of Independence in 1947, her father, Jawaharlal Nehru, became Prime Minister. Since her mother had died in 1936, Indira Gandhi acted as hostess and confidante of her father and travelled with him all over India and abroad. In 1959, Indira Gandhi became the president of the Indian National Congress, the fourth woman to hold this office.

After her father's death in 1964, Indira Gandhi was appointed a minister in the cabinet of Congress Prime Minister Lal Bahadur Shastri. When Lal Bahadur Shastri died in 1966, Indira Gandhi was chosen by Congress Party to succeed him as Prime Minister. Congress Party won the following general elections in 1967 and Indira Gandhi was elected to head the Congress government. Being short on words, initially she was dubbed as *goongi gudiya* (dumb doll). Initially, it was also said that, being a woman occupying the high position, Indira Gandhi would be a passive leader and a puppet in the hands of senior Congress leaders. But, as time passed, she not only turned out to be a fluent and effective speaker but also emerged to be one of the strongest leaders in the history of the independent India. Her strong personality gave rise to a rift between her and certain senior Congress leaders which came to head In 1969. The Congress party, which was then controlled by her opponents, expelled her for "indiscipline", an action that split the party into two factions: the Congress (O)—for Organisation—under Morarji Desai, and the Congress (R)—for Requisition—under Indira Gandhi. She continued as Prime Minister with support from communists and regional parties.

In the fifth general elections in March 1971, Indira Gandhi campaigned fiercely on the platform "Banish poverty" (*garibi hatao*) and Congress (R) gained a large majority in Parliament paving way for her re-election as Prime Minister. In August 1971, Indira Gandhi signed the twenty-year Treaty of Peace, Friendship, and Cooperation with the Soviet Union. Then came the war with Pakistan in December 1971. India's decisive victory over Pakistan in the war leading to the creation of Bangladesh as an independent nation separate from Pakistan generated a national surge in her popularity.

Indira Gandhi nationalised the banks for which she received immediate approval from the masses. She also took the initiative of discontinuing privy purses-personal allowance payments to India's princely states, which she felt were anachronistic given India's democratic post-independence character. Her efforts at achieving self-sufficiency for India in food grains production—the Green Revolution—achieved consummate success. In 1971, India sent its first satellite into space. Victory in war against Pakistan and other achievements led to her party, the Congress (R), sweeping the state legislative assembly elections in a number of states in 1972. Indira Gandhi gave a push to India's nuclear programme and under her leadership India carried out its first nuclear tests in 1974.

In 1975, Indira Gandhi's election to Lok Sabha was set aside by Allahabad High Court, but the High Court ruling was over-turned by Supreme Court. In view of many anti-government agitations started by the opposition parties, Indira Gandhi declared a State of Emergency in the country on June 26, 1975, assumed extraordinary powers and suspended civil rights. Emergency rule lasted nineteen months. It was lifted in January 1977 and in the general elections held a couple of months later, she and Congress Party were voted out of office.

During the period she remained out of office, she faced a judicial inquiry and went through difficult times at the hands of the then government. But, with the re-gained support and sympathy of the people, she emerged unscathed out of all that turmoil.

In the next general elections held in January 1980, Indira Gandhi and her party, renamed Congress (I)–'I' for Indira-campaigned on the slogan "Elect a Government That Works!" and made a spectacular comeback. Indira Gandhi was once again elected Prime Minister, this time as leader of the Congress (Indira) party.

As part of strong action against terrorist outfits in Punjab, Indira Gandhi launched "Operation Blue Star" to flush out terrorists taking shelter in the Golden Temple. This action against their holiest shrine caused deep distress among the Sikhs. On October 31, 1984, Indira Gandhi's Sikh bodyguards assassinated her to avenge what had happened in Golden Temple.

Indira Gandhi's regime was marked by some radical developments in political field. Economically, Indira Gandhi led India to one of the fastest growing economies in the world. She acquired a formidable reputation as a "statesman" who possessed extraordinary skill in national and international politics. She was a brilliant political strategist and thinker who met all the problems and challenges head-on and succeeded. Her charm, intelligence and charisma made her a powerful leader, much loved and admired by her people.

25

Indra Nooyi (1956-)

President and Chief Financial Officer of PepsiCo, the world's third largest food and beverage company, Indra Nooyi was born in 1956 in Chennai, previously Madras, India.

Indra Nooyi's academic career began with her graduation from Madras Christian College in India, where she earned a bachelor's degree in Chemistry, Physics and Math, followed by an MBA in Finance and Marketing from the Indian Institute of Management in Calcutta. She also holds a master's degree in Public and Private Management from the Yale School of Management in New Haven, Connecticut, in the United States. At Yale, Indra was a member of the President's Council on International Activities, and recently served as a featured speaker at Yale's Tricentennial celebration and the Yale School of Management's 25th anniversary.

Prior to attending Yale, Indra Nooyi spent time in southern India where she challenged traditional roles as a guitarist with a rock band and involvement with a women's cricket team. After completing her MBA in Calcutta, she began her career in India, where she held product manager positions at Johnson & Johnson and at Mettur Beardsell, Ltd., a textile firm. It was while working for Johnson & Johnson that Indra decided to continue her education at Yale.

Indra Nooyi is President and Chief Financial Officer of PepsiCo, as well as a member of the company's Board of Directors, a position she assumed in May 2001. She is responsible for PepsiCo's corporate functions, including finance, strategy, business process optimization, corporate platforms and innovation, procurement, investor relations and information technology. Previously, from February 2000 through April 2001, Indra was Senior Vice President and Chief Financial Officer of PepsiCo, when she played an instrumental role in PepsiCo's merger with The Quaker Oats Company. From 1996 to 1999, she was Senior Vice President of Corporate Strategy and Development.

Before joining PepsiCo in 1994, Indra Nooyi served as Senior Vice President of Strategy and Strategic Marketing for four years at Asea Brown Boveri, a leading global supplier in the electric power industry. She was part of the top management team responsible for the company's U.S. business and its worldwide industrial businesses.

From 1986 to 1990, Indra Nooyi was at Motorola, joining the company as the business development executive for its automotive and industrial electronic group and becoming its Vice President and Director of Corporate Strategy and Planning. Before that, she directed international corporate strategy projects for six years at Boston Consulting Group.

In addition to her role as a member of the Board of Directors of PepsiCo., Inc., Indra Nooyi serves as Successor Fellow at Yale Corporation. She is a member of the boards of Motorola, the International Rescue Committee and Lincoln Center for the Performing Arts in New York City. Indra is a member of many other boards, including the advisory boards of Yale School of Management, PlaNet Finance and Greenwich Breast Cancer Alliance, and the Board of Trustees of Eisenhower Fellowships and Asia Society. She is a member of The Trilateral Commission, which is a group dedicated to addressing leadership issues and responsibilities across North America, Asia and Asia-Pacific, as well as Europe.

Indra Nooyi is committed to expanding multi-cultural and diversity awareness, as well as to providing leadership and achieving high performance and excellence in all that she does. Two of the factors she cites as contributing to this mindset are her exposure to various cultures and her parents' teachings that "if you do a job, do it better than anybody else."

She is proud of her Indian origin and attends many of PepsiCo events in her traditional *sari*. Indra believes the corporate world appreciates people who are genuine, and because of this has made "Be Yourself" one of her life principles. She attributes her success to many factors, including upbringing, motivation, dedicated employees– and lots of hard work.

Indra Nooyi's personal passions include two daughters; one in college and the other in grade school. She and her husband live in Fairfield County, Connecticut. Indra Nooyi has been ranked as one of the 50 most powerful women in America by *Fortune* magazine. She is the highest-ranking Indian-born woman in corporate America.

26

Indrani Rehman

One of the greatest dancers of our time, Indrani Rehman was among the luminous names of sixties and seventies who carried the glory of Indian classical arts to all corners of the world, through her varied performances imbued with grace of body and spirit, and her mastery over several dance forms. She had studied with leading gurus in India to master the contrasting styles of Bharata Natyam, Kuchipudi, Mohini Attam and Odissi in the 1950's. She was disciple in Bharatnatyam of Pandanallur Chokkalingam Pillai; studied Mohini Attam at Kerala Kalamandalam with Chinnammu Amma. To Indrani Rehman goes the credit for bringing the Odissi to the national and international dance scene. When this form was languishing in Orissa, she took the initiative to study it from Guru Debaprasad Das. Her role in giving Odissi a national and international profile is unmatched. From her childhood, Indrani Rehman had been brought up in an atmosphere conducive to the study of dance.

While Indrani Rehman's name is well known to admirers of Indian classical dance, it is a lesser known fact that her husband Habib Rehman, a leading architect, was the designer of Rabindra Bhawan, the building that houses the Sangeet Natak, Sahitya and Lalit Kala Akademies in Mandi House, New Delhi. Indrani Rehman's story has an interesting twist relating to her devotion and commitment to dance. When she got married at the age of 15, she had her husband sign a contract that he would not stop her from dancing.

In the year 1952, she won the Miss India title. At that time, this contest was something of a novelty, and pictures of Indrani in a classical dance pose were on the front pages of almost every newspaper. Indrani Rahman, a married Muslim mother of one, was elected by the country's press to represent India at Miss Universe pageant when it was first held in 1952 in Long Beach, California.

After her dance debut in New York in 1960, Indrani became a highly respected figure in the dance world there. By 1975, she was giving performances at leading universities across the United States. She taught at the Juilliard School, the New York State University College of Arts, and at Harvard University's Summer Dance Center. As a teacher at the Juilliard School, she played a vital role as a producer of Indian classical dance concerts, having her own troupe and featuring younger exponents. Her mother, Ragini Devi, and her daughter, Sukanya, were also gifted performers. In New York in 1979, they performed together in "Three Generations of Indian Classical Dance." Indrani followed naturally the footsteps of her mother who was internationally known for her leading role in the revival of Indian classical dances in the the 1930's.

Indrani's repertoire consisted of compositions, choreographic creations and traditional numbers as taught to her by her guru. Her repertoire reflected the earlier versions of Odissi when it was emerging as a classical dance form.

Indrani was an artist of international repute, often appearing before heads of state in her native India and abroad. In 1961 she performed for John F. Kennedy and Prime Minister Jawaharlal Nehru during Nehru's official visit to Washington. She also performed for such figures as Queen Elizabeth II, Chou En Lai, Gamal Abdel Nasser and Nikita Kruschev. Indrani Rehman did not let advancing age stop her from promoting Bharat Natyam overseas. Having settled in the United States, Indrani had become a distant legend for dance enthusiasts in India.

Indrani received numerous awards which included the Indian Government's national award, the Padma Shri; the Sangeet Natak Akademi Award; Natya Kala Bushan; Sahitya Kala Parishad Award; the Key to the City of New York.

Indrani Rehman passed away on 5 February 1999 in New York.

27

Jaya Bachchan (1948-)

Jaya Bachchan (nee Bhaduri), daughter of noted author-journalist Taroon Kumar, was born on 9 April, 1948 at Kolkata. She married the legendary star of Indian cinema Amitabh Bachchan on 3 June 1973.

Acting opportunites came Jaya's way early. She was still in her teens when she got her first break in Mahanagar in 1963, a Satyajit Ray film. At the close of the decade, she won rave reviews for her role as Uttam Kumar's sister in the Bengali film, Dhanni Meye. After graduating from the Film and Television Institute of India at Pune, Jaya landed in Mumbai with a role in Hrishikesh Mukherjee's film Guddi in 1971 in which she played the role of a star struck fan. As the giggly Guddi who relieves her boring school days with fantasies of a film star, Jaya etched a persona that the whole country could identify with–and love. Her success in 'Guddi' brought her offers in several Hindi movies. In a short span she figured in several films most of which proved big hits. She has acted with almost all the superstars of her time, but her films with Sanjeev Kumar and Amitabh Bachchan were spell-binding and highly applauded. Her talents were well exhibited in films like Koshish, Kora Kagaz, Bawarchi, Sholay, Milli, Chupke Chupke, Parichay, Silsila, Nauker and Abhimaan. She has worked with the best directors of the Hindi cinema from Yash Chopra, Ramesh Sippy, Govind Nihalani to Karan Johar.

Jaya Bachchan has always been involved with quality cinema and is a highly respected figure in the Indian Film industry. She now takes up only a few select films and she is currently actively involved in doing theatre. Live, energetic and versatile Jaya is not a mere name in film industry but is a living legend. She is one of few actresses who has consistently shunned female glamour. Glamour and artificiality have been anthema to Jaya, professionally and personally. She would begin each film trying to look the conventional glamorous heroine but would, as the story unfurled, revert back to the normal self. In real life too, Jaya is labeled as conservative icon with the '*saree pallu*'. Since starring in Satyajit Ray's *Mahanagar* (The Big City 1963), she has come to be recognised as a rare champion of naturalistic performance on the Indian screen.

In October 2003, Jaya Bachchan was appointed the chairperson of State Film Development Corporation of U.P. with cabinet rank. She was elected to Rajya Sabha from U.P in 2004. Jaya has engaged herself actively in several social causes besides spearheading the Children's Film Society some years ago. She has also worked actively towards the upliftment of her *alma mater,* The Film and Television Institute of India, Pune. The other issues that have been engaging her attention have been education and healthcare for women and children and facilities and care of mentally and physically challenged children.

She bagged Best Actress awards for her performances in Kora Kagaz (1975) and Nauker (1980). Jaya has also won awards for her stylised performances in Fiza (2000) and Kabhie Khushi Kabhie Gham (2001). In 1998, Omega, the prestigious Swiss watch company, presented "The Lifetime Achievement" award for India's legendary couple Amitabh and Jaya Bachchan. Jaya Bachchan headed the Alexandria Film Festival jury 2001.

28

Jhumpa Lahiri (1967-)

Jhumpa Lahiri, an Indian-American of Bengali descent, was born 1967 in London, England, and raised in Rhode Island. Her given name is Nilanjana Sudeshna. It is said that a school teacher found this name too long and used her nickname *Jhumpa* instead by which name she is now known.

She is a graduate in English literature of Barnard College (1989). She did her M.A. in English, M.A. in Creative Writing, M.A. in Comparative Studies in Literature and the Arts, and Ph.D. in Renaissance Studies from Boston University.

She has taught creative writing at Boston University and the Rhode Island School of Design. Her first book, *Interpreter of Maladies*, a collection of nine stories, was published as a Mariner original paperback in June 1999 to overwhelming acclaim. Her stories concern the lives of Indian-Americans and the nuances of their lives. *Interpreter of Maladies* won the 2000 Pulitzer Prize for Fiction, the PEN/Hemingway Award, the American Academy of Arts and Letters Addison M. Metcalf Award, was a Los Angeles Times Book Award finalist, and was named Best Debut of the Year by The New Yorker. Lahiri was awarded a Guggenheim fellowship in 2002. It was translated into twenty-nine languages and became a bestseller both in the United States and abroad. She has been hailed as a writer of uncommon elegance and poise.

Her second book and first novel, *The Namesake,* was published in 2003. In May 2000, "The Third and Final Continent," a story by Lahiri that ran in a summer 1999 fiction issue of The New Yorker was one of three stories that won the magazine a National Magazine Award for Fiction.

In 1999, she was named by The New Yorker as "one of the 20 best writers under the age of 40." She was a recipient of Transatlantic Review Award from Henfield Foundation and fiction prize from the Louisville Review, and was fellow at the Fine Arts Work Center in Province town.

Currently, Jhumpa Lahiri lives and works in Brooklyn, New York with her Guatemalan-American husband and their son Octavio.

29

J. Jayalalithaa (1948-)

J Jayalalitha is the Chief Minister of Tamil Nadu, India (since March 2, 2002). She was also Chief Minister from 24-06-1991 to 12-05-1996 and from 14-05-2001 to 21-09-2001. In 1981, she joined the AIADMK (All India Anna Dravida Munnetra Kazhagam-a regional party in the state) and became its Propaganda Secretary. In 1984 she became member of the Rajya Sabha. She was Deputy Leader of the Party. In 1989, she was elected to the Tamil Nadu legislative assembly where she became the first woman to be elected Leader of the Opposition. In 1991, she was re-elected to the legislative assembly and became Chief Minister for the first time. She is the General Seceretary of AIADMK). She has earned the sobriquet of 'Iron Lady' and came to be known as 'Puratchi Tallaivi' (Tevolutionary Leader). She is also popularly called "amma" (mother) by her followers.

Jayalalitha was born on February 24, 1948 in Mysore to actress Sandhya. She was educated at the Bishop Cotton Girls High School in Bangalore and later at the Presentation Convent Church Park in Chennai. On completion of Matriculation in 1964, she won a scholarship from Government of India for higher studies but did not accept it as she took up a career in films in Tamil, Telugu, Kannada, Hindi, English and Malayalam. Although she hails from Karnataka, she has identified herself with Tamil Nadu.

She was trained in classical dance (Bharata Natyam) and Carnatic Music from the age of 4 onwards. She is proficient in other dance-forms such as Mohini Attam, Kuchipudi, Kathak, Manipuri. She made a debut in Bharatnatyam at the age of 12. She has given performances in Bharatha Natyam all over India and has sung several songs herself in her films. She is proficient in English, Tamil, Telugu, Kannada, Hindi and can understand Malayalam also.

Prior to her venture into politics, she had a successful career in the film industry as an actor. *Chinnada Gombe,* her first film (in Kannada) was a major hit. Her first Telugu film *Manushulu Mamathalu* made her a superstar. She has played leading roles in 115 films in Tamil, Telugu, Kannada and one each in Hindi and English and won several awards. In 1972, she was honoured by the Tamil Nadu Government with the award *Kalaimamani.*

J Jayalalithaa has been honoured with a number of Degrees by various Universities: Doctor of Literature (D. Litt) by University of Madras in 1991; Doctor of Science by TN Dr MGR Medical University in 1992; Doctor of Letters by Madurai Kamaraj University in 199; Doctor of Science by Tamil Nadu Agricultural University in 2003. Doctor of Letters by Bharathidasan University in 2003.

30

Jijabai (1594-1674)

Jijabai was the mother of Shivaji. She was married to Shahaji Bhosle who was in the service of Ahmednagar kingdom. She was born in 1594 in the town of Sindhkhed in Maharashtra to Maratha Sardar, Lakhuji Jadhav Rao, and Malasa Bai. Her father was a descendant of the Yadava kings of Devagiri and a powerful Sardar of the court of Nizam Shah of Ahmednagar.

Jijaji gave birth to two sons, Sambhaji and Shivaji. In 1630, Shahaji contracted a second marriage with Tukabai. After this Jijabai seems to have broken all but formal relations with her husband.

In course of time, her father Jadhav Rao, who was with the Moghuls, and her husband Shahaji who was with the Nizam happened to be in opposite camps. Jijabai had to choose between her loyalty to her father and that to her husband. She threw in her lot with her husband. Jijabai was indignant with the Maratha Jagirdars and Sardars serving under Moghul and Nizam rulers. She was unhappy because both her father and her husband were also spending their lives in the service of the those rulers. She used to pray "Oh Rudramba, give me the strength of one of your arms. I want to see an independent and powerful Maratha Emperor shining in the glory of his own flag and his own army." She used to wish how blessed she would be if only she could give birth to a son like Bhima or Arjuna and her son could put begin a new chapter of liberty and self-respect in the country. When Shivaji was born she deemed it to be her prime mission to make him the saviour of his country. Jijabai narrated stories of bravery to her son Shivaji and gave him training in martial arts and equipped him for the role he was to play in the years to come. Jijabai was a woman of austere and religious temperament. Her constant companionship, advice and reading of Hindu scriptures and especially the Mahabharata and the Ramayana, instilled in young Shivaji's mind a burning hatred for wrong and injustice, a pride in the past glory of his country and an intense desire to liberate it from foreign rule. Shivaji's bravery, skill and exploits were the direct result of the training he received from his mother Jijabai and she remained the silent source of strength inspiration and power behind him. She also imbued him with religious tolerance, justice and fair play.

Jijabai had a high sense of self-respect, a heart as strong as steel, and a deep religious consciousness. Under her orders many temples were built in Pune. Whenever holy men came to Pune, Jijabai used to make Shivaji offer them service. There great refinement, their teachings and blessings infused new strength into Shivaji's body. Jijabai laid foundations for the prosperity of the neighbouring villages by her orderly administration. She herself settled disputes and meted out justice in the open court. The far-sighted Jijabai brought up her son in such a way that his father's aloofness did not cause young Shivaji unhappiness or pain. Love of his country, his religion, freedom and justice were the firm foundations on which she raised the structure of Shivaji's life. Jijabai taught Shivaji to honour all women and he rigidly enforced it. Jijabai was opposed to forcible conversions. She did not subscribe to the view that a convert was lost to his religion for ever.

In January 1664 Shahaji fell from his horse and died. The news of Shahaji's death was a bolt from the blue to Shivaji and Jijabai. She was so overcome by sorrow that she decided to perform 'sati', burning herself on the pyre. But Shivaji begged of her to give up the decision and finally she agreed. In 1666, when, at Emperor Aurangzeb's invitation, Shivaji left for Agra, Jijabai was appointed head of the council of regency for the little kingdom of Poona during his absence.

Shivaji wanted his mother to be by his side when a free state, for which he and Jijabai were working, would be born. The auspicious day dawned soon. Jijabai advised Shivaji to take the royal crown not from the hands of a Moghul but from a priest of Benaras. On the thirteenth day in the month of Jyestha of the Hindu year Ananda (1674), Jijabai witnessed the coronation of her son Shivaji. But fate was cruel. On the twelth day after the coronation of Shivaji, the great and noble mother Jijabai passed away. She was 80 then.

Jijabai's life is an example of how a mother can transform the lives of individuals, society and even a nation.

31

Kalpana Chawla (1961-2003)

Astronaut Dr Kalpana Chawla was born on 1 July 1961 in Karnal (India). She died on February 1, 2003 over the southern United States when Space Shuttle *Columbia* and her crew perished during entry.

Kalpana Chawla graduated from Tagore School, Karnal, India, in 1976 and acquired Bachelor of Sience degree in aeronautical engineering from Punjab Engineering College, India, 1982. She did Master of Science degree in aerospace engineering from University of Texas, 1984 did Doctorate of Philosophy in aerospace engineering from University of Colorado, 1988.

Kalpana Chawla was an avid maker of aero-models as a child. She considered it her birthright to be a 'resident of the milky way' becoming the second Indian after IAF officer Rakesh Sharma to go to Space. She wanted to go the Mars. Her motto was 'follow your dreams'. A naturalised American, She never forgot the pull of her roots. For the Indian American community, she epitomised the indomitable spirit of Indian womanhood. In answer to a question about her original identity she quoted the philosopher Seneca "I was not born for one corner; the whole world is my native land." The central element of her success in one word was perseverance.

In 1988, Kalpana Chawla started work at NASA Ames Research Center. In 1993 she joined Overset Methods Inc., Los Altos, California, as Vice President and Research Scientist to form a team with other researchers specializing in simulation of moving multiple body problems.

Selected by NASA in December 1994, Kalpana reported to the Johnson Space Center in March 1995 as an astronaut candidate in the 15th Group of Astronauts. In November, 1996, she was assigned as mission specialist and prime robotic arm operator on STS-87. In January 1998, she was assigned as crew representative for shuttle and station flight crew equipment, and subsequently served as lead for Astronaut Office's Crew Systems and Habitability section. The 16-day flight of STS-107 *Columbia* (January 16 to February 1, 2003 was a dedicated science and research mission. The STS-107 mission ended abruptly on February 1, 2003 when Space Shuttle *Columbia* and her crew perished during entry, 16 minutes prior to scheduled landing.

She was posthumously awarded the Congressional Space Medal of Honor, the NASA Space Flight Medal, and the NASA Distinguished Service Medal.

32

Kamladevi Chattopadhyaya (1903-1988)

A Gandhian, a reformer, an orator and an author who always cherished to work for upliftment of the socio-economic standard of women, Kamaladevi Chattopadhyaya was born in 1903 in a wealthy Saraswat family of Mangalore in South Karnataka. She had her education at a Catholic Convent and St. Mary's College, Mangalore, and later at Bedford College and London School of Economics.

She was married in 1914 when she was yet in her teens. Tragically, her young husband passed away within a year. In 1919 at the age of sixteen she married Harindranath Chattopadhyaya, the poet-musician-actor brother of well-known leader Sarojini Naidu.The marriage broke up not long after but not before Kamaladevi bore a son. In 1933, when she took divorce, few upper-class women would have dared do so. The divorce exposed her not only to the wrath of her sister-in-law Sarojini Naidu but also to the displeasure of Mahatma Gandhi.

Kamaladevi's exposure to politics came from icons of the freedom struggle like Gopalakrishna Gokhale, Ranade and Annie Besant, who were friends of her family. After her meeting with Margaret Cousins, a key figure in the Suffragist movement in the West, Kamaladevi joined active politics and became the first woman to contest in 1926 a seat in the Legislative Assembly of Madras province, only to be defeated.

Kamaladevi was a member of the All India Congress Committee, and also of its Working Committee. She participated in the Civil Disobedience movement and was imprisoned on several occasions for her anti-imperialist stand and strong speeches. In 1936, Kamaladevi became president of the Congress Socialist Party, which had leaders like Jayaprakash Narayan, Ram Manohar Lohia and Minoo Masani. Throughout her long involvement in the freedom movement, she stood up for women's rights. When Mahatma Gandhi opposed the inclusion of women in the salt satyagraha march, Kamaladevi spoke out against this stand.

Kamaladevi was a front rank leader in women's movement in India. She played great role in the growth of All India women's conference. She was Organising Secretary, Vice-President and President of All India Women's Conference. She pressed for a uniform civil code as a means to promote gender justice and worked hard for the prevention of child marriage.

After a much talked about debut on stage-considered thoroughly improper for women from respectable families at that time-she blazed a trail for women all over the country. With her poet-playwright second husband Harindranath Chattopadhyay, she performed across India, experimented with regional drama, and even acted in two silent films. In 1944 she set up the Indian National Theatre for the promotion of a 'nationalist theatre'. She stressed on the folk heritage in the performing arts, and set up a theatre crafts museum in Delhi to preserve these forms. She set up the National School of Drama in Delhi, and later headed the Sangeet Natak Akademi.

After Independence, Kamaladevi entered a new phase in her life. Refusing offers of posts such as Union Minister, Governership, Ambassadorships and even Vice-Presidentship, she immersed herself in causes that stirred her spirit of service. Kamaladevi threw herself into humanitarian service, drawing up a refugee rehabilitation model based on the principle of cooperation. The Indian Cooperative Union, despite huge obstacles, finally managed to create an industrial township called Faridabad on the outskirts of Delhi, founded entirely on community effort.

When Kamaladevi was looking for other causes which would combine artistic creativity and public service, another opportunity came her way in 1952. At the behest of the Planning Commission, the Cottage Industries Board was divided and Kamaladevi was appointed chairman of the All-India Handicrafts Board. She travelled to remote corners of India to revive handicrafts traditions that were in danger of dying out and made it a vigorous industry. Equating artisans with artists, she constituted several awards for these master craftsmen. She was also appointed Chairman, All India Design Centre, Vice-President, World Crafts Council and President, Indian cooperative union. Another institution which flowered under her is the India International Centre.

Many of her ideas that seemed radical then are accepted today, like the right to maternity leave and child care and the need to consider women's unpaid household labour an economic activity. Her study on the abject situation of women in the mining industry led to her deep association with labour unions.

Kamaladevi won several honours such as Magsaysay Award, the World Crafts Council award, UNESCO recognition and the Padma Vibhushan.

Kamadevi passed away on 29 October 1988. On her death in 1988, President R. Venkataraman said he found it difficult to prefix the word 'late' to Kamaladevi's name, because "hers was, and will always be a palpable presence". The truth of that statement seems undeniable today, as so many of the cultural institutions in India are a gift of her vision.

33

Kamala Nehru (1899-1936)

Kamla Nehru (nee Kaul)-born 1899-was the daughter of Pandit Jawaharlal Mul, a businessman of Delhi. She was married to Jawaharlal Nehru who was later to become the top Congress leader. Her selection as bride was made by Jawaharlal's father, Motilal Nehru, before Jawaharlal returned to India from England where he had been sent for higher studies. Motilal Nehru had informed his son that his wife-to-be was a twelve year old girl named Kamla Kaul-"A little beauty and...very healthy". All JawarharLal had to do was give his assent.

In 1915 when Kamla was sixteen, she came to live in Allahabad in order to be groomed as Jawaharlal's wife. Coming from a traditional Kashimiri family, Kamla was not conversant with of European manners and habits. The Nehru daughters' governess, Miss Hooper, undertook Kamla's training in the use of cutlery and speaking English. Kamla was a serious and intense girl of beauty but she was shy and withdrawn. The marriage date was selected by family astrologers: 8 February 1916 which was Basant Panchami. At the age of 17 she gave birth to the only daughter Indira Priyadarshini in Anand Bhawan, Allahabad.

Kamala was a woman of great courage and determination who played a notable part in the freedom struggle. With Jawaharlal away in prison, Kamala took to social work to begin with. She started a dispensary in her house in Allahabad and also started a movement for women's education and to get them out of *purdah*. As a member of the Rashtriya Stree Sabha Kamala Nehru worked for the entry of Harijan into temples.

In March 1930 Mahatma Gandhi organized 'Salt Satyagraha and civil disobedience' movement. Kamala, who was ill but had been longing 'To play her own part in the national struggle and not to be merely a hanger-on and a shadow of her husband', put on a white Khadi congress volunteer uniform and went with her daughter Indira and a band of congress women to picket the British-staffed Ewing Christian college in Allahabad. Kamala fainted in the mid-day sun and was brough back home. Kamala Nehru was first among the group of volunteers to sell contraband salt during the Salt Satyagraha. All through the long months of 1930, the Desh Sevika Sangh which she led along with Kusturba Gandhi and Sarojini Naidu, did hard jobs like policing disturbed areas in Bombay. While the men were in jail, they took over. On new year eve (1930) Kamala was arrested by the British police and lodged in Mallaca jail in Allahabad. She was released on 26th January 1931. Her brave and heroic role in the freedom struggle left an imprint on the nationalist movement.

Because Kamla was relatively unsophisticated, reserved and could not speak fluent English, she did not receive attention from the ladies of the house which was due. She suffered intensely in this atmosphere and this affected her health. She fell ill with cough and high fever which persisted and in course of time was diagnosed as pulmonary Tuberculosis. When the treatment at Lucknow could not control the disease, she was taken to Switzerland in 1926 for specialist treatment. Noticing some improvement in her health, she was brought back to India towards the end of 1927. In 1935, her condition again became bad and she was taken to Vienna (Austria) then to Berlin (Germany) for surgery. On receiving disturbing reports on Kamla's condition, Government of India released Jawaharlal Nehru from jail on compassionate grounds and he was with Kamla in Switzerland in September 1935. Kamala Nehru died in clinique Sylvana in Lausanne (Switzerland) on 28 February 1936 at a very young age of 37. She was cremated there and her ashes were brought to India by Jawaharlal Nehru.

34

Karnam Malleswari (1979-)

First Indian woman ever to win an Olympic medal in weight lifting, Karnam Malleswari was born on 1 June 1979 at Voosavanipeta village of Srikakulam district in Andhra Pradesh. She had her school education from Z.P.P.G. High School in the nearby town of Amadalavalasa. Third in a family of six children of Rarndas, a constable with the Railway Protection Force, she took to the sport at the age of 12 at her village gymnasium, following her elder sister Karnam Narasamma. Her younger sister Krishna Kumari is also a national level lifter. Her mother, Shyamala, gave her daughter full moral and worldly support in her sporting career and accompanied her to competitions.

It was in Sydney Olympics 2000 that weightlifter Karnam Malleswari won Bronze medal in the 69-kg category finishing close behind China's Lin Weining and Hungary's Erzsebet Markus. Not only did she become the first woman from India to win an Olympic medal but also the third individual medal winner since the country started taking part in the Olympics. It was the only one medal obtained by India in the Games. Prime Minister Atal Behari Vajpayee hailed Malleswari's world-class performance "a tribute to Indian womanhood".

Earlier, she had won Gold in Istanbul World Championship (1994) and Asian Championship (54-kg category) at Pusan, Korea (1995). In World Weightlifting Championship at Guangzhou (China) on November 19, 1995, Malleswari set a new world record by winning three Golds in 54-kg category. She broke her own record in the Senior National Weightlifting Championship in 1997, and won India's first medal, a weightlifting Silver, in the 1998 Asian Games. She ranked No. 5 in the world.

Malleswari was married in 1997. She took a break from competitive weightlifting, to return in 1998 for the Bangkok Asian Games. She participated in the Athens Olympics in 2004 but was unable to win a medal.

Karnam Malleswari was honoured with Arjuna Award in 1994 and 'Rajiv Gandhi Khel Ratna Award' in 1995-96.

35

Kasturba Gandhi (1869-1944)

Kasturba Gandhi, affectionately called Ba later in life, was born on 11 April 1869 at Porbandar (Gujarat). Her father, Gokuladas Makharji, was a well-to-do businessman and she was one of his four children. She was only seven years old when she was formally betrothed to Mohandas Karamchand Gandhi who was six months younger to her. She was illiterate at the time of her marriage (1982). They were both aged 13. Gandhi was an English-educated gentleman always on the fast track, often drastically changing his thinking and living. Kasturba was illiterate. It was indeed an ordeal for her to keep pace with him but she did so with dignity and without reservation. He taught her to read and write. She alone had the opportunity to see Gandhiji's life in all its completeness. She was the sole witness of his spiritual progress from over-indulgence in sensual pleasure to perfect *brahmacharya*. Gandhiji s living was very simple, but her living was even simpler. She had five children, of whom four grew up to manhood. In consultation with her, Mahatma Gandhi took the vow of Brahmacharya in 1901. She took to austere simplicity when he decided to change his life. She adapted herself to Ashram life without any difficulty. Although Kasturba identified herself with the work of her great husband throughout her life, she did not accept his ideas unless she understood them and considered them right. Gandhiji often had to work hard to convince her.

Kasturba Gandhi was a deeply religious Hindu wife. In early life, she considered untouchability a part of religion. Later she renounced all caste distinctions and brought up a Harijan girl as her own daughter. A delicate, small but elegant lady, she was simple, straightforward and methodical. Her simplicity had an elegance, all its own. She was ready to lay down her life for her principles.

Kasturba Gandhi showed an independence of spirit, and Gandhi's autobiography records an incident when he was almost tempted, in a moment of acute anger, to throw her out of the home. He had asked that she should contribute, as did everyone else at their ashram, to menial tasks; and though she agreed, she balked at having to clean the toilets, and flatly refused to do so. There were also disagreements between them on the care of their sons, whom Kasturba (like some others) was inclined to believe had been neglected by their father. Gandhi, on the other hand, took the view that as his sons, they were entitled to no special privileges. Harilal, in particular, caused her great sorrow, and when he once arrived at her bedside during her last illness, she burst into tears.

Her public life began after she joined her husband in South Africa in 1897. From 1904 to 1914, she was the soul of the Phoenix Settlement and became Kasturba-'mother'-to the inmates, a role continued at Kochnab, Sabarmati and Sevagram Ashram in India. She led the women's *satyagraha* in the final fight in South Africa. She was imprisoned and came out of jail in an emaciated condition. After his return to India in 1915, Mahatma Gandhi took up the cause of the indigo workers against the oppression of the white planters in Champaran in Bihar. Kasturba joined him and taught cleanliness, discipline and reading and writing to the village women and children. In 1918, she took an active part in the Kaira Satyagraha-'No Tax Campaign'-and taught the village women the art of non-violent resistance. Later during India's non-violent fight for freedom, she took up the leadership of the movement whenever Gandhiji was arrested.

In 1930 and again in 1932, she courted arrest by picketing liquor and foreign cloth shops. In 1939, she participated in the Rajkot Satyagraha for political reforms and was kept in detention at Tramba. In 1942, Gandhiji was arrested early in the morning of August 9 at Birla House, Bombay. Kasturba decided to address the meeting which Gandhiji was to have addressed that afternoon. She was arrested as she was proceeding to the meeting and taken to Arthur Road prison at Bombay, from where after two days she was taken to the Aga Khan Palace detention camp at Poona to join her husband. In February 1943, Gandhiji went on a 21-day fast and Kasturba looked after him day and night. She took only one meal a day of fruit and milk. She had done the same during all his previous fasts. This enabled her to have the strength to nurse him while she shared his ordeal. Her health began to fail soon after Gandhiji's fast in detention. The strain, physical and emotional, was too great. She suffered from chronic bronchitis, with heart failure, and a terminal pneumonia carried her away. She attended prayers morning and evening till the end. She gave up all food except 'Ganga Jal' (Ganga water) on the last day. She wanted to hear nothing but 'Ram Nam'. She died on 22 February 1944 on Maha Shivratri Day as the sun went down, with her head on her husband's lap. Her wish that she would like that a sari specially made for her out of the yarn spun out by Gandhiji be used as a shroud when she was dead, was fulfilled.

36

Kiran Bedi Dr. (1949-)

The first and the most celebrated and widely known woman officer of Indian Police Service (IPS), Kiran Bedi was born on 9th June 1949 in Amritsar, (Punjab) to Prakash Lal Peshawaria and Prem Lata. Her father was an ace Tennis player. They had four daughters—Kiran being the second of the four. The parents had a vision ahead of their time and were in no way conventional in the upbringing of their daughters. They believed in giving them the best of the education which was not the trend of the times. Kiran completed her schooling from the Sacred Heart Convent School, Amritsar, and obtained her B.A. degree (1964-68) in English from the Government College for Women, Amritsar. She was judged Best Athlete and Best cadet–National Cadet Corps (NCC, won honours in debates, declamations and dramatics) and was awarded All Rounder Trophy in her college. She then earned a Master's degree (1968-70) in Political Science from Punjab University, Chandigarh. She received Academic and Sports Scholarships, was conferred Awards in debates and declamations, headed the Youth Leadership Camp and represented the University in the III Commonwealth Expedition (COMEX III) held at New Delhi in 1971. In 1972, Kiran married Brij Bedi who was a University tennis player, a former farmer and a textile engineer by profession. They have a daughter.

Even while in active service in the Indian Police, She continued her educational persuits, and obtained a Law degree (LLB) in 1988 from Delhi University, Delhi. She earned Ph.D. in 1993 from Indian Institute of Technology, New Delhi. The topic of her thesis was ***Drug Abuse and Domestic Violence***.

She won many sports titles including the Junior National Lawn Tennis Championship in 1966, the Asian Lawn Tennis Championship in 1972, and the All-India Interstate Women's Lawn Tennis Championship in 1976. She also won three gold, as well as two silver, medals at the Women's Festival Sports held in 1976 in Delhi.

She began her career as a Lecturer in Political Science (1970-72) at Khalsa College for Women, Amritsar. In the year 1972, she was selected for the Indian Police Service (IPS). She stated that she joined the police service "***because of my urge to be outstanding***". She was the first woman police officer in India when she joined the Indian Police Service. In her career in the police, she has handled many challenging assignments in the Delhi Traffic Police during the Ninth Asian Games in Delhi and Special Traffic in Goa during Commonwealth Head of Governments meet, Narcotics Control Bureau and as Deputy Inspector General (Range) Mizoram. She has been Inspector General of Prisons, of Tihar Jails, Delhi, Special Secretary to the Lt. Governor of Delhi and Joint Commissioner with Delhi Police. She was also Inspector General of Police, Chandigarh and Joint Commissioner of Police (Training), Delhi Police. For her, role of a police officer is not only to apprehend wrong-doers but also to help people and show them the way to a better life. In 1994 when she was appointed Inspector General of Prisons and given the responsibility of managing Tihar jail (Delhi) which was amongst the most notorious prisons, she succeeded in two years in transforming this "ugly hellhole" into an "ashram", a site of inter-disciplinary learning, introducing radical reforms and returning human dignity and creativity to the prisoners. In January 2003, Secretary-General of United Nations appointed Kiran Bedi as the Civilian Police Adviser in the UN Department of Peacekeeping Operations. She held the position of Special Commissioner (Intelligence) with the Delhi Police prior to her UN appointment. On the conclusion her assignment with UN, in 2005, she was appointed Director General, Home Guards and Commandment, Civil Defence.

She is today the most celebrated police officer, having been conferred President's Gallantry Award (1979), the Ramon Magsaysay Award for Exceptional Government Service (1944) and the Joseph Beuys Award (1997) for Holistic and Innovative Management by a German foundation (1997). She was declared "Woman of the Year" 1980 and awarded the Asia Region Award for Drug Prevention and Control (1991) by the International Organization of Good Templars (IOGT), a Norwegian organization. She has also been honoured with Mahila Shiromani Award (1995), Father Machismo Humanitarian Award (1995) and Lion of the Year award (1995) and Pride of India award (1999). She received International Award from Associations of Christian Colleges and Universities : International Ecumenical Forum (ACCU-IEF) for promotion of quality of life through the campaign against Alcohol, Drugs, AIDS and Tobacco in September 1998. She was conferred the first IIT–Delhi Alumni Association 1999-2000 ; award for outstanding contribution to National Development; the WESTERN SOCIETY OF CRIMINOLOGY USA, THE 2001 Morrison, Tom Gitchoff Award for actions that have significantly improved the quality of justice in India. She received Chinmoy Award 2003 for Welfare Policing.

Besides her professional contributions, two voluntary organizations—*Navajyoti* (which literally means *New Enlightenment*), set up in 1988, and *India Vision Foundation*, set up in 1994, were established by her with the objectives of improving the condition of the drug addicts and the poor people. Navjyoti and India Vision Foundation reach out to thousands of poor children daily for primary education and women for adult literacy. They provide vocational training and counselling services in the slums, rural areas and inside the prison apart from treatment for drug addiction. Her efforts have won national and international recognition, and her organizations were awarded the Serge Soitiroff Memorial Award for drug abuse prevention by the United Nations.

She was placed in the 5th position amongst 'Ten Most Admired Indians 'as per an exclusive opinion poll amongst a list of 100 eminent Indians conducted jointly by *The Week* and marketing research and opinion polling agency TNS Mode and published in *The Week* in its issue dated 10 September, 2000. She was voted 1st amongst "Ten Most Admired Women" through a nation-wide TN Sofres Mode Poll and published in "The Week" in its issue dated 15 September 2002.

Kiran Bedi is an author and subject of various books and films. She has written: A Biography 'I Dare!'; Another Biography "The Kindly Baton", 'It's Always Possible' (a book on the transformation of one of the largest prison in the world; "Government@net" (a book on e-governance)

Indian women see Kiran Bedi as a role model and a hero.

37

Kiran Mazumdar-Shaw (1953-)

Chairman and Managing Director of Biocon India, Kiran Mazumdar-Shaw, 51, was born in Bangalore and educated in Bishop Cotton Girls School and Mount Carmel College, Bangalore (1973). She went on to Ballarat College, Melbourne and did master brewer's degree in 1975, specializing in Malting and Brewing Technology, and became India's first woman brew master. She was Technical Consultant, Jupiter Breweries, Calcutta and Technical Manager, Standard Maltings Corporation, Baroda (1975-77). In 1978, she was Trainee Manager, Biocon Biochemicals, Cork, Ireland. In 1978, she founded Biocon India, Bangalore, a company that has evolved from a maker of enzymes to a major pharmaceutical enterprise producing everything from insulin to antibodies, with annual revenues of $122 million. She has been Chairman and Managing Director of Biocon, India's No. 1 biotech company in terms of revenue and reach. She is married to John Shaw, a Scotsman and Indophile, who headed a leading textiles MNC, Madura Coats from 1991-1998 as Chairman and Managing Director. John Shaw has since joined Biocon as Director, International Business and is the Vice Chairman of the Board.

Since 1994, she has been Chairman, Syngene Int'l, Bangalore; and since 2000, Chairman, Clinigene Int'l, Bangalore. Within 25 years of founding of Biocon India, Kiran Mazumdar-Shaw-who along with her British economist husband John Shaw owns 61.5 per cent of the post-IPO company-has emerged as the wealthiest woman in India. When her company went public in 2004, its shares were oversubscribed by 33 times on opening day, and it now has a total stock-market value of over $1.2 billion. The company, which now focuses on biopharmaceutical clinical research and enzymes, reported revenues of $168 million in 2004, with a profit of $45 million in 2004. Kiran Mazumdar-Shaw aims to make Biocon one of the world's top-five biotech companies in the not-too-distant future.

Kiran Mazumdar-Shaw is the recipient of several prestigious awards including the Best Woman Entrepreneur, Ernst & Young's Entrepreneur of the Year Award for Life Sciences & Healthcare, Leading Exporter, Outstanding Citizen, Technology Pioneer. She has been described as "India's Biotech Queen" by The Economist while the New York Times calls her "India's mother of invention".Biocon was singled out as a World Economic Forum Tech Pioneer in 2001.

Kiran Mazumdar-Shaw was chosen as the BioSpectrum Person of the Year 2003 for her outstanding contribution in the field of biotechnology. She was honoured with Sir M.V. Memorial Award, instituted by the Federation of Karnataka Chambers of Commerce and Industry, for the year 2002 in recognition of her significant achievements as an industry leader as well as her contribution to the society at large in various fields. In 2000 Kiran Mazumdar Shaw was appointed Chairperson of the Vision Group on Biotechnology to draw up the Karnataka State's Biotech Policy. Ms. Shaw is also a Board member of BVGH (Bio-Ventures for Global Health). She has been invited to join the Prime Minister's Council on Trade and Industry in India.

Kiran Mazumdar-Shaw has been Vice-President, Association of Women Entrepreneurs of Karnataka (AWAKE) and has won Rotary Award for Best Model Employer and National Award for Best Small Industry. She won the Economic Times Award for Corporate Excellence and was declared the Businesswoman of the year (2004).

Her most cherished awards are the PADMASHRI (1989) and PADMA BHUSHAN (2005) presented to her by the President of India, for her pioneering efforts in Industrial Biotechnology.

She is known for her art collection and as the hostess with the 'mostest' in Bangalore. She has recieved an honorary Doctor of Science, University of Ballarat, 2004. in recognition of her pre-eminent contribution to the field of Biotechnology. She is held to be a role model for young women.

Kiran Mazumdar-Shaw has actively campaigned for civic amenities, roads and cleanliness in Bangalore. She contributed Rs. One Crore towards starting the Swachcha Bangalore programme of door-to-door collection of garbage. She has written a coffee table book 'Ale and Arty' on brewing beer.

Kiran Mazumdar-Shaw says she draws inspiration from her late father. "He made me believe that scientific knowledge is hard currency," she says. For her especially, those words couldn't ring more true.

38

Kishori Amonkar (1931-)

Born on 10 April 1931, Kishori Amonkar, a music genius from Goa widely considered the finest female vocalist of her generation, has attained such mastery over her art that she can justifiably claim to be the sole heir to the exacting standards set by her predecessors-her illustrious mother, Mogubai Kurdikar, and the formidable Surashree Kesarbai Kerkar. Kishori Amonkar owes her standing as a female vocalist par excellence to her mother's persistent efforts to give her an all round musical education which included, besides the classical, the teaching which she received from her *guru* on light classical, ghazals, bhajans, quwwalis. She taught her not merely to aim at audience applause but to see that her singing had a sacred quality. Kishori was known in her teens to be engrossed in film music. She wanted to be a play back singer. She learnt ghazals and *thumris* from Pandit Husnaram of the once famous pair of film music directors. But she soon got disillusioned and devoted whole-heartedly to classical music.

Although she hails from the Jaipur Gharana and in her early years she absorbed the approach and repertoire of her distinguished mother's teacher Ustad Alladiya Khan, Kishori developed her own style and moved away from Alladiya Khan's "Jaipur gharana" style in some respects. As a mature artist her approach is usually regarded as an individual, if not unique, varient of the Jaipur model. While her mother was essentially a purist, Kishori Amonkar has ventured into light classical music as well, without compromising on the principles of her gharana. Her devotional fare includes Hindi and Marathi *bhakti geets* (Prayer songs), as well as *bhajans* in Kannada and Sanskrit.

Kishori has studied 'Natya Shashtra' extensively and has gained new, meaningful expressions through her music. She has an enchanting and intellectual approach to raga interpretation and development. She is endowed with beautiful and highly expressive voice capable of communicating any emotion she wants to portray. She is a versatile singer, and her repertoire ranges from 'Khayals' and exquisite 'Thumris' to spiritually elevating 'Bhajans'. She is greatly inspired by the teachings of the ancient Vedic *ragas,* written at a time when vocal music was highly devotional in character.

Kishori Amonkar has been criticized for being temperamental but, despite criticism, Kishori is much sought after for her mellifluous and enthralling music. Kishori Amonkar is not fond of ostentation and leads a simple life at Prabhadevi, Mumbai. She loves Goa and she has worked for advancement of classical music there. The prestigious "Goa Today" (January 1994) declared Kishori Amonkar "Woman of the Year 1993".

Kishori Amonkar has travelled extensively and has participated in major prestigious festivals in India and abroad. She has been awarded numerous honours and titles and has, like her mother, also been awarded the 'Padma Bhushan', but the honour she cherishes the most is the title of 'Gana Saraswathi' that was given by the Jagadguru Mahaswamiji of Sringeri Matt. Other awards bestowed on her include the Sangeet Natak Akademi Award (1985), the coveted Sangeet Samradhini Award (considered as one of the most prestigious awards in Indian Classical Music) in 1997 and "Kala Shiromani" award of the Calcutta Critics' Association.

39

Kittur Rani Chennamma (1778-1830)

One of first Indian women crusaders for independence, Kittur Rani Chennamma was daughter of Dhulappa Gowda, the Desai of Ketki Karnataka). She received training in horse riding, sword fighting and archery in her young age. She was married to Raja Mulla Sarja of Kittur, a princely state of Belgaum in Karnataka. Mulla Sarja had a son, Shivaling Rudra Sarja from his first wife, Veeranama. On Malla Sarja's death in 1816, Shivaling Rudra ascended the throne. But he too died in 1824, without any child of his own though a little before his death, he had adopted a child. The British refused to recognize the adoption. Rani Chennamma showed remarkable courage and intelligence. She composed her differences with her Sardars and proclaimed the continuance of the State. This was not to the liking of the British who had intended to annexe the State. Determined to save the State in peaceful manner, if possible, and through war, if inevitable, Rani Chennamma first made an appeal to the Governor but to no avail. The Chief Agent of Dharwar, Thackerey, on the other hand, conveyed to the Rani that the gates of Kittur should be opened within 24 minutes, failing which the gates would be blown open. All this while, Rani Chennamma had fortified the place and addressed the neighbouring princes for help. She was directing the military operations herself from the rampart. When Thackerey advanced towards the gate, he was struck by a sally made by the Rani's escort. Rani's troops seized the enemy guns, cut the British officers to pieces and executed the traitors. Rhe Rani's soldiers also arrested a few hiding Englishmen and forty servants of the East India Company and would have executed them but for the Rani's intervention. The defeat of Thackerey's army was a humiliation for the British.

When Elphinstone, the British Governor of Bombay, heard of the defeat, he ordered Rani's troops to surrender and the annexation of the State. Rani did not lose nerve. As a measure of goodwill, she released the prisoners and treated them with courtesy. Rani Chennamma communicated to Wilhem Chaplin, the Commissioner of Deccan, that she was wholly averse to war but that the Company was showing hostile postures. Rani defined the writ of the East India Company and offered stiff resistance to the Company's army. On 30 November 1824, the British attacked the Kittur fort with 200 guns. There was heavy fighting. The British had to seek reinforcement. Unfortunately for the Kittur troops, they ran out of ammunition. With no hope of success and not prepared to sacrifice the lives of the people in the fort, Rani's garrison, at her instance, surrendered on 4 December 1824. The British arrested the leaders of the Kittur troops and Kittur passed into British control. Rani Chennamma was also taken prisoner, detained in Balihongal and she died in captivity in 1830. According to another version, Rani Chennamma was also captured and killed by the British in 1829.

Kittur Rani Chennamma's heroic resistance is still commemorated locally in song and story. Her statue stands as sentinel over Belgaum at a prominent square there.

40

Kunjarani Devi (1968-)

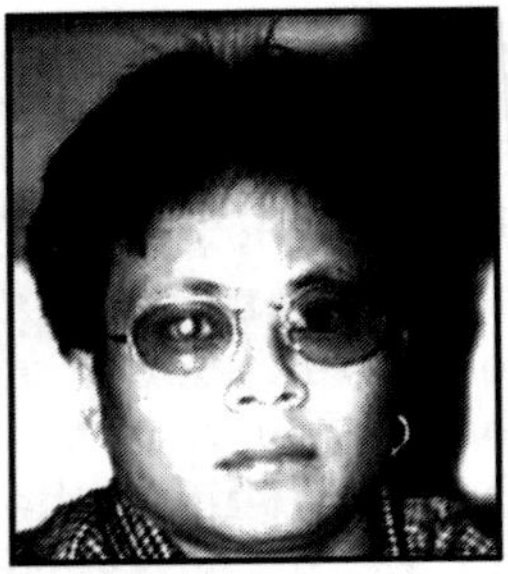

Ranked No. 5 weightlifter in the world, Nameirakpam Kunjarani Devi was born on 1 March 1968 at Kairang Mayai Leikai in Imphal in Manipur. Kunjarani Devi started taking interest in sports while still in Imphal's Sindam Sinshang Resident High school in 1978. She finished her graduation from the Maharaja Bodha Chandra College in Imphal. Joining the Central Reserve Police Force she went on to make mark in the Police Championships and captained the Indian Police team from 1996 to 1998. Beginning 1985, she has been consistently winning medals, mostly Gold, in the National Weightlifting Championships in 44-kilogram, 46 kilogram and 48-kilogram, the latter now her consistent weight. She created two new National Records in Trivandrum in 1987. Changing her weight category to 46-kilogram she claimed a Gold in Pune in 1994 but was relegated to Silver when she tried to compete in the 48-kilogram class four years later in Manipur.

Her first World Women's Weightlifting Championship was the Manchester edition in 1989 in which Kunjarani won three Silver Medals. Since then she has taken part in seven successive World Championships and with the exception of the Melbourne edition in 1993, she has won Silver Medals at every one of those competitions Kunjarani won Bronze Medal in the Asian Games at Beijing in 1990 and Hiroshima in 1994. She has been a regular participant in the Asian Weightlifting Championships. Starting with one Silver and two Bronze Medals in the 1989 edition in Shanghai, she progressed to three Silver Medals in the 44-kilogram class in the 1991 edition in Indonesia. She retained her second spot in the next one in Thailand in 1992 and China in 1993. Her best performance came in the 1995 competition in South Korea where she won two Gold and one Bronze in the 46-kilogram category. But in the championship held in Japan in 1996, she could win only two Silver and one Bronze.

Nameirakpam Kunjarani Devi has the distinction of being the first Gold Medallist in the Commonwealth Championships held at Nauru in 1995 in the 48-kilogram category. She finished runner-up in the women's Commonwealth weightlifting championship in Melbourne 1999. Returning to international competition after serving a six-month ban for testing positive during random tests carried out during the July 2001 Senior Asian Weightlifting Championships, N. Kunjarani Devi created history by becoming the first winner in the newly-introduced women's weightlifting competition in 17th Commonwealth Games 2002, sweeping all the three Gold Medals in 48 kg weight category. In Athens Olympics (2004) Kunjarani Devi could get only the fifth place.

She has won 61 medals on the international competitions. Both Kunjarani and Malleswari are ranked No 5 in the world, the highest by an Indian sportsperson in the Olympic events. In addition, Kunjarani is ranked among the 10 greatest lifters of the century. Holding the rank of an Assistant Commandant in the Central Reserve Police Force, Kunjarani has received due recognition for her achievements in weightlifting. She was honoured with the Arjuna award in 1990, the Rajiv Gandhi Khel Ratna Award in 1996 and the K.K. Birla Sports Award, also in 1996.

41

Lakshmi Sahgal, Captn (INA) (1914-)

Lakshmi Sahgal was born Lakshmi Swaminadhan on October 24, 1914 in what was then called Madras. Her father was Dr S Swaminadhan, a leading criminal lawyer of the Madras High Court. Her mother was Ammu Swaminadhan, a social worker, freedom fighter and campaigner for women's rights, who successfully contested elections to the Madras Municipal Corporation, the Constituent Assembly, the Lok Sabha and Rajya Sabha. She also served as national president of the All India Women's Conference. As a young girl, Lakshmi participated in nationalist programmes of burning of foreign goods, including her own clothes and toys, and picketting of liquor-vends.

After graduating from the Madras Medical College in 1938 and doing her diploma in gynaecology and obstetrics, in 1940, Lakshmi left Madras for Singapore where she established a clinic and served the poor, especially migrant Indian labour. While working in Singapore, she played an active role in the India Independence League which had been in the forefront of Indian freedom movement. In 1942 when Japanese overran the Singapore island, Lakshmi was drawn to Netaji Subhas Chandra Bose's vision of freeing India and joined his Indian National Army, commanding the women's regiment, Rani of Jhansi Regiment. On October 21, 1943, when the Provisional Government of Azad Hind was announced, Lakshmi was the sole woman member of its cabinet. The Rani of Jhansi Regiment performed active duty on the front. Lakshmi, who was given the rank of Colonel, although in the popular imagination she remained 'Captain Lakshmi', was active both militarily and on the medical front. She played a heroic role not only in the fighting but during the terrible days when INA personnel were hunted by the British troops.

It was during this period that she met three Indian Army officers, Shah Nawaz Khan, G. S. Dhillon and Prem Kumar Sahgal, who had been taken prisoner by the Japanese and who had helped Subhash Chandra Bose found the Indian National Army (INA). Captn Lakshmi Swaminadhan was captured by the British troops and brought to India on March 4, 1946 when she received a heroine's welcome. Realising that keeping her a prisoner would be counter-productive, the British authorities released her. Lakshmi Swaminadhan campaigned for the release and rehabilitation of imprisoned and de-mobilised INA personnel, and for the freedom of India. She travelled throughout the country and collected large funds for the INA soldiers and mobilized people against the colonial power.

After the War and after the trial of Shah Nawaz Khan, G. S. Dhillon and Prem Kumar Sahgal for treason and their release, Lakshmi Swaminadhan caught up once again with the three. Not long afterwards, she married Col. Prem Kumar Sahgal and settled in Kanpur. (Col. Sahgal was the son of Justice Achhru Ram Sahgal, a Judge of the Punjab High Court and who was one of the judges in the Gandhi Murder Case.)

In Kanpur, Lakshmi intensified her medical work for the refugees from west Pakistan and worked tirelessly among them for several years. Later on, she established a small maternity home in a hired premise where it continues till today. In 1971, when large number of refugees came from what was East Pakistan into West Bengal, Lakshmi Sehgal worked at a camp in Bongaon for several months. In October 1984, when anti-Sikh riots broke out in Kanpur in the wake of Indira Gandhi's assassination, she came out in the defence of Sikh families and property.

Lakshmi Sahgal has been active in Left politics, trade unions and women's movement without neglecting her medical work. When the All India Democratic Women's Association was formed in 1981, she became vice-president of the organisation and has participated in its activities. Her daughter, Subhashini Ali, reflected her mother's leftist views and won the Kanpur parliamentary seat in 1989 on a Communist Party (Marxist) ticket.

In 1998, Lakshmi Sahgal was awarded Padma Vibhushan by the President of India. In 2002, Lakshmi Sahgal was nominated by Left parties to fight for the office of President of India against NDA's candidate APJ Abdul Kalam. She lost.

42

Lata Mangeshkar (1929-)

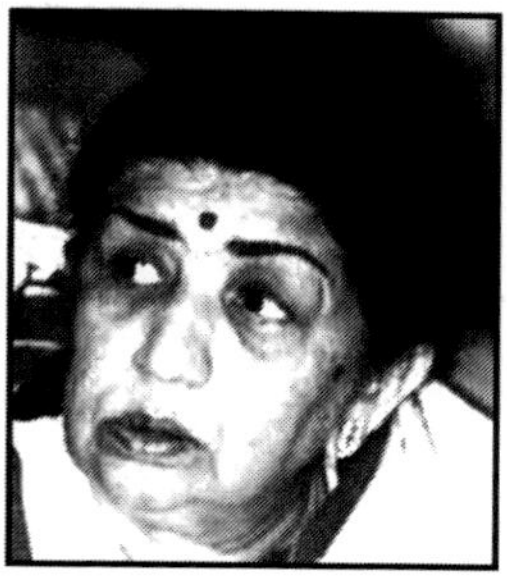

The "Nightingale of India", Lata Mangeshkar, has charmed her fans with over 50,000 songs she has sung as a playback singer in films and out of films. She is variously called as "The Pride of India", "The Melody Queen", "The Voice of the Millennium".

Latabai Mangeshkar was born on 28th September, 1929, at Sikh Mohalla, Indore, Madhya Pradesh, India. Her father, Pt. Deenanath Mangeshkar, a classical singer and stage actor, who came from Mangeshi in Goa, was a classical singer trained in the colourful Punjabi school of Baba Mushelkar. He gave her singing lessons from around the age of five. She also studied with Aman Ali Khan Sahib and later Amanat Khan. When her father died in 1942, the onus of being the breadwinner of the family fell on Lata. Lata, only 13 at that time, acted as heroine's sister in Pahili Mangalagam, a Marathi film by Master Vinayak Rao, and sang three songs. Satisfied with her performance in 'Pahili', Vinayak signed her as a staff artiste on a monthly salary of Rs. 60 per month which was raised to Rs. 350 by 1947.

Between 1942 and 1948 she acted in as many as 8 films in Hindi and Marathi to take care of the family's economic problems. She made her debut as a playback singer in the Marathi film *Kiti Hasaal (1942)* but the song was edited out. Her first Hindi song was in a Marathi Film (1943)-Gajabhau (*maata ek sapoot ki duniya badal de tu...*) In Badi Maa (1945), starring Noorjehan, Lata acted, sang for herself and for younger sister Asha. The first Hindi film in which she gave playback was *Aap ke Sewa Main (1947)* but her singing had gone unnoticed. Lata was even rejected for *Shaheed (1948)* by producer S. Mukherjee who complained that her voice was too thin! However Ghulam Haider unable to use her in *Shaheed* gave Lata her breakthrough song with *Dil Mera Toda* from *Majboor (1948)*. 1949 saw the release of four films. *Barsaat, Andaaz (1949), Dulari* and *Mahal*. The songs of all four films were runaway hits particularly *Aaega Aanewaalaa* from Mahal. Lata's initial style of singing was reminiscent of Noorjehan but she soon got over that to evolve her own distinguished style. The film industry in those days was dominated by Urdu writers and lyricists. With her search for perfection she improved her Urdu by hiring a tutor. Her phenomenal success made Lata the most powerful woman in the Film Industry.

She waged battle with Mohd. Rafi in the 1960s and stopped singing with him over the issue of royalty to playback artistes. She refused to sing for S.D. Burman from 1957-62 and such was her clout that she had her way and they came back to her.

Lata has sung under the baton of all the top composers barring O.P. Nayyar and with all the top playback artistes of the day. The 1960s and 70s saw Lata go from strength to strength For some time Lata Mangeshkar has sung infrequently but even today the songs of some of the biggest hits of today *Dil To Paagal Hai (1997), Maachis (1997), Hum Aapke Hain Kaun (1994)* and *Dil Se (1998)* were sung by her.

Lata Mangeshkar has been active in all shades of Indian popular and light classical music having sung *ghazals, bhajans* and pop. She has sung over 50,000 songs in 20 Indian languages for three generations of heroines, ranging from Nargis to Zeenat Aman to Kajol. She even made it to the Guinness Book of Records as the most recorded artist in the world. Lata Mangeshkar's songs have captured the hearts and imagination of millions of her admirers around the world.

Apart from her film songs, Lata Mangeshkar has personally adapted the works of leading Marathi poets and set them to music for private recordings. She has recorded devotional songs by Sant Tukaram, and her recording of the Bhagwat in Sanskrit is recognised as her crowning achievement.

Lata Mangeshkar was awarded Filmfare Awards for her songs in 1958 (Madhumati), 1962 (Bees Saal Baad), 1965 (Khandaan), 1969 (Jeene Ki Raah). After 1969, she announced that Filmfare Awards should be given to fresh talents. In 1994, however, she accepted the Filmfare's Lifetime Achievement Award. In 1980, she was presented key of the city of Georgetown, Guyana, and Honorary Citizenship of the Republic of Suriname. In 1985, 9th June was declared as Asia Day in honour of her arrival in Toronto, Canada. In 1987, Honorary Citizenship of the U.S.A (Houston, Texas) was bestowed on her. In 1998, Lux Zee Cine Lifetime Achievement Award was given to her. Shivaji University, Kolhapur and Hyderabad University have honoured her with the Degrees of Doctor of Literature. Lata Mangeshkar felt most honoured with the title of *Asthaan Sangeet Vidwaan Sarloo* (Court Musician of the Shrine) in Triputi. She was given Swar Bharati award by Shankaracharya of Sankeshwar.

A Dada Sahib Phalke Award winner for her contribution to Indian Cinema, Lata Mangeshkar was honoured first with India's 2nd highest civilian award Padma Vibhushan (1999) and later the highest civilian award-Bharat Ratna. She was nominated to Rajya Sabha in 1999.

43

Lila Poonawalla (1944-)

The first woman CEO of a Multinational Engineering Company, in India's business history, Lila Poonawalla was born in Hyderabad (Pakistan) on September 16, 1944. She came to India as a refugee with her grand parents, mother and four brothers. They stayed at a refugee camp in Lonavala and then moved to Pune and made this city their home. The entire family had to survive on the pension from their father's Life Insurance Policy, who had died in a train accident when Lila was only two and a half years old. Inspite of limited financial resources, Lila, due to her determination was the only one amongst her siblings to go in for higher education. She was the only girl in the family of nine boys, her four brothers and five cousins.

Lila studied at the Mount Caramel Convent High School. She took keen interest in extra-curricular activities like girl guide, baseball, basketball and other sports. After completing her Intermediate from the Ferguson College, she joined Government College of Engineering, Pune and graduated in mechanical engineering with a First Class Degree, in 1967. She became the first woman mechanical engineer in Pune.

In 1967 Lila joined Ruston & Hornsby as a trainee engineer. She met Firoz, her husband-to-be on the first day that she joined Ruston & Hornsby. Firoze was the Quality Control Manager there. Despite opposition from their families, they married. By mutual consent and after taking their parents into confidence, they decided not to have children. After their marriage, Lila left Ruston to join Vulcan Laval.

Lila rose to become Exports Manager in 1978. She had to work hard to get the Indian operations of Vulcan Laval recognised for both performance and quality. In 1986, she was appointed the Executive Vice-President. This was also the year when she appeared on the cover of the International Business Magazine "Svensk Export". She was appointed the Managing Director of Vulcan Laval in 1987. With this appointment, she became the first Indian woman to be appointed MD of a multinational company. She also became the first woman in the Alfa Laval group to reach that position. She remained the only woman managing director in the entire group until her retirement. The Swedish press gave huge coverage to the `lady in the sari' when she took over as the Managing Director of the Indian operations she was appointed Executive Chairperson of Tetra Pak India Ltd. and Vice-Chairperson and Managing Director of Alfa Laval in 1992. In 1996 she was appointed Chairperson Alfa Laval India and CMD Tetra Pak (India). She stepped down as the CMD in 1999 but retained the portfolio of Chairperson of Alfa Laval India and Tetra Pak India. She is the Chairperson of DeLaval. She has recently been appointed as the Government's nominee on the Board of IDBI Lila has been on the governing body of organizations like the CII (Confederation of Indian Industries), and TIFAC (Technology Information Forecasting and Assessment Council formed by the Government of India) as the Chairperson for Agro Food Processing. She is member of the Scientific advisory board of the Central Cabinet (SAC-C) and as Chairperson of the Herbal And Floriculture Taskforce of SAC-C.

Lila has always been ready to take risks. She has been a stickler for punctuality and discipline. And her resourcefulness has paid off on all occasions. In 1993, King Carl Gustaf XIIV of Sweden visited India and inaugurated the company's new technology centre in Pune. Under her management, the company grew from a Rs. 50 crore to a Rs. 250 crore company in less than six years.

Lila has managed her career and home with equal ease, largely due to her emphasis on Time Management. She also takes time off from her own leisure to indulge herself in a wide variety of interests, which bring her great happiness. Lila has a penchant for collecting everything under the sun. She has an exquisite collection of crystal-ware from different parts of the globe, and a variety of clocks, all giving perfect time, a vast collection of trinkets and souvenirs from all her journeys. Collecting matchboxes is another obsessive interest She is the member of British Match Club. Her collection includes a foot long matchbox from the Swedish Match Factory. She has a collection of chessboards of varied descriptions. One of her most unique and lovable collection is of COWS, smiling, mooing, dancing, grazing, playing, fighting, in fact, showcasing them in every mood and action.

Lila has received innumerable awards and honours some of which are: Royal Order of the Polar Star Award by the His Majesty, the King of Sweden (2003); Lifetime Achievement Award from India Women Scientists Association (2001); Udyog Bhushan Award from Annasaheb Magar Foundation; PCMC (2000); Mahila Jeevan Gaurav 1998); In 1995, she received Pune's Pride, International Business Council award, Special Lady of the Decade award, Best Citizen, Udyog Ratan, Rashtriya

Udyog, Global India Excellence; Indira Gandhi Memorial National and Vijay Ratna (1994); Vikas Jyoti and International Excellence Gold (1993); International Woman Award By the Indian High Commissioner in U. K., Rajiv Gandhi Excellence and Hind Gaurav (1992); in 1991 Industrial Excellence, Special Executive Magistrate, Indira Gandhi Priyadarshini, Gem of India, Udyog Jyoti, Kohinoor Ratna and FIE Foundation; in 1990 Mahila Shiromani by the Vice President of India, Marketing Man of the Year, and Post Independence Excellence Award 1947-89; Padmashree by the President of India (1989); Best Lady Executive by the President of India (1983).

As Chairperson Emeritus of the Maharashtra Chapter of Quality Circle Forum of India (QCFI), and Vice President of the QCFI (India), Lila Poonawalla has been propagating the Quality Circle Technology via countless presentations and by organizing Quality Conventions all over the country. Another project spearheaded by Lila and Firoz Poonawalla, which has been their dream project since long, is the Quality Circle Excellence Center, located in the heart of Pune's industrial belt–Pimpri-Chinchwad

On her 50th birthday in 1994, Lila received from the Rausing family, ownersof the Tetra Pak Worldwide group a special birthday gift–100,000 Swiss francs with which she established in 1994 the Lila Poonawalla Foundation to promote education among women. The Foundation has supported more than 300 girls to reach their goals.

Lila Poonawalla is on the board of trustees of three Pune-based NGOs (non-governmental organizations): namely, World-wide Fund For Nature, India, Indo Swiss Vocational Training Trust, Ashta No Kai-The Women's Literacy and Development Project

Lila Poonawalla is the Vice Chairperson of Poona Blind Men's Association. She is a Promoter Trustee on the Board of Trustees of Pune Citizens Police Foundation. She is the Programme Director for Fair & Lovely Foundation's *Project Saraswati,* which is one of the several projects undertaken by the Foundation to encourage economic empowerment of Indian women.

She is associated with education and is on the Board of International Institute of Foreign Trade, International Institute of Information Technology, Science and Technology Park Pune University, Symboisis Management Institute, and Pune University Management Acadamy.

She is also on the Board of IDBI, DeLaval India, Beeyu Overseas, Neilsoft, BioImagene, Filarozil Exports, LaRoz Elegance, and Pragati Leadership Institute,

Lila Poonawalla is one of the Sweden's best-known ambassadors in India and she is amongst the most widely recognised Indians in Swedish memory.

44

Madhubala (1933-1969)

The Venus of Indian screen, Madhubala (real name: Mumtaz Jehan Begum Dehlavi) was born on 14th February 1933 in a poor, conservative family of Pathan Muslims in Delhi. She was the fifth of eleven children. Her father Ataullah Khan a coach man in Delhi migrated to Bombay in search of better future. Madhubala began life in the film world as a child artist, Baby Mumtaz, in Bombay Talkies' Basant (1942) when she was only 8 years old. Devika Rani, the proprietor of Bombay talkies and a leading actress of those days impressed by her performance re-christened her Madhubala. In 1947, when she was barely 14 years, she got her first break as a heroine against another debutant Raj Kapoor in 'Neel Kamal' directed by Kedar Sharma. In the next four years she worked in as many 24 films which secured her financially. It was the suspense thriller, 'Mahal' (1949), again a Bombay Talkies movie, with Ashok Kumar 20 years her senior and a leading star at that time, that catapulted her to stardom. Mahal's success gave her roles with most of the leading men of the time like Ashok Kumar, Dev Anand, Rehman and Dilip Kumar. She was a thorough professional, hard working and punctual throughout her career.

During the 1950's, on a routine check-up it was discovered that she had a major heart problem. Madhubala endured her fate bravely and her sickness was kept a secret from the industry for many years. Professionally too by the mid fifties her career suffered a set back with some of her major films flopping at the box office. On the top of them all, she passed through a very bad period on personal, matrimonial front. Despite the flops, Madhubala bounced back career-wise, looking as glamorous and sparkling as ever and in the 1958-60 period she had a string of hits in Mr and Mrs 55, Phagun (1958), Howrah Bridge(1958), Kala Pani (1958), Chalti Ka Naam Gaadi (1958) and the all time classic Mughal-E-Azam (1960).

She was proposed by many, but she chose Kishore Kumar, her co-star in a number of musical comedies. It is believed that Kishore knew she had a health problem but in spite of that they had a civil marriage. After her marriage she went to London for an operation but the doctors refused to operate on her as the chances for survival were remote. She stayed with her own family. Her marriage lingered for nine long years till her death on February 23, 1969, when she was only 36 years of age.

Madhubala was without doubt the most beautiful Hindi Film heroine ever. And also perhaps the most under-rated actress ever with her beauty attracting more attention than her performances.

A film journalist wrote of her: "Till madhubala came, most of the heroines were only-eyed, weeply-faced and had cranky, theatrical style of acting. This girl (Madhubala) with her infectious laughter, the twinkle in her eyes and a bubbling personality was like a ray of sunshine.......Madhubala had the most beautiful hands, with tapering fingers."

45

Madhuri Dixit (1967-)

Born on May 15, 1967, in Maharashtra to Shankar and Snehlata Dixit, Madhuri Dixit married Shri Ram Nene, a Los Angeles based surgeon, on Oct 17, 1999. She was a top-line model in India before entering the Hindi film industry.

Madhuri wanted to become a micro-biologist but that was not to be. She was a student of Parley College, An offer from Rajishri Productions brought Madhuri her first role in the film 'Abodh' (1986) which was released but it flopped. It wasn't until Director Subhash Ghai saw Madhuri and gave her a tiny dance sequence in 'Karma' (1986), that things improved.

In her efforts to build up her career in films, Madhuri had no qualms about accepting second fiddle roles and even participated in a TV serial. She struggled on for some time in this fashion. Her efforts paid off in 1988 when she was suddenly catapulted to heights of fame and success. Subhash Ghai gave Madhuri a proper launch in 'Ram Lakhan' (1988). And then N.Chandra's 'Tezaab' and 'Ek, do, teen char' took the nation by storm and she got rave reviews. 'Tezaab' went on to complete a golden jubilee and turned out a bigger hit than 'Ram Lakhan'. A great performance followed in Dil (1990) which brought Madhuri her first Filmfare award. 1990 onwards, a hit film per year followed including Saajan, Khalnayak, Prem Pratigaya, culminating in Hum Aapke Hain Koun (1994), Hindi cinema's biggest blockbuster. The 'Choli ke peechhe' song in Khalnayak caused a stir with women liberation groups asking for a ban on Madhuri. Prakash Jha's 'Mrityudand' (1997) ensured critical acclaim. Madhuri went on to win a handful of awards for her performances in Mrityudand and Dil Toh Pagal Hai, 1999 was Madhuri's golden year. This year had Madhuri in a number of different characters. MF Hussain's 'Gajagamini' was an art film that had Madhuri playing a range of characters. Madhuri's first south Indian film, 'Engineer', was a techno thriller.

Awards and Achievements: Nominated for Filmfare Award 1989 for Tezaab; Nominated for Filmfare Award 1990 for Prem Pratigya; Filmfare Award 1991 for Dil; Filmfare Best Actress Award 1993 for Beta; Fimfare Best Actress Award 1995 for Hum Aapke Hain Koun; Filmfare and Lux Zee Cine Awards Best Actress 1997 for Dil To Pagal Hai; Screen Videocon Best Actress Award 1996 for Raja; Lux Zee Cine Awards Best Supporting Actress Award 2002 for Lajja.

Madhuri Dixit has continued to act in films after marriage though she has cut down on her assignments.

Madhuri Dixit has built for herself a screen image which is not only that of a siren full of sensuous songs and dances, but also one of an adult woman full of substance and maturity. Her personal life has been admirable. She has handed her success with level-headed sobriety and is known for her discretion and modesty.

46

Mahadevi Verma (1907-1987)

Mahadevi Verma was born in 1907 in an enlightened family of Farrukhabad, Uttar Pradesh. After doing Masters in Sanskrit from Allahabad University, she started teaching. She founded the 'Prayag Mahila Vidyapitha', Allahabad, an educational institution for promoting the education of girls which also maintained widowed and helpless women. She was its first Principal. She also founded Sahityak Sansad, an organization of literatures.

Mahadevi had a cloistered life all through with exclusive dedication to art and letters. Quite at the threshold of her literary career, Mahadevi was appointed Hony Editor of the famous Hindi monthly 'Chand' and was awarded Seksaria Prize in recognition of her poetic talent. This award was followed by a number of other honours, such as, Mangal Prasad Prize of Hindi Sahitya Sammelan, the coveted Jnanpeeth Award, the title of Padam Bhushan and Degree of Literature (honoris causa).

An active freedom fighter, Mahadevi Verma is regarded as one of the four pillars of the great Romantic movement in modern Hindi poetry, Chayavada, the other three being Suryakant Tripathi 'Nirala', Jaishankar Prasad and Sumitranandan Pant. Her five poetical works which have made her immortal are–*Nihar* (Dewy mist before dawn), *Rashmi* (Morning sun-beam), *Niraja* (Water lily), *Sandhya-git* (The evening song) and *Deep-Shikha* (Flame of the earthen lamp). The main theme of Mahadevi Varma's poetry is love. Her love is not sensuous or psych-physical love; nor is it the love of deity-couples. The object of love in Mahadevi Varma's works is an ideal figure who symbolizes the highest cultural and aesthetic values of life. Mahadevi's poetic style is tastefully ornate. Her central theme is *Virah* or the unfulfilled or dejected love. Mahadevi's art is pictorial art. She is a painter in words as also in line and colour. Her poetic diction has Sanskrit base but she has also made use of indigenous words and phrases. Her poetic canvas intense mystical quality. Her mysticism led to the birth of a movement called Rahasyavada. Mahadevi Verma has often been compared with Mira Bai, the great 16th century devotional poetess, in her lyrical mysticism and deep devotional offerings to God. She is more popular for her poems than her stories and novels. Mahadevi Verma is held to be one of the greatest Hindi poets of all times.

Basically a poet by spiritual make-up, Mahadevi also made a mark as a painter and a writer of exquisite pen-portraits in prose. Her four prose works which have earned her admiration are: *Shrinkhala ki kadiyan* (The fetters), *Atit ke chalchitra* (Glimpses from the past), *Smriti ki rekhayen* (Silhouetes from memory), *Path ke saathi* (Fellow-writers) *and Mera Parivar* (My kith and kin dealing with her pets).

Mahadevi Varma was a nominated Member ofUP Legislative Council, representing literature. She was the first woman to be made a Fellow of the Sahitya Akademi, in 1979. She was honoured with Padma Bhushan by the President of India.

She died on 11 September 1987.

47

Maharani Gayatri Devi (1919-)

Gayatri Devi was born on 23 May 1919 to Maharaja Jitendra Narayan and Maharani Indira Devi of the "Koch" dynasty of Cooch Behar. Her mother Maharani Indira Devi was a renowned beauty of her times. Gayatri Devi studied at Shantiniketan, Laussane, Switzerland, London School of Secretaries, Brilliantmont and Monkey Club London. Gayatri Devi had an adventurous childhood. She was a tomboy and shot her first panther when she was only twelve-year-old. She travelled extensively with her mother and family in Europe and speaks several languages. At the age of 19, she fell in love with Man Singh, the heir to the Jaipur throne when she happened to meet him in London. Their marriage was initially opposed by her parents, as Man Singh already had two wives. Ultimately the parents yielded and in 1940 Gayatri Devi married Man Singh, to be appropriate, HH Saramad-i-Rajahai Hindustan Raj Rajendra Shri Maharajadhiraj Sir Sawai Man Singh II Bahadur of Jaipur. It was held to be an ideal match–the Maharaja handsomely dangerous and the Maharani ravishingly beautiful. It was an eloquent example of emotional integration and hearty mutual admiration for one another. Man Singh was the last ruler of Jaipur before India's Independence. After Independence it merged with the State of Rajasthan. Maharaja Man Singh served as India's first ambassador to Spain. He died in 1970 while playing polo.

Maharani Gyatri Devi took active interest from the outset in cultural, educational and social activities and sports. Her first remarkable public activity was to establish Maharani Gyatri Devi Girls Public School in jaipur in 1943. After Partition in1947, she raised funds for helping the refugees. When Queen Elizabeth II visited Jaipur in 1961, Maharani Gyatri Devi was her host.

Maharani Gayatri Devi was listed by Vogue as one of the world's most beautiful women, and was a favourite of society columnists and photographers. To date she is a picture of vivid beauty and her grace and charm still have a majestic appeal. Harper and Qyeen magazine has placed her amongst the 100 most beautiful women of the past century.

In 1962 she entered politics and was elected to Lok Sabha by an astounding majority which was entered in the Guiness book of records. She won the seat again in 1967 and 1971 on the Swatantra party ticket against Congress Party candidates. It is said that her political successes earned her the wrath of the persons in power. Gayatri Devi was accused of breaking tax laws and served 5 months in Tihar jail. The term in jail brought to an end her political career that had begun in 1962. After this unpleasant experience, Gaytri Devi quit politics and devoted her time in writing her memoirs which was published *in 1976* as an autobiography" *A Princess Remembers"*. She also wrote "A Government's Gateway". She was also the focus of a film called *Memoirs of a Hindu Princess,* directed by Francois Levie.

Maharani Gyatri Devi was President of Rajasthan Mahila Parishad, Rajasthan Bal Vikas Samiti, Red Cross

Society (Rajasthan), Indian National Committee for Children (Rajasthan), Social Welfare Board (Jaipur). She was Chairman of Sawai Jai Singh Benevolent Fund, Lady Patron of Ashoka Club (Jaipur), Chand Shilpshala–asewing school for the help of the destitute women. She took keen interest in fine arts. She promoted the dying art of blue pottery. She was President of the All India Badminton Association, and Rajasthan State Swatantra Party; Vice-President of the All India Lawn Tennis Association and All India Swatantra Party.

48

Maharani Jindan (Jind Kaur) (1817-1863)

Maharani Jind Kaur, popularly addressed as Rani Jindan, was the youngest wife of Maharaja Ranjit Singh and mother of Maharaja Duleep Singh (1838-1893), the last sovereign of the Punjab before British rule. Wielding much authority in Punjab, she was known for her beauty as well as strength of will and art of diplomacy.

On the death of Maharaja Sher Singh, elder son of Maharaja Ranjit Singh, in September, 1845, Rani Jindan became Regent for her young son Duleep Singh, foster brother of Maharaja Sher Singh. Rani Jindan cast off her veil and became the symbol of the sovereignty of the Khalsa ruling the Punjab in the name of her son. She reviewed the troops, held court and transacted state business in public. The army generals treated the Rani with deference and addressed her as Mai Sahib or mother of the entire Khalsa Commonwealth. Rani Jindan resisted the efforts of the British to annex Punjab. She decided on a policy of aggression and planned to avenge the wrongs done by the British. The army entered the war with British troops with enthusiasm and fought bravely but was defeated. (Rani Jindan has been accused by some historians of working against the Khalsa army in the war with the British but this view is controversial.) When the treaty of Bharowal was signed in 1846, Rani Jindan was deposed as 'Regent' and banished to Sheikhupura near Lahore. Henry Lawrence, the British Resident at Lahore, not only imprisoned her in the Sheikhupura jail but also dethroned Maharaja Dalip Singh. He first expelled the prince to Fatehgarh fort in Uttar Pradesh, and then to London. From Sheikhupura jail, Rani Jindan was exiled to Benares and then transferred to the old red-stone fort of Chunar in the district of Mirzapur in Uttar Pradesh. She escaped from the Chunar fort and arrived on 29 April 1849 at Kathmandu where Prime Minister Jung Bahadur granted her asylum as a mark of respect to the memory of the late Maharaja Ranjit Singh, in spite of the objections raised by the British Resident there. The British Government promptly confiscated her jewellery and stopped her pension. Nepal Government assigned to her a residence at Thapathall, on the banks of the Vagmati river and settled upon her an allowance for her maintenance. She patiently bore her exile and built a Sikh shrine in Kathmandu. Under constant pressure firm the British, the Nepal Darbar turned hostile lowards the Maharani and levied humiliating restrictions on her. The breach between her and Nepal Darbar widened. Towards the end of 1860, it was signified to Maharani Jind Kaur that her son, Maharaja Duleep Singh, was about to return to India and that she could visit him in Calcutta. She travelled to Calcutta to meet her son, who took her with him to England.

Maharani Jind Kaur died at Kensington, England, on 1 August 1863.

Paying a tribute to the Maharani, Colonel Alexander Gardener, who was a close associate of Maharaja Ranjit Singh, said: "Maharani Jind Kaur was the most brave queen of Punjab who did the kingdom of Punjab proud." Mulk Raj Anand, a scholar of eminence, has remarked: "Rani Jindan, a woman of beauty from a modest household, whom Maharaja Ranjit Singh married late in his life, rose to be a heroine. She resisted the efforts of the British to annexe Punjab for sometime. She came out of the *purdah*, held *durbar* with the chiefs of the army, daily took counsel with the nobles, and conducted the State with uncommon commonsense, in some of the most difficult situations facing the kingdom of the Punjab".

49

Mahasweta Devi (1926-)

A leading writer of modern Bengali fiction and champion of tribal communities, Mahasweta Devi was born at Dhaka (now in Bangladesh) on 14 January 1926 to literary parents. Her father Manish Ghatak was a poet and a novelist, and her mother Dharitri Devi was also a writer and a social worker. She is the sister of Ritwik Ghatak, the celebrated film director. She was married to Bijan Bhattachariya, a dramatist-actor. She joined Vishvabharati University in Santiniketan and completed B.A. (Hons) in English. Mahasweta started her career as a school teacher in 1948. She did her Master'degree in English literature in 1963 from Calcutta University. In 1964, she joined Bijoygar College, Calcutta, as a lecturer. In 1984, she took retirement from Calcutta University to concentrate on her writing. She was a roving Reporter of a Bengali daily (1982-84).

Mahasweta Devi started writing at a young age and contributed short stories to various literary magazines. Her first book, Jhansir Rani (The Queen of Jhansi), was published in 1956. This work marked the beginning of a prolific literary career. Her first novel, Nati, was published in 1957. Among her masterpieces are Hazaar Chaurasi

Ki Maa, Rudali, Bioscoper Baksho, and Chatti Munda O Tar Tir. She writes about the lives of ordinary men and women, particularly Adivasi (tribal) people like the Santhals, Lodhas, Shabars and Mundas, and other topics of social and political relevance. Her novel Hazaar Chaursai ki Maa has recently been filmed. She has also written children's storie and text books and translated foreign literature into her native Bengali language. She knows Hindi, Oriya and Santhali apart from English.

Mahasweta Devi, 71, has been a writer for more than 40 years. She has published twenty collections of short stories and nearly hundred novels, primarily in her native language, Bengali. She has also been a regular contributor to several literary magazines such as Bortika, a journal dedicated to the cause of oppressed communities within India. She has also been writing about the downtrodden and the tribles in Economic and Political Weekly (Planning Commission's journal). Her books have been translated into Hindi, Oriya, Telegu, Malayalam, Kannada, Gujrati, Marathi and Panjabi. One of her stories has been translated into Japanese, Italian and French.

From early stage in her life, she has worked for the welfare of aboriginal societies like All Indian Vandhua Liberation Morcha, West Bengal Kheria-Sabar Welfare Society and West Bengal Oraon Welfare Society. She is a founder member of 'Aboriginal United Association' and, since 1980, has been editing an aboriginal-magazine 'Bartika' which is concerned with the unprivileged of the society.

Unusual for most writers, she is also an activist and for the last 30 years she has been working with more than a dozen organizations devoted to the uplift of branded labour of tribals of West Bengal, Bihar and Orissa. She is called 'the mother of Sarbars', branded a criminal tribe in West Bengl's Purilia District.

Mahasweta Devi has been the recipient of several awards. In 1995, she won the Jnanpath award, India's highest literary award and donated the prize money to a tribal welfare society. In 1996, she won the Magsaysay award, the Asian equivalent of the Nobel Prize, for journalism, literature and creative communication. She has also been honoured with Padmashri, Sahitya Akademi Award (1979), Saratchandra Memorial Award, Tarashankar Memorial Award, Leela award, Bhuban Mohini Desi Medal (Calcutta University) and Amrita Award (1968). She was chosen for the Indira Gandhi Award for National Integration for 2004 for her commitment to social and economic uplift and sensitizing the society towards communal harmony and national integration.

She lives and works in Kolkata, India.

50

Mallika Sarabhai (1953-)

Mallika Sarabhai, one of the leading exponents of Bharatnatyam and Kuchipudi, is the daughter of the great dancer Mrinalini Sarabhai and the renowned scientist Vikram Sarabhai. After completing her graduation with honours in Economics (1972), Mallika went on to do her Masters in Business Administration from the Indian Institute of Management, Ahmedabad, in 1974 and Ph.D. in Organisational Behaviour from Gujarat University in 1976. She received D.Lit (Honoris Causa) in 1998 from University of East Anglia, Norwich for contribution to the arts.

Mallika has learned both the theory and practice of dance. She started her acting career when she was fifteen. She has acted in over 20 films–both Gujarati and Hindi and also in a French-Shri Lankan movie. She played the role of Draupadi in Peter Brooke's film 'Mahabharata' (1989) which was made in English and French and which brought her international recognition.

Mallika has been lead soloist since 1977 at the Darpana Academy of Performing Arts; specializes in *Bharata Natyam* and *Kuchipudi*; also a contemporary dancer with the Darpana Performance Group; the Pan

Project, London; the Battery Dance Company, New York; the National Dance Institute, New York. She has performed throughout India as well as Western Europe, North and South America, East and South East Asia, Australia, Africa and the Middle East. She has led her dance group to prestigious festivals at *Sadlers Wells-Festival des Champs Elysees*-Festivals of Perth, Singapore, Hong Kong, Japan, Israel, Egypt and to all major festivals held in India.

While dance is her first love, Mallika is also a noted film-maker, internationally known choreographer, an actress, a TV anchor, an editor and a publisher. She has choreographed over 36 performances. She has directed over six series of documentaries and short films on subjects from arts to science to education. She was CEO of a TV channel and has been anchor of numerous TV programmes. She has been author and editor of several monographs on arts and literature.

Mallika, along with her mother co-directs the Darpana Academy of Performing arts in Ahmedabad. The academy now has many faces. There is Darpana for Development, which makes performing arts modules for development issues; Janavak, an authentic Indian folk dance group that aims at folk revival; Chitrakathi, a film unit that prepares educational films and TV material; Mapin Publications that publishes books on Indian heritage; Kritikranti, a trust for inter-disciplinary work in the arts and crafts; Jagruti, a project for environment empowerment; the Value Project that familiarises children with moral dilemmas; Parivartan which seeks to bring about changes in the life of Bhil women; and Centre for Non-violence through the Arts.

Mallika has received several awards. She received Critics Award for best actress (Muthi Bhar Chawal-1974); best actress award (Mena Gurjari (1975); Critics Award for best supporting actress-Katha (1983); Critics Award for best supporting actress, Sheesha (1984); Gold Medal at the folk festival, Dijon(1984), for leading best folk dance group; Gaurav Puraskar (1992), for contribution to arts, Government of Gujarat; FIE Foundation, Ichlkaranji (Maharashtra) award 1996 for outstanding contribution to the cause of Indian classical dance. She was the recipient of the "French Palme D'or", the highest civilian award by the French Government and in Paris she was honoured as the 'Best Soloist Artist' from among 400 dancers from 25 countries.

Mallika Sarabhai was the subject of three documentary films-Pride of India, Mallika Sarabhai and Fatal Reaction-made by Ministry of External Affairs (2002), Films Division (2001) and Jongbloed, a Dutch Director (1996).

51

Mamta Banerjee (1955-)

Known as the tigress of Bengal for her guts and fiery speeches, Mamta Banerjee, was born in Calcutta on January 5, 1955. Her father, Promileshwar Banerjee, was a freedom fighter and a Congressman. He died when Mamta was still in school. Her teenage brother had to find a job to sustain the family. Despite financial difficulties, she continued her studies, raising resources for her studies by giving tuitions. She did her M.A., B.Ed and LL.B from Calcutta University. As a college student,she often outwitted the then Democratic Students Organisation, a front of CPI(M) dominated Socialist Unity Centre of India. She set up a unit of Chhatra Parishad, Students wing of the Congress Party. She formally joined the Congress Party in 1969. She worked as a teacher in a school.

Mamta Banerjee was the General Secretary of Mahila Congress (I), West Bengal, from 1976 to 1980; Secretary of District Congress Committee (I), Calcutta South from 1978-81; General Secretary of All-India Youth Congress (I) 1985-87; Member of Executive Committee of Congress Party (I) 1988; Member of Executive Committee of West Bengal Pradesh Congress Committee (I) 1989; President of Youth Congress, West Bengal 1990. She played an active role in organizing the AICC session in Calcutta in 1984. In 1984, she was elected to the 8th Lok Sabha and in 1985, she became a member of the committee on the Welfare of Scheduled Castes and Scheduled Tribes. She was re-elected to Lok Sabha in 1991 and became a minister in Narasimha Rao's Cabinet for HRD, Youth Affairs and Sports. Due to differences with Congress leadership, she left the Congress party in 1998 and floated a new party-the Trinamool Congress-of which she has, ever since, been the President. She was elected to Lok Sabha again in 1998

She became the Railways Minster in the N.D.A. government in 1999. When Tehelka.com exposed corruption in the government, she left the government. Her main field of work is West Bengal.

Mamta Banerjee is a firebrand leader. She has a reputation for honesty and sincerity and is known as 'messiah' of the poor.

Mamta Banerjee has published a number of books : Uplabdi, Jantar Darbare, Maa, Pallabi, Manabik (in Bengali), Struggle for Existence, Motherland, Crocodile Island (in English). Her hobbies are music and writing.

52

Maneka Gandhi (1956-)

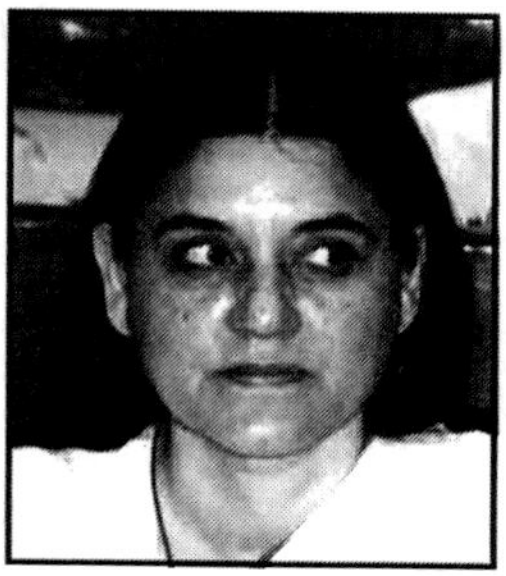

Maneka Gandhi is a leading environmentalist, animal activist and a crusader for vegetarianism. She, herself, is vegan, an author, political commentator, columnist, television and radio personality. Daughter of Lt Col. T S Anand, She was born on 26th August 1956 in Delhi. She was educated at Lawrence School, Sanawar (Himachal Pradesh) and Jawaharlal Nehru University. She married Sanjay Gandhi (younger son of Mrs Indira Gandhi). She lost her husband at a young age when Sanjay was killed in a plane crash. They had a son. Maneka Gandhi entered politics in 1982 after her husband's death. She formed the Sanjay Vichar Manch in 1983 and joined the Janata Dal in 1988 and was its General Secretary. She was elected to Lok Sabha from Pilibhit in 1989, 1996 and 1998. She has been Minister for Environment and Forests (1989-91), Minister for Welfare (1998) and Minister for Social Justice and Empowerment of the Government of India. She was elected to Lok Sabha fourth time in 2004. As India's Social Welfare Minister, she simplified and shortened procedures. Controversy followed her everywhere because of her strong stands and no-nonsense attitude.

Maneka Gandhi has been actively participating in various political and non-political activities, from social service to writing books, fighting to preserve wild life and nature, a cause very dear to her heart.

Maneka Gandhi was the Editor of political monthly magazine, 'Surya', 1976-80. She is a columnist writing on animal welfare and environment and creator and presenter of T.V. shows on on animals and environment. She is Founder Member of People for Animals, Patron, Worldwide Fund for Nature (WWF), Chairperson, Delhi Society for Prevention of Cruelty to Animals (DSPCA) and Managing-Trustee, Ruth Cowell Foundation (animal care shelter and hospital). Often accused of putting animals above people, few know that Maneka Gandhi is Chairperson of Rugmark, an organisaton that works to rescue and rehabilitate child labour in the carpet industry. She has received many awards including Lord Erskine Award from the RSPCA, 'Prani Mitra Award', 1996 and "Maharana Mewar, Foundation Award" 1996 for Environmental work. Her writings include (i) 'Sanjay Gandhi', (ii) 'Stories for Children' (iii) '1001 Animal Quiz', (iv) 'Penguin Book of Hindu Names', (v) 'Complete Book of Parsi and Muslim Names' (vi) 'Brahma's Hair', (vii) 'Heads and Tails', (viii) 'Animal Laws of India' and (ix) 'First Aid for Animals'.

Maneka Gandhi in many ways changed the face of modern India. She won landmark decisions in environment and animal protection. She passed pathbreaking legislation protecting coastal areas and historical buildings. She laid the legal basis for environmental tribunals and initiated the ecomark scheme for environment-friendly products. Internationally, she negotiated the Montreal Protocol for India and brought about the Polluter Pays system. She was a member of the Schumacher Committee, the Eurosolar Board and Wuppertal Institute Board.

MP and Animal Welfare Board member Maneka Gandhi dispatched a letter to more than 250 top Indian companies to ask them to make the decision not to use Australian wool until two abusive practices of Australian sheep, "mulesing" (live flaying) and live exports, are ended. Maneka Gandhi's letter was in support of PETA's (People for the Ethical Treatment of Animals') international campaign against lamb mutilations and live sheep shipments.

53

Mata Amritanandamayi (1953-)

Mata Amrananathamayi the great spiritual personality lovingly known as Amma or Ammachi, was born on September 27th, 1953 to parents Sugunandan and Damayanthi in the small village of Parayakadavu, near Kollam, Kerala. She is widely respected as a loving humanitarian and revered by some as a saint. Sudhamani, as she was earlier named, was born to a family of fisher folks. Her schooling ended when she was nine and she had to take care of the domestic work full-time. She did not have a spiritual mentor or guru. From these humble beginnings started the journey of a young fisher woman on the path to 'universal motherhood', which took her even to the United Nations General Assembly, where she addressed the world.

Amma is a devotee of Krishna. Her devotees claim that she had many mystical experiences as a child. In 1975, during a religious function in the neighborhood, Sudhamani had a vision and showed her 'Krishna Bhava'. From then onwards she devoted herself to serving humanity. Slowly people began to flock to the village and seek her blessings. She started a small seaside hamlet where some of her disciples came to live with her. The

Vallikkavu ashram, also called Amritandanmayi Math started off in 1981 as a soul-soothing spiritual tourism centre The *Math* has now developed into a full-fledged institution known as Mata Amritanandamayi Mission Trust with branches in many Indian cities and in several Asian countries, the US, Europe and Mauritius. The Trust is now the headquarters of various charitable projects such as Amrita Niketan (orphanage), Amrita Balamandiram (hostel for scheduled caste students), Amrita Bhavanam (hostel for tribal children), Amrita Kripa Sagar (hospice for the terminally ill cancer patients), Amrita Medical Centre and Amrita Medical Mission of Ayurveda. The trust has built 25,000 houses for the poor in 12 Indian States.

The gist of her teachings is: God is compassion and love. Compassion and love—those are the two things the world needs. There are many people who don't get love. As for compassion, is there any person in this world who has not sinned? That's what Christ also said, isn't it? To me, compassion is forgiving, compassion is giving people even when they don't deserve. According to her all religions are good: Compassion and love are taught by all religions. Mata Amritanandamayi's guidance for the seeker of liberation is simple and absolute: Serve God and surrender the ego and all its desires. She says, as many of the most revered saints and sages throughout history have also proclaimed, "Contentment ensues from egolessness. And egolessness comes from devotion, love and utter surrender to the Supreme Lord." In Ammachi's teachings, the role of the guru is to "break the ego of the disciples" so that "they can know reality." Ammachi believes that the path to liberation is a path of humility and obedience.

In 1993, Amma was one of the three persons who represented Hinduism at the Parliament of the World's Religions in Chicago. Amma was presented with the 2002 Gandhi-King Award for Non-Violence by The World

Movement for Nonviolence at the UN General Assembly Hall (Palais Des Nations) in Geneva in recognition of her lifelong work in furthering the principles of non-violence Amma mostly draped in a white sari travels around the country and abroad, giving *'darshan'*, bringing solace and peace to an increasing number of devotees black, brown and white, with her divine hug She is known to the world as 'the hugging saint'. She offers warm hugs to everyone who approaches her and in India she has been known to individually hug over 50,000 people in a day, sitting sometimes for over 20 hours. Amma travels all around the world, and is said to have hugged at least 21 million people in the past 30 years. Through her extraordinary acts of love and self sacrifice, Amma has endeared herself to millions.

Amma is also well known for her soul stirring bhajans, or Indian devotional chants. Music is a big part of the Ashram and Amma herself has composed hundreds of beautiful bhajans. The senior swamis are accomplished musicians in both vocal and instrumental areas of music. Other Ashram devotees are also accomplished musicians, many of them not even studying vocal music, harmonium, keyboard and tabla.

54

Mayawati (1956-)

Mayawati was born to Prabhu Das and Ram Rati on January 15, 1956 in Badalpur village of Ghaziabad (U.P). She was educated at Kalindi College (Delhi) and Ghaziabad, Meerut University (Uttar Pradesh) and received the degrees of B.A. and B.Ed. During her school and college days she participated in debates and youth programmes and greatly interested in the betterment of the lot of Dalits, backward and minority communities. She worked as a teacher in various schools of Delhi Administration from 1977-1984. She took her law degree at Delhi University. She was an articulate and confident advocate. She was involved in several organization of backward and minority communities and employees' federation. Mayawati, who shares her birthday (January 15) with American civil rights leader Martin Luther King Jr, had once aspired to join the civil services after her college but she was drawn towards BSP supremo Kanshi Ram who founded Bahujan Samaj Party (BSP) on April 14, 1984. Under the inspiration of Kanshi Ram, she entered politics in 1984 and joined his Party (BSP) and soon became the powerful face of Dalit politics.

Mayawati's initial brush with politics was rough when she lost two bye-elections to the Lok Sabha from Bijnore and Haridwar in 1985 and 1987. But, fighting third time in 1989 general elections, she made her Parliamentary debut winning from Bijnore. She has never looked back since then. She was Member of Rajya Sabha from 1994-96. In 1998 she was elected to Lok Sabha 2nd time and in 1999 elected to Lok Sabha third time. Her party's impressive performance of improving its tally from 4 seats in 1998 to 14 seats in 1999 Lok Sabha elections established her as one of the strongest Dalit leaders in U.P. In 2004 general elelctions she was elected to Lok Sabha fourth time.

In 1995, at the age of 39, Mayawati became the first Dalit chief minister to head the UP government. She was also the youngest politician to assume the chief minister's office in Uttar Pradesh, India's most populous state. She was the first and only Dalit to become the Chief Minister of any of India's states. Although her government did not last more than four months (June-October 1995) the first time, Mayawati's political journey had come full circle. Through her leadership she became an icon and a symbol of dignity for millions of Dalits. "Behenji" (sister), as she is endearingly called by her supporters, was returned as chief minister two years later at the head of a BSP-BJP coalition government, this time for six months (March-September 1997). She was Member of UP Legislative Assembly from 1996-98.

She was re-elected to U P Vidhan Sabha in 2002 and announced that her party would take care of the interests of not only the Dalits, minorities and backwards, but also work for a *sarvjan samaj*. In 2002, Mayawati became the chief minister of a coalition government in Uttar Pradesh for the third time in seven years. She had worked assiduously to shed the image of being just a Dalit leader after making inroads into the upper caste bastion in the recent elections.

Mayawati was Vice-President of Bahujan Samaj Party during 1995-2002 and Party Leader from 2002. Under her leadership the Party has broadened its support base to include upper caste Hindus and Muslims. In the last elections to Assembly and Lok Sabha, She fielded a large number of Muslims and upper-caste members as party candidates.

55

Medha Patkar (1954-)

Medha Patkar, founder of the Narmada Bachao Andolan and the National Alliance of People's Movements, was born on 1 December 1954 in Bombay. Her father was a freedom fighter and later a trade unionist. Her mother works in a women's organisation named Swadhar. After earning an M.A. in Social Work from the Tata Institute of Social Sciences, she worked with voluntary organizations in Bombay slums and tribal and rural areas of North-East Gujarat, Maharashtra and Madhya Pradesh.

Medha Patkar has been a central organizer and strategist of Narmada Bachao Andolan (NBA), a people's movement organized to stop the construction of a series of dams planned for India's largest westward flowing river, the Narmada, which would submerge more than 37,000 hectares of forest and agricultural land and displace some 320,000 villagers, and to fight for just rehabilitation of lakhs of people who would be ousted by the dams. She led numerous marches and rallies against construction of the dams and for the rehabilitation of oustees. She has also been working to obtain just compensation for people affected by dams. She has undertaken fasts and has been arrested a number of times in the course of her fight against authority.

Linking the Narmada Bachao Andolan with a number of peasant, tribal, dalit, women and labour movements throughout India, Medha Patkar has helped establish the National Alliance of People's Movements-a secular political alliance opposed to globalisation-liberalisation based economic policy and for alternative development paradigm and plans. She has served as a Commissioner to the World Commission on Dams, the first independent global Commission constituted to enquire on the water, power and alternative issues, related to dams, across the world.

Medha Patkar and several others from the National Alliance of People's Movements (NAPM) have now announced their plan to form the People's Political Front (PPF) to contest the Lok Sabha elections. The PPF's decision to enter electoral politics is stated to be aiming at "changing the nature of politics." PPF, it is stated, is not a part of any established party or even of any alliance.

Medha Patkar has received numerous awards, including the Deena Nath Mangeshkar Award, Mahatma Phule Award, Right Livelihood Award, Goldman Environment Prize, Green Ribbon Award for Best International Political Campaigner by BBC, and the Human Rights Defender's Award from Amnesty International.

56

Meena Kumari (1932-72)

'Tragedy Queen' of Indian cinema, Meena Kumari, originally named Mahjabeen Ali Bux, was born in 1932 to the Parsee theatre actor and music teacher Ali Bux and the dancer Iqbal Begum. Having hit upon hard times and living near Rooptara Studios, Ali Bux sought to get his daughters into films. Under the name of Baby Meena, Mahjabeen entered film line at the age of six. Her early adult work was mainly in mythologicals. She shot into stardom in the early fifties with the release of Vijay Bhatt's *Baiju Bawra (1952)* in which the suffering Indian woman found a new face in Meena Kumari. It was a strong performance and fetched her the inaugural Filmfare Award for Best Actress.

She became Film Director Kamal Amrohi's second wife and with *Parineeta* (1953), *Daera (1953), Ek Hi Rasta (1956), Sharda (1957)* and *Dil Apna Aur Preet Parayi (1960),* Meena went from strength to strength playing the suffering woman. Meena was known for her tragic roles and she too chose more such roles to cultivate her image of being the great tragedienne. In this her greatest ever performance that immortalized her was in Sahib Bibi Aur Ghulam (1962) produced by Guru Dutt. That year Meena made history as she garnered all the three Best Actress nominations for the Filmfare Award-For *Aarti (1962), Main Chup Rahoongi (1962)* and of course *Sahib Bibi Aur Ghulam* for which she won the award.

While on the professional front, the emphatic success of certain films like *Dil Ek Mandir (1963), Kajal (1965)* kept her at the top, her marriage with Kamal Amrohi ended in 1964. Therafter Meena increasingly took to alcohol to dull her pain. With heavy drinking she lost her looks and began playing character roles.

Meena's best film which became a cult classic-Pakeezah (1972)–was jointly planned by her and her husband Amrohi in 1958. But it was held up when the couple split. Realizing that she had limited time left, Meena went all the way to complete this film. Taking 14 years to complete, Pakeeza was released in February 1972, barely a month before Meena's death on 31st March 1972. The film went on to become a huge success at the box-office and has since acquired a legendary status

A talented poetess in her own right, a collection of her poems, *Tanha Chand,* under the pseudonym Naaz was compiled by Gulzar and published after her death.

Meena Kumari, the legendary 'Tragedy Queen' of Indian cinema, was one of the most beloved actresses in Bollywood cinema. Her studied reserve, chaste diction and extraordinary voice, that struck the right balance between the erotic and the pathetic, ensured her a lasting place in the hearts of the Indian movie-goers.

57

Meera Behn (1892-1982)

Meera Behn was born as Madeleine Slade in 1892 in England. Her father, Admiral Sir Edmond Slade, came of a traditional aristocratic family. Her mother was a beautiful and artistic and came of aristocratic but unconventional parentage. In her family there was a strain of gypsy blood which, according to her, was responsible for her wander lust. Madeleine was a solitary child who hated school and was educated at home by a governess. She loved flowers, birds, trees and animals. She was fond of riding and gardening and learnt French, German and later Egyptian. Madeleine was six feet tall with attractive features, a sharp hooked nose and beautiful eyes. She was much sought after by young men but she felt bored by London society. She did not go to dancing but loved music.

Madeleine read Romain Rolland's Book 'Mahatma Gandhi' at one sitting and it changed her life-"Now I knew what that something was, the approach of which I had been feeling". In order to prepare herself to come to Gandhiji, she gave up alcoholic drinks, became a vegetarian and studied the Bhagvad Gita. She came to India in 1925 and remained with Gandhiji. Life at Gandhiji's ashram was hard but she adjusted herself to life there. She adopted Indian dress, learnt Hindi and mastered spinning and carding. She never married, though she fell in love twice–once in England and once in India. She took a vow of Brahmacharya, shaved off her head and in later years adopted saffron robes. She wanted to become a Hindu but Gandhiji dissuaded her. Gandhiji gave her name of Meera in view of her devotion to him and her dedication to the service of India. She was sent to the Kanya Gurukul, Dehra Dun, where she taught English, Spinning and Carding, and studied Hindi and the Scriptures. At first Gandhiji did not allow her to join political struggle. She toured Bihar, Bengal and Madras to propagate Khadi and to teach improved methods of spinning and carding. She accompanied Gandhiji to the Second Round Table Conference in 1932 and acted as his interpreter on the Continent on his way back home. She said that India was her home and she felt like a foreigner in England. Asked about her religion in London, she said: "She followed Gandhiji's religion but was not a Hindu. There was a Christ and a Buddha. Now there is Gandhi." To a New York correspondent she said: "You have your Christ; to me Gandhi is Christ."

During Second World War, Gandhi ji sent Mera to Orissa, Assam and Bengal and it was on the basis of her reports that he worked out a scheme of non-violent civil defence against Japanese invasion. She went to see the Viceroy but he would not meet her. She met his Secretary and told him that the time had come for the british to end their rule and quit India. Gandhiji sent her to the AICC at Allahabad with a draft on Qyit India movement which was later accepted at AICC Bombay in August 1942.

She joined the Satyagraha movement and was in prison once with Kasturba, and twice by herself. She was arrested alongwith Gandhiji on the morning of 9 August, 1942 and was in the Aga Khan Palace Detention Camp from August, 1942 to May, 1944. In the Detention Camp,she played Carroms, Badminton and Table Tennis.

She narrated her discussions with Gandhiji in her biik "The Spirit's pilgrimage". After her release, she set up a center for the service of villagers and old cows and bullocks near Rishikesh, called Kisan Ashram, later re-named as Pashulok. She worked as Hony Advisor to the UP Government in connection with newly launched "Grow more food" campaign for some time. Later she did similar work in Kashmir.

After Gandhiji's death, the pull for India was not the same. On 18 January 1959, Meera left India for good and settled in a small village about 30 miles out of Vienna. She was awarded Padma Vibhushan in January1982. She passed away on 29 July, 1982.

58

Mirabai (1504-1550)

Mirabai is the most famous of the women *bhakta* poets of north India. There are differences about the precise details of her life. According to one version, she was born in 1504 at Medata, Nagaur District (Rajasthan) and was the only daughter of a Rajput chieftain Ratan Singh. Her mother died when Mirabai was only four or five years old. Mirabai is said to have been devoted to Lord Krishna from a very early age.

Mirabai was married to Bhoja Raj, the heir apparent to the throne of the famous warrior Rana Sanga of the House of Sisodiya in 1516. There were no children from this marriage, and in the event Mirabai took no interest in her earthly spouse, since she believed herself to be married to Krishna. By 1527 A.D. she lost her father, her husband and her father-in-law. Mira, who had dedicated her life to Lord Krishna, accepted these bereavements stoically. It is said that her relatives expected her to commit *sati* (self-immolation), after the death of her husband. But Mira did not. She wrote: "*sati na hosyan girdhar gansyan mhara man moho ghananami*", "I will not commit *sati*. I will sing the songs of Girdhar Krishna." Having lost all interest in life, her devotional activities intensified without caring for the family's prestige and the sneers of the society. She held religious gatherings and sang and danced in the presence of saints and religious-minded persons. She was considered to be a blot on the name of the Rana's family.

After Rana Sanga's death and after the death of his son Ratansi, his other son Vikramjit ascended the throne. He was a despot. He troubled Mira and even tried to administer poison to her. This made her all the more devoted to Lord Krishna. Her love for Lord Krishna not of the life then but a continuity of ages and numerous lives. This spirit of complete surrender to Lord Krishna found expression in various glorified ways. She tried to generate fearlessness in men around her and attempted to making them rise to a higher level.

Mira began to devote most of her time in prayer and worship and, when things became too uncomfortable for her in the palace, she left the palace for good and went to the pilgrimage of Mathura, Vrindavana and finally to Dwarika where she lived till her death in 1547. Mira composed hundreds of poems in praise of her God, Lord Krishna. They are full of vivacity and feelings. Her writings have left a strong imprint on the Indian life. Her original language must have been Rajasthani with slight influence of Brij and Gujarati here and there. Her poems have gained a unique popularity and are sung by the rich and the poor alike, even to this day. She spent her life dancing in trance and singing the attributes of her Beloved Krishna till she left this mortal world in 1547.

A devoted poetess of the Bhakti *yug*, Mirabai belonged to no particular sect; not did she start one of her own. Mira's life was marked by a series of mishappenings and trouble which she could win over only with patience and confidence in herself. This intense agony was the driving force behind her compositions full of eternal bliss, everlasting beauty of heart and mind. She never lost her courage, endowed as she was with the strength of devotion to Lord Krishna. Mirabai had grown into a legend in her own life-time.

59

The Mother (of Pondicherry) (1878–1973)

Mirra Alfassa, later known as the Mother, was born in Paris on the 21st of February 1878. Her mother was Egyptian and her father was Turkish. Mirra had divine visions from her childhood. Mirra received her early education at home and at a private school. She attended an art studio in Paris and became an accomplished painter. She was also a talented pianist and writer. A series of psychic and spiritual experiences are believed to have revealed to her not only the existence of God but one's possibility of uniting with Him, of realising Him. of manifesting Him upon earth in a life divine. One day in the year 1912 Mirra had a first vision of the future: "the advent of universal harmony, the realization of human unity and the establishment of ideal society".

She came to India in 1914 and met Sri Aurobindo in Pondicherry. She at once as recognised him the one who for many years had inwardly guided her spiritual development. She was associated with the work of Shri Aurobindo when he started a philosophical monthly named *Arya* on August 15, 1914, to express his vision of man and his divine destiny. After a stay of eleven months in

Pondicherry, she returned to France for a year and then went to Japan for a period of nearly four years.

In 1920 the Mother rejoined Sri Aurobindo in Pondicherry where Sri Auribindo had established an Ashram, a celebrated spiritual centre. She took charge of Ashram in Pondicherry in 1926. She was the inspirer of Auroville, the international town near Pondicherry. It was to serve as a meeting place for the followers of Shri Aurobindo. Sri Aurobindo and the Mother jointly developed, what they called, "Integral Yoga" in which the Divine Power in us uses all life as the means of our upward evolution and then every experience becomes a step on the path to perfection. The number of disciples around them gradually increased. Under her guidance, which covered a span of nearly fifty years, the Aurobindo Ashram grew into a large and multi-faceted community of about 1400 persons. Among the Mother's other accomplishments during this period were the creation of the Sri Aurobindo International Centre of Education and the initiation of Auroville.

After Sri Aurobindo passed away in 1950, the Mother continued their mission to bring down upon earth the spiritual consciousness they called the Supramental. The Mother personally directed the daily activities of the Ashram until the age of eighty-four. From March 1962 she remained in her room, but from there continued to guide the Ashram and receive people regularly. On 17th November 1973, at the age of ninety-five, the Mother left her body.

60

Mother Teresa (1910–1997)

Mother Teresa was born Agnes Gonxhe Bojaxhiu on August 27, 1910 in Uskub, a town in the Ottoman province of Kosovo (now Skopje in the Republic of Macedonia), where her father was a successful contractor. Her parents had three children, and Teresa was the youngest. The family was ethnically Albanian. Her parents, Nikolla and Dranafila Bojaxhiu, were Catholic, though the majority of their native Albania was Muslim, with a large Orthodox Christian minority.

At the age of twelve, she felt strongly the call of God. She knew she had to be a missionary to spread the love of Christ. At the age of eighteen she left her parental home in Skopje and entered the order of the Sisters of Our Lady of Loreto, an Irish community of nuns with missions in India. After a few months training at the Institute of the Blessed Virgin Mary in Dublin she was sent to Darjeeling in India as a novice sister. In 1931, she made her first vows there, choosing the name Sister Mary Teresa in honour of Teresa of Avila and Thérèse de Lisieux. She took her final vows in May 1937, acquiring the religious title *Mother Teresa.*

From 1929 to 1948 Mother Teresa taught geography and catechism at St Mary's High School in Calcutta, becoming its principal in 1944. The poverty all around left a deep impression on her. In September 1946, by her own account, she received a "call within a call" from God to serve Him among the poorest of the poor.

In 1948 she received permission from Pope Pius XII, via the Archbishop of Calcutta, to leave her community and live as an independent nun. She quit the high school and, after a short course with the Medical Mission Sisters in Patna, she returned to Calcutta and found temporary lodging with the Little Sisters of the Poor. She then started an open-air school for homeless children. Soon she was joined by voluntary helpers, and she received financial support from church organisations and the local authorities.

In October 1950 Teresa received Vatican permission to start her own order, which the Vatican originally labeled as the *Diocesan Congregation of the Calcutta Diocese*, but which later became known as the Missionaries of Charity, whose mission was to care for (in her own words) "the hungry, the naked, the homeless, the crippled, the blind, the lepers, all those people who feel unwanted, unloved, uncared for throughout society, people that have become a burden to the society and are shunned by everyone."

With the help of Indian officials she converted an abandoned Hindu temple into the Kalighat Home for the Dying, a free hospice for the poor. Soon after she opened another hospice, Nirmal Hriday (Pure Heart), a home for lepers called Shanti Nagar (City of Peace), and an orphanage. The order soon began to attract both recruits and charitable donations, and by the 1960s had opened hospices, orphanges and leper houses all over India.

In 1965, by granting a Decree of Praise, Pope Paul VI granted Mother Teresa's request to expand her order to other countries. Teresa's order started to rapidly grow, with new homes opening all over the globe. The order's first house outside India was in Venezuela, and others followed in Rome and Tanzania, and eventually in many countries in Asia, Africa and Europe, including Albania. In addition, the first Missionaries of Charity home in the United States was established in the South Bronx, New York.

Mother Teresa's work inspired other Catholics to affiliate themselves with her order. The Missionaries of Charity Brothers was founded in 1963, and a contemplative branch of the Sisters followed in 1976. Lay Catholics and non-Catholics were enrolled in the Co-Workers of Mother Teresa, the Sick and Suffering Co-Workers, and the Lay Missionaries of Charity. In answer to the requests of many priests, in 1981 Mother Teresa also began the Corpus Christi Movement for Priests.

By the early 1970s, Mother Teresa had become an international celebrity. In 1971 Paul VI awarded her the first Pope John XXIII Peace Prize. Other awards bestowed upon her included a Kennedy Prize (1971), the Albert Schweitzer International Prize (1975), the United States Presidential Medal of Freedom (1985) and the Congressional Gold Medal (1994), honorary citizenship of the United States (November 16, 1996), and honorary degrees from a number of universities. In 1972 Mother Teresa was awarded the Nehru Prize for her promotion of international peace and understanding. In 1979 Teresa was awarded the Nobel Peace Prize. In the same year, she was also awarded the Balzan Prize for promoting peace and brotherhood among the nations.

From 1983 onwards, Mother Teresa started having health problems : heart attack, pneumonia, fracture of collarbone, malaria, failure of the left heart ventricle. She underwent heart surgery, but it was clear that her health was declining. On March 13, 1997, she stepped down from the head of Missionaries of Charity. She passed away in September 1997 in Calcutta at the age of 87.

Mother Teresa was granted a full state funeral by the Indian Government in gratitude for her services to the poor of all religions in India. The former U.N. Secretary-General Javier Pérez de Cuéllar, said: "She is the United Nations. She is peace in the world."

At the time of her death, Mother Teresa's Missionaries of Charity had over 4,000 sisters, an associated brotherhood of 300 members, and over 100,000 lay volunteers, operating 610 missions in 123 countries. These included hospices and homes for people with HIV/AIDS, leprosy and tuberculosis, soup kitchens, children's and family counseling programs, orphanages and schools.

Until her death, Mother Teresa continued her work among the poorest of the poor, depending on God for all of her needs. Despite years of strenuous physical, emotional and spiritual work, Mother Teresa seemed unstoppable. Though frail and bent, with numerous ailments, she always returned to her work, to those who received her compassionate care for more than 50 years.

Mother Teresa is already revered as a modern-day saint by Christians from all corners and denominations. On Oct. 19, 2003, Pope John Paul II beatified Mother Teresa. The beatification took place in Rome, and her popularity has remained strong in the months since. Many believe Blessed Mother Teresa will be named a saint of the Catholic Church someday, and her beatification is the latest step in that path to sainthood.

61

Mridula Sarabhai (1911–1974)

Mridula Sarabhai was born to Ambalal and Sarladevi Sarabhai at Ahmedabad on 6 May 1911. She received schooling at "The Retreat" in the school conducted by her parents for their children. Mridula was born with a silver spoon in her mouth and was reared in extreme comfort and luxury, traveling to Indian hill stations or going to Europe for her holidays. Mridula first met Mahatma Gandhi in 1918 when she was 7 years old and from then onwards she was a changed person. She matriculated in 1928 and joined the Gujarat Vidyapeeth started by Mahatma Gandhi but discontinued her studies after one year in 1930 and joined the national freedom movement. She was Congress Seva Dal volunteer, 1930-46, participating in the Salt Satyagraha, organizing the boycott of foreign cloth and British goods. During 1934-37, she was a delegate to the Indian National Congress and was an AICC member for some time. In 1937, she participated in the Rajkot Satyagraha as a Praja Mandal volunteer. During 1941-42, she acted as Secretary of the Ahmedabad Congress Committee. In 1945, she became organizing Secretary, Kasturba Gandhi National Memorial Trust. She was offered membership of the Bombay Legislative Assembly but, under Gandhiji's advice, she did not accept the offer and continued to work as a Shanti Sainik. In 1946, when Jawaharlal Nehru became Congress

President, Mridula was nominated as a member of the Congress Working Committee and a General Secretary of the Congress.

During struggle for Independence, Mridula was arrested a number of times for participating in Satyagrahas and other freedom movements. In 1930 she underwent 3 weeks imprisonment. In 1932 she was detained for 6 months. During 1932-33 she was externed from Ahmedabad and placed under house-arrest; arrested and convicted for six months. In 1937 she was detained for 3 months for participating in Rajkot Satyagraha. She was kept under detention from August 1942 to December 1944.

As Shanti Sainik, she worked hard in bringing about normalcy during communal disturbances in Ahmedabad (1941), Garh Mukteshwar-Meerut-(1946), Bihar (1946-47), East and West Punjab (1947-48), Delhi (1948-50), East and West Bengal (1950-51), Aligarh (1961) and Ahmedabad (1969). Before and after Partition, she worked in both India and Pakistan for communal peace, recovery of abducted women and in the care of minorities. From 1948-53, Mridula was in-charge of special rehabilitation schemes of the Jammu & Kashmir Government on behalf of the National Conference. In early years after Independence, she unofficially functioned as Personal Assistant to Prime Minister Jawaharlal Nehru. In 1968, she played an active role in the starting of Indian branch of Amnesty International and functioned as one of its Secretaries till her death During 1970-73, she associated herself with Khan Abdul Ghaffar Khan, the Frontier Gandhi, and worked with him in the formation of the Insani Biradri, an organization dedicated to communal harmony.

During 1953-74, after Sheikh Abdullah, Chief Minister of J & K, was arrested, Mridula devoted herself to Kashmir and stood by Sheikh Abdullah even when he was accused of anti-national plans and pleaded for him and his cause vigorously. In that struggle, she had to resign or leave every organization she was connected with. She was removed from Congress Party membership in 1958, and detained under Preventive Detention Act in Tihar jail for about a year and later put under 'House' detention in her home in Ahmedabad under Defence of India Rules. Following a long campaign, Sheikh Abdullah was released and was due to be re-installed as Chief Minister of J & K but Mridula did not live to see that day as she passed away in October 1974 after a sudden illness.

Mahatma Gandhi had great affection for Mridulas. She worked with Mahatma Gandhi and imbibed many values from him. But she also had the courage of conviction to differ from Gandhiji on certain matters. Despite her deep personal loyalty and regard for Jawaharlal Nehru, she did not toe his line always. Jawahrlal Nehru admired her as "an extraordinarily brave girl", "a tremendous worker, a great organizer with amazing grit and courage". Sarojini Naidu described her as the 'Joan of Arc' of Gujarat. The shopkeepers of Ahmedabad used to call her *Pathan*. "She is the bravest man in the Indian army', said General Thimayya. At home her family and friends called her 'Boss'.

All through her stormy life, her liberal and fond parents quietly stood behind her and supported her in every way. Her wealthy parents had made her financially independent. She spent her money on the causes she worked for.

Of all the prominent Congress women who took part in the freedom struggle, Mridula Sarabhai was the only one who did not accept any office in the Government. Before 1947 her main objective was to work towards India's Independence. After Independence it was for achieving harmony and national integration.

62

Mrinalini Sarabhai (1918-)

A world renowned exponent of Indian classical dance, Mrinalini Sarabhai came from the well-known Swaminadhan family of Madras. Her mother was a member of Parliament. Her husband Vikram Sarabhai was space and nuclear scientist who was from Sarabhai family of Ahmedabad, among the 10 richest industrial families of the country. Her sister Captain Laxmi Pandit was with Netaji's INA. With this background, she had interesting experiences and met many famous people, from Gurudev Tagore to Bertrand Russell, Homi Bhabha, John Rockefeller III and American dance pioneer Ruth St Denis and politicians, painters, poets, musicians, a good many big names of the 20th century at home and abroad.

Trained in the Pandanallur tradition by Sri Meenakshi Sundaram Pillai, Mrinalini has retained the purity of Bharatanatyam and yet invested it with her creative and stylish fragrance. Her guru for Kathakali was the great artisan Asan Kunja Kurup and for Mohiniattam, Kalyanikutty Amma, the doyen of this ancient tradition. Much of her world-view and philosophy was learnt at Shantiniketan where she spent her youth under the inspiration of Rabindranath Tagore. She was trained in

Java and the United States, studying acting at the American Academy of Dramatic Arts.

Mrinalini was among the first to explore *Tantra* in dance. She created "*Maya* and the Disciple" and an abstract dance-drama "The Song of Creation" televised by CBS, New York.

Mrinalini Sarabhai set up the Centre for Non-Violence Through Performing Arts, the first of its kind, seeking to spread the message of peace and non-violence through performing arts. And Darpana, an academy founded by her in Ahmedabad in 1948 does that through dance, drama, music and puppetry. Mrinalini and her friends recently set up Prakriti, an organisation concerned with environmental protection.

Mrinalini Sarabhai is internationally recognized as a Bharatnatyam and Kathakali dancer and choreographer. She has solo performances in India and abroad. She has travelled extensively with her troupe, and has received many distinguished awards and citations in recognitions of her artistic eminence. Sarabhai is a director as well as an author of books on dance, scholarly books, novels and children's books. Age has not slowed her down. She speaks with absolute conviction, clarity, and eloquence. And she still dances.

Veteran dancer-choreographer and exponent of Bharatnatyam and Kathakali, a writer, poet, environmentalist, humanist, teacher and founder of institutions, Mrinalini Sarabhai has lived her life with tremendous fortitude and courage. Her reputation the world over as one of India's most celebrated Bharatanatyam dancer is unquestioned.

Mrinalini Sarabhai was the first woman to receive "*Veera Shrinkhala*". She received Padma Shri from Government of India in 1965 in recognition of her standing in the world of classical dances, Natya Kala Shikshamani 1960 and Gold Medal for Choreography at Olympic Cultural Festivalin Mexico in 1968. She was bestowed the 'Knight of the Order of Arts and Letters' by the Government of France as a "tribute to her myriad talents in the field of culture and for changing lives of people around her for the better."

63

M S Subbulakshmi (1916–2004)

Madurai Shanmukhavadivu (M.S) Subbulakshmi, the great Carnatic singer was born in Madurai, Tamil Nadu on September 16, 1916 to noted Veena player Shanmukhavadivu Ammal and Advocate Subramania Iyer. Hailed as the nightingale of Carnatic music, she was popularly known as M S. Young Kunchamma, as M S was called in her childhood, was brought up in a musical environment. Music was in her blood. Her grandmother Akkammal was a violinist. Her mother used to play and rehearse constantly and Kunchamma used to listen and hum ragas along with the Veena and the Nadaswaram recitals frequently heard from the nearby temple. Kunchamma accompanied her mother in local concerts and later gave solo performances. At the age of 10, she cut her first album for HMV. In 1929, she began attending concerts with her mother. By the time she moved to Chennai in 1936, she was already a popular Carnatic vocalist. She was hailed as the child prodigy of Madurai. Starting with 'Seva Sadan' in the 1930s, M S had a brief stint in Tamil films. She played the male role of Narada in 'Savitri' (1941) to raise money for launching Kalki, her husband's nationalist Tamil weekly. Her title role of the Rajasthani saint-poetess Meera in the eponymous film

(1945) gave her national prominence. This movie was re-made in Hindi in 1947.

In 1940 she married T Sadasivam, a senior executive in *Anand Vikatan,* a Tamil weekly. The same year she was awarded the Isai Vani, conferred by Semmangudi Srinivasa Iyer and Raja Mannikaran Pillai. After her big hit 'Meera', she quit films and concentrated solely on Carnatic music as a whole time passion, bagging highest awards and honours climaxing with the highest civilian awatrd of 'Bharat Ratna' in 1998, the first musician to receive this honour.

M S was the first woman to be awarded Sangeetha Kalanidhi by the Music Academy, Madras. The other honours conferred on M S include the Padma Bhushan (1954), Padma Vibhushan (1975), Kaalidas Sanman (1988). the Ramon Magsaysay award (1974), Indira Gandhi Award for National Integration (1990), Konarak Samman (1991), Raja Sir Annamali Chettiar award on her 80th birthday (1996), Chandrasekharendra Sarawati award and Swaralaya award (1997).

She gave concerts all over the world-at Edinburgh festival (1963), United Nations on UN Day (1966), Carnegie Hall in New York, Royal Albert Hall in Britain and also performed in Tokyo, Bangkok, Hong Kong, Manila, Singapore and Malaysia. She gave the inaugural concert in the India Festival, London in 1982. M S, who had been performing regularly at the Thyagaraja Festival, was given the title of "Sapthagiri Sangeeta Vidwanmani".

In recognition of her divine voice and her contribution to Carnatic music, she was conferred degrees of Doctor of Letters by many Universities including Sri Venkateswara University (1971), Delhi University (1973, Benares Hindu University (1980), University of Madras (1987) and the Viswa–Bharati University, Shantiniketan. Shas earned acclaim from big and famous personalities like Mahatma Gandhi, Rajaji, Pandit Jawarharlal Nehru, President A P J Abdul Kalam as well as top ranking musicians both in the Carnatic and Hindustani sphere in the country.

In real life, Subbulakshmi was an extremely traditional and conservative woman of her generation.With husband Thiagarajan Sadasivam to guide her, M S Subbulakshmi raised over Rs. 30 million for charity through her concerts, the first charity concert being for the Kasturba Memorial Fund in 1944.

Millions of homes in India start their day with the soul-stirring voice of this legendary Carnatac vocalist singing to the melody of 'Venkateswar Suprabhatam' sung in praise of Lord Balaji of Triputi and 'Bhajgovindam' all in praise of God. She was one of the greatest musicians who aroused spiritual consciousness through soulful music.

M S passed away on 11 December 2004.

64

Mumtaz Mahal (1593-1631)

Arjumand Banu Begam, better known by her other name, Mumtaz Mahal, daughter of Asaf Khan, the brother of Emperor Jehangir's wife Noor Jahan, was born in 1593 in Agra. She was married to Shah Jehan (then Prince Khurram), the fifth Mughal Emperor at the age of 19 in the year 1612. She was the Emperor's second (some say third) wife but she was the principal wife who was his inseparable companion on all his journeys and military expeditions. She was his counsellor and inspired him to acts of charity and benevolence towards the weak and the needy. For the love and sincerity she showed to her husband, Mumtaz Mahal received highest honor of the land-the royal seal-Muhr Uzah-from Shahjahan, the emperor.

Mumtaz Mahal was woman of legendary beauty and virtue, who had a very deep and loving relationship with her husband. Even during her lifetime, poets would espouse her beauty, gracefulness and compassion. It was said that even the moon would hide in shame from her beauty. She enjoyed watching elephant and combat fights performed for the court. Stories of her virtue spread all over the Mughal Empire.

Mumtaz Mahal bore Shah Jehan fourteen children, seven of whom died young. She died in childbed in 1631 (only three years after his accession to the throne) in Burhanpur in the Deccan where she had accompanied him on a military campaign. She was at first buried in Buhanpur in a garden called Zainabad but afterwards her remains were removed to Agra. Legend has it that on her deathbed, her last wish to the emperor was for a symbol or a monument to their love. Inconsolable, the emperor promised immediately. After her death, it is said, Shah Jahan went into secluded mourning for a week. When he appeared again his hair had turned white, his back was bent, and his face worn out. He kept his promise and built, in the memory of his beloved wife, the finest sepulchre ever-a monument of eternal love. The sad circumstances in which Mumtaz Mahal died inspired all his subjects to join in the Emperor's pious mission to build an everlasting symbol of love. It took twenty-two years for over twenty thousand workmen and master craftsmen to build the unparalleled monument of love, purity and beauty, called the Taj Mahal, on the banks of the River Yamuna in Agra, the capital of Mughal monarchs. It was completed in 1648 (some say in 1645). It stands on a raised, square platform (186 × 186 feet) with its four corners truncated, forming an unequal octagon.

65

Nafisa Ali (1958-)

Nafisa Ali was born to a Roman Catholic mother and a Muslim father, Ahmed Ali, one of the oldest living photographers. She is married to Col. Ravinder 'Pickles' Sodhi, a dashing polo player, and has three children. She believes in Vedanta.

Nafisa Ali is winner of the Miss India crown (1976) at 19, runner up at the subsequent Miss International contest, model, actress, celebrity wife, TV star and the recipient of the Rajiv Gandhi Excellence Award. Before she bagged the Miss India title, she was the national swimming champion from 1972-1974. She was a Calcutta Gymkhana jockey in 1979.

Nafisa is actively involved with the non-governmental organisations—Action India and The Naz Foundation. She worked for the rehabilitation of quake victims in Kutch district of Gujarat and child welfare schemes.

Nafisa Ali is chairperson and founder of 'Action India' which set up Action India (Trust) AIDS Projects Holsitic Care Centre, known as "Ashraya" (sanctuary) in New Delhi for people suffering from HIV/AIDS, as a pilot project with the assistance of the Government of Delhi under the "Bhagidari" (citizen-government) scheme. 'Action India' opened a 10-bedded, in-patient facility, Ashraya, which is run by a team of doctors, nurses, counsellors and volunteers. Nafisa Ali is working on its expansion into a 60-bed facility through donor support.

Nafisa Ali organised a charity ball with a fashion show by six leading designers, in March 2000. The proceeds went towards funding a 12-bedded facility for AIDS patients run by the NAZ Foundation. Another event along with Hollywood hunk, Richard Gere, and Bina Ramani, raised funds for Sahara's hospice for the HIV positive, the Michael Care Home.

She was originally against religion because she thought religious heads created divisions among people. While attending a discourse by an architect-turned-swami of the Chinmaya Mission, she realized that she had shut spirituality out of her life. In her home, she has set up an altar for gods from all religions and she teaches her children that it does not matter by what name you call him–"Allah or Christ–God is God."

Nafisa acted in a number of films and won acclaim : Bewafaa (2005), Yeh Zindagi Ka Safar (2001), Major Saab (1998), Aatank (1996), Kshatriya (1993), Tum Karo Vaada (1993), Junoon (1979)

Nafisa Ali fought Parliamentary election on Congress ticket in 2004 but lost. She has been nominated to the Film and Television Institute of India, Pune. In 2005, she was appointed Chairperson of the Children's Film Society of India (CFSI).

Nafisa Ali is a woman at ease with herself, who has enjoyed her life in its various phases. "For 15 years, I was an army wife, because I felt my husband and children needed me...I loved it, because in the army, it is possible to have such a happy life with so little."

66

Naina Lal Kidwai (1957-)

One of the two Indians picked by Fortune magazine in its list of 50 most powerful businesswomen in 2003 and ranked 47, Naina Lal Kidwai, is probably the highest paid women executive in India. She is the only Indian to figure among six most powerful businesswomen in Asia.

Naina Lal Kidwai got her first notion of business success from her father, the CEO of a prominent Indian insurance company. One of two accomplished daughters (her sister is India's leading female golfer and represents the country in international tournaments), Naina Kidwai, raised in Mumbai and Delhi, went to School in Shimla and finished first in her class every year at secondary school and was chosen school captain. In 1977, she studied in Lady Shri Ram College of Delhi University and graduated from there in Economics. In the college she was actively involved with debates and plays and inter college events. She was Secretary and later President of the LSR Students' Union and won the college's leadership award. After doing Chartered Accountancy, she spent three years at Price Waterhouse, gaining invaluable audit and control experience, before enrolling at Harvard Business School and in 1982 became the first female Indian citizen to graduate from HBS. Naina Kidwai has established herself as one of India's best bankers, a shrewd negotiator with a talent for anticipating new sectors of growth.

Nina Lal Kidwai joined ANZ Grindlays Bank (now Standard Chartered Bank) in India in 1982, rising through the ranks in a variety of merchant, retail, and investment banking assignments. She joined JM Morgan Stanley in 1994 where she became Vice Chairman and Head of their investment banking business. At that time, Morgan's operations in India were relatively small. She engineered a joint venture with investment bank JM Financials, making the resulting firm one of the largest in that industry in India. She also aggressively pursued opportunities in technology, nabbing the accounts of Wipro and Infosys, among others, and brokered a joint venture between AT&T and two conglomerates, owned by the Birla and Tata families, to create a telecom company offering cellular service throughout India. By 1999, JM Morgan Stanley was the No 1 investment bank in India in terms of M&A, with deals worth nearly $700 million. It attributed the astonishing turnaround in large part to Kidwai.

In November 2002, Nina Lal Kidwai became vice chairman and managing director of The Hongkong and Shanghai Banking Corporation's (HSBC) investment banking and securities business in India. In addition to her role as vice chairperson and managing director of HSBC Securities and Capital Markets, she was appointed Deputy CEO of HSBC in India in 2004.

In 2000, Naina Lal Kidwai was ranked 3rd by Fortune Magazine in their first ever listing of the world's top women in business in Asia. Fortune magazine also placed her amongst the top 50 Women in Business, internationally, in the years, 2001, 2002 and 2003. She was selected as one of 2002's fifteen emerging "Global Influentials" by

Time magazine. She has figured in Wall Street Journal's list of the world's top 50 businesswomen in 2004. She was the winner of the third Teacher's Achievement Award (Business) in 2004. She is stated to be the highest-paid women executive in India. She believes that gender has rarely been a barrier to her success.

She is held to be an epitome of elegance in her stylish sarees and pearls. Married and the mother of two children, Naina Kidwai, a devotee of Western and Indian classical music, enjoys returning to the Himalayas for trekking and to observe wildlife.

67

Najma Heptulla (1940-)

Najma Heptulla, daughter of Syed Yusuf Ali, was born on 13 April 1940 in Bhopal in a conservative Sunni family. She is grand-niece of Maulana Abdul Kalam Azad, the famous Congress leader. She earned an M.Sc. (Zoology) in 1960, First Division, First in the University. At the age of 22, she obtained a doctoral degree in Cardiac Anatomy. She was Research Fellow, CSIR, for 2 years and Senior Fellow for 3 years. She married Akbar Heptulla, a Bohra Muslim, in December 1966 and has three daughters. After three years of marriage, she plunged into politics.

Najma Heptulla was first elected to Rajya Sabha in 1980 and has held the office of Deputy Chairman of the Rajya Sabha for three terms (January 1985 to January 1986 and 1988 to 2004). Najma Heptulla has been a member of the Executive Committee of the Inter-Parliamentary Union and Vice-President of that body before she was elected as President of the IPU Council, which office she held from 1999-2002. At the end of her term, the IPU Council conferred upon her the title of Hony President of IPU Council. Najma. Heptulla presided over the Conference of Women Parliamentarians of the Commonwealth Parliamentary Association in New Delhi in 1992. In 1997 she headed the Indian delegation to the UN Commission on the Status of Women.

Najma Heptulla started her political career as Joint Secretary of Bombay Pradesh Congress Committee. She served as General Secretary of the All India Congress Committee (I) in 1986-87 and Spokesperson for that same Party from 1986-87 and in 1998. She was Secretary, Science Forum in Parliament and Treasurer, Society of Latin America.

Najma Heptulla is the Founder and President of the Parliamentarians' Forum for Human Development, sponsored by UNDP, and a Distinguished Human Development Ambassador for UNDP. She was President of Indian Council of Cultural Relations, Government of India (2002-05).

Najma Heptulla is President of the Azad Foundation for Research and Development, President of the Indo-Arab Society, Member of the Board of Trustees of the India Islamic Cultural Centre.

68

Nargis Dutt (1929–1981)

Born in 1929, Nargis, one of the greatest romantic heroines of Indian cinema, was the daughter of Jaddanbai, a Muslim *thumri* singer from Allahabad, and Mohan Babu, a Hindu from Rawalpindi. The convented-educated Nargis wanted to be a doctor. But at a time when she was too young to decide for herself she was offered a job as an actress, which she accepted and shot up to become a great star.

Nargis married the famous actor Sunil Dutt. Nargis and Sunil Dutt first met on the sets of Balraj Sahni's *Do Bigha Zameen* Then he was a student and an aspiring actor and she was already an established star. But they did not get married until several years later, soon after they starred as mother and son in Mehboob Khan's 1957 classic, *Mother India*. Their son Sanjay Dutt is also a famous actor.

Nargis made her *debut* in Mehboob's *Taqdeer* (1943). In course of time what Nargis brought to the Indian screen was a charisma that grew from her innate strength and self-assurance. More than Raj Kapoor's debut film *Aag*, it was Mehboob Khan's *Andaaz* in 1949, that saw her star in the ascendant. Her winning streak continued with a variety of roles in *Barsaat, Anhonee* and *Jogan*. But it was the special chemistry between Nargis and Raj Kapoor that made for that memorable winning combination and after *Awara* Nargis worked exclusively with Raj Kapoor for 15 films. Even so, it was Mehboob's *Mother India* that fashioned her role as earth goddess, that made her an icon for all time. Nargis was a legendary figure even in her lifetime as a film artiste, and social worker. She had acted in more than 50 films and almost all her films received both critical and popular acclaim.

She was the first Indian artiste to receive the Inernational award for the Best Actress at the Karloy Vary Film Festival, Czechoslovakia in 1958 for her role in 'Mother India'. She was also the first actress to receive the Urvashi Award, India's highest acting honour in 1968. She won the National Award for *Raat Aur Din*. She was also the first actress to be decorated with the title Padma Shri in 1958. She won Soviet Land Nehru Award in 1974.

Nargis's charitable work for Spastics saw her nominated to the Rajya Sabha (1980). She became the first patron of the Spastics Society.

While undergoing specialized medical treatment for cancer in New York, Nargis Dutt repeatedly expressed her regret about the lack of such treatment and facilities in the Indian subcontinent. She articulated a dream of providing affordable cancer-related medical care to communities that had no access to even basic diagnostic capabilities. Unfortunately Nargis Dutt did not live to see her dreams realized, herself falling victim to the illness in 1981. Pursuant to her wish her husband Sunil Dutt spearheaded the creation of the Nargis Dutt Cancer Foundation to improve cancer-related medical care in impoverished areas of the Indian subcontinent.

69

Nelli Sengupta (1886-1973)

Social worker and freedom fighter, Nelli Sengupta was an English lady born in 1886. She married Jatindra Mohan Senguta in 1909 and came to India to live in Chittagong. She joined freedom struggle in 1921. She supported her husband whole heartedly in his role in the National Movement. Nelli Sengupta was imprisoned in 1933 for participating in civil disobedience movement. She promoted social and cultural activities organized by the youth of Calcutta (1925-31). She was Alderman, Municipal Corporation of Calcutta 1933-39. She was elected unopposed to Bengal Legislative Council in 1940 and 1946. She was the president of Indian National Congress in 1922. After partition she opted to live in East Pakistan and became a Member of its Legislative Assembly in 1947 and 1954. She was associated with relief committees formed at Chittagong in 1948-48 in connection with riots, floods, cyclones and famine. Later she came to India for medical treatment and died in Calcutta in 1973.

70

Noor Jahan (1577-1645)

Favourite wife of the powerful Mughal Emperor Jahangir, Noor Jahan was the daughter of a Persian immigrant, Mirza Ghiyas Baig of Tehran. Originally named Mehr-un-Nisa, Noor Jahan was born when her parents were migrating to the Sub-continent in the 16th century during the time of the Mughal Emperor Akbar. Her father Mirza Ghiyas Baig entered into Mughal Emperor's service and rose rapidly by sheer merit. Noor Jahan received her early education in Quran and the Persian language and had a special flare for poetry. It is believed that Prince Salim (later Emperor Jahangir) first met Noor Jahan in a garden of the Royal Palace when her girlish innocence, ready wit, beauty, grace and wisdom captured the young prince's heart. She was, however, married at the age of seventeen to a Mughal officer, Sher Afghan Quli Khan who had a much admired military career. Upon later suspected to be siding with the Emperor Jahangir's enemies, Sher Afghan Quli Khan was executed in 1607, leaving Noor a widow with a young daughter called Ladli.

In 1607 Noor Jahan was brought to court to serve as a lady-in-waiting to one of Jahangir's court women. she was a remarkable beauty. Jehangir fell in love with Noor Jehan and married her in 1611. She was 34 then. He first gave her the title Noor Mahal which he changed in 1616 to Noor Jahan, or "Light of the World."

After marriage, Noor Jahan won Jehangir's complete confidence. She dominated her royal husband as no woman in Indian history has done. Emperor Jahangir left most of the State affairs to her care, himself leading a life of ease and comfort. Her father was promoted to the rank of Prime Minister with the title of 'Itmad-ud-daula' while her brothers were appointed to high posts and they dominated the court. A number of historians believe that Noor Jehan became the real power behind the throne and became the virtual ruler of the whole empire until the Emperor died in 1627. Coins were struck in her name. She ruled through trusted males. She controlled all domestic and foreign trade. She took special interest in the affairs of women, giving them land and giving dowries for orphan girls. She herself owned ships which took pilgrims as well as cargo to Mecca.

Noor Jahan was an excellent conversationalist, a fine judge of Persian poetry and a poet herself. Her accomplishments made her an irresistible companion for the emperor. The key to her success was Jahangir's addiction to drugs and alcohol and his adoration of Noor Jahan above everyone else

Noor Jahan also ruled the emperor's vast *zanana* which housed hundreds of people including Jahangir's wives, ladies-in-waiting, concubines, servants, slaves, female guards, spies, entertainers, crafts people, visiting relatives. eunuchs, and all the children belonging to the women. Noor greatly influenced the *zanana's* tastes in cosmetics, fashions, food, and artistic expression. She spent money lavishly, experimenting with new perfumes, hair ointments, jewelry, silks, brocades, porcelain, and cuisine from other lands. Fashions at court, highly influenced by Persian culture, began to blend into local styles.

Both Jahangir and Noor Jahan were devotees of the elegant and sophisticated Mughal artistic style. The Emperor owned an admirable collection of exquisite miniature paintings, and together with Noor constructed beautiful gardens, notably in the court's summer retreat in Kashmir. Noor used some gardens for official functions. Others were opened up for the people for general use.

Noor Jahan enjoyed the height of her power when she was surrounded by loyal men which included members of her own family. Struggles between Jahangir's sons for power, however, slowly chipped away at her reign. The ultimate winner was Jahangir's third son, Shah Jahan. By this time Noor Jahan's influence had waned considerably. Shah Jahan had been allied with Noor Jahan through most of his father's reign, but when she swung her support to others, he rebelled. An old and trusted general, Mahabat Khan, disgusted with the direction of court politics, and particularly the role of Noor Jahan, also joined the rebellion. According to another account, Noor Jahan's decision to marry her daughter from her first husband to Shah Jehan's younger brother Shahryar, and her consequent support to his candidature to the throne made Shah Jehan rebel against his father Emperor Jehangir. Emperor Jehangir was captured by rebels in 1626 while he was on his way to Kashmir. Noor Jahan intervened to get her husband released. Jehangir was rescued but he died on October 28, 1627.

Upon his succession to the crown, Shah Jahan arrested her. Her imprisonment ended her influence at court, and she spent the last years of her life in exile in Lahore. Here she spent a quiet time living with her daughter until her own death in 1645. Her tomb lies in Lahore next to Jahangir's.

71

Padmaja Naidu (1900-75)

Padmaja Naidu, daughter of Sarojini Naidu, the legendary Congress leader, was born in 1900 at Hyderabad. She was educated at Hyderabad and Mussoorie. She devoted herself to the cause of nation like her mother. At the age of 21, she entered the national scene and became the joint founder of the Indian National Congress of Hyderabad. She was founder of Hyderabad Swadeshi League. She spread the message of Khadi and inspired people to boycott foreign goods. She was jailed for taking part in the "Quit India" movement in 1942.

Padmaja Naidu was the Governor of West Bengal (1956-67). During her public life spanning over half a century, she was associated with the Red Cross. On 21st November 1975, Himalayan Zoological Park in Darjeeling (India) was dedicated by Indira Gandhi, the then Prime Minister of India, to the memory of Padmaja Naidu. Since then the zoo is known as "Padmaja Naidu Himalayan Zoological Park".

Padmaja Naidu was Hony Secretary, Hyderabad Khadi Prachar Sangh; Founder of Plague Relief

Association, 1929, Food Relief Association 1943, Indian Conference of Social Work, Hyderabad, 1949. She was member of Provisional Parliament of India 1950-51. She was associated with Senate of Osmania University; was Member, All-India Handicrafts Board; Vice-Chairman, Jawaharlal Nehru Memorial Fund; Chairman, Executive Council of Nehru Memorial Museum and Library Society, 1968-74 and Indian Red Cross Society 1971-72.

She passed away in 1975.

72

Promila Dandavate (1929-2002)

A fiery politician and crusader for women's rights, Promila Dandavate was born in 1929. She studied in the J J College of Arts, Mumbai. During her college days, she was initiated into the Rashtriya Seva Sangh (a rival to Rashtriya Swayamsevak Sangh) by her friends. As a member of Seva Sangh, Promila was involved in various social and constructive activities like digging of wells and constructing of roads in villages.

Promila was married to Professor Madhu Dandavate, a socialist. In 1973, after her husband became a member of Parliament, she shifted to Delhi with him. Promila Dandavate had participated in anti-price rise movement in Mumbai. She took the movement to Delhi.

Promila Dandavate was a member of Seventh Lok Sabha from 1980 to 1984 representing Bombay North Central Parliamentary Constituency of Maharashtra. Earlier Promila Dandavate was elected to Bombay Municipal Corporation from Dadar Constituency from 1968 to 1973. She initiated her political career through participation in the Samyukta Maharashtra movement in 1956. She was a founding member of the PUCL and a member of its National Council and the National Executive

Committee for a number of years. She was also a founding member of the Mahila Dakshata Samiti. An active member of Lok Sabha, Promila Dandavate upheld and pleaded the cause of the deprived sections of the society particularly the destitute women. She was jailed during the emergency for 18 months. She was a member of Joint Committee of the Houses of Parliament to examine the question of the working of the Dowry Prohibition Act, 1961 during 1981-82.

Popularly known as 'Promilatai', she was a vocal activist of the rights of women and was actively associated with various women's organizations. She worked for the setting up of National Commission for Women which was eventually set up in 1991. She involved herself in educating economically backward women through *Stree Vimochan Sabha*. She represented International Council of Social Democratic Women in the Seminar on Adult Education in Ceylon (Sri Lanka) in 1971. She was a member of South Asian Association for Regional Co-operation and was a member of the team of observers during national elections in Bangladesh in 1996. She organised the Socialist International Women's Conference in Delhi in 1997. A person of literary bent of mind, Promila Dandavate authored a book, namely "Widows, Abandoned and Destitute Women in India".

Promila Dandavate passed away on 1 January, 2002 at New Delhi at the age of 73

73

P.T. Usha (1964-)

Hailed as "Sprint Queen", "Golden Girl", "Payyoli Express", "Running Machine" and with many other salutary names, PT Usha was born on 20 May 1964 to Paithal and Lakshmi, a family of cloth merchants, at Payyoli, a small village in Kozhikode in Kerala. She began her athletics career by winning the school junior championship in 1974. She followed it up by winning four Gold Medals at the National School Meet in 1977-78 and four Gold, one Silver and one Bronze at the National Amateur Meet at Quilon. At the National School Games at Nagpur in 1979, she set new record in three events. Moving to Mercy College in the Palghat and to Providence College in Calicut, she was spotted by coach O.M. Nambair who shaped her into a great athlete.

Her first international performance came in the 1982 Asian Games in which she won two Gold medals in 100 meters and 200 meters. At the Los Angels Olympics held in 1984, Usha missed a medal by 1/100 of a second and she had to remain content with 4th place. Usha won the most medals at a single championship-six at Jakarta in 1985. In the 10th Asian Games held at Seoul in 1986, Usha kept the flag of India flying high by winning 4 Gold and 1 Silver medal in the track and field events. Here she created new Asian Games records in all the events she participated. She won four Golds and two Silvers at the Asian Track Federation meet in Delhi, 1989. She won 17 medals-13 Gold, 3 Silver and a Bronze in four Asian Track and Field Championships during the period from 1983-89. Usha has won 101 international medals so far. No other athlete in India has achieved as much as she has.

At present Usha is an officer in the Southern Railway. In 1991, she married V. Srinivasan, then a Central Industrial Security Force Officer and a State level *Kabaddi* player, and their son Ujjwal was born the following year. In 1999, Usha at age 34, mother of 7-year old son, participated in the Asian Track Federation Meet in Japan and astonished everybody by winning two Bronze medals in the 200 m and 400 m. She set a new national record for the 200 m, improving on her own previous record.

P.T. Usha's athletics career spanned nearly two decades. She was adjudged the Best Sportsperson of Asia in 1985, 1986, and 1989. She was named sportsperson of the century by the Indian Olympic Association. She was awarded the Arjuna Award in 1983, and the Padma Shri in 1985. She is the winner of Adidas Golden Shoe for the Best Asian Female Athlete for the year 1986. In Cochin, a road has been named after her. Usha has set up an academy in Koyilandi (Kerala) to train young athletes.

74

Rajkumari Amrit Kaur (1889-1964)

Rajkumari Amrit Kaur was born on 2nd February 1889 in Lucknow. She was the daughter of Raja Sir Harnam Singh of the Kapurthala royal family. She had her higher education in England. On her return from England she came in touch with Gopal Krishna Gokhale and Mahatma Gandhi, under whose influence she entered politics and became one of Mahatma Gandhi's close followers. Her participation in Salt Satyagraha landed her in Bombay jail. In 1937, she went to Bannu in Northwest Frontier Province to promote the cause of the Congress and was arrested there on the charges of sedition. She participated in the Quit India Movement (1942).

Rajkumari Amrit Kaur was President of Women's Association, 1930-33. In 1938 she became the president of All India Women's Conference. In 1945 (London) and 1946 (Paris), she participated in the UNESCO's conferences as a member of Indian delegation. After India attained freedom in 1947 she joined the Central Cabinet as Minister for Health, the first woman to hold Cabinet berth, and served as such till 1957 after which she remained Member of Rajya Sabha until her death on 2 February 1964.

Rajkumari, who did not marry, was equally active in social work. She spent most of her time for the uplift of women and the eradication of social evils. She was a strong champion of female education and equally concerned with the upliftment of Dalits.

Rajkumari Amrit Kaur was the driving force behind many an important welfare organisation. She was Founder Chairperson of the All India Women's Conference and the Indian Red Cross. She was President of the Governing Body of the Lady Irwin College, New Delhi, Founder President of the Delhi Music Society and the Indian Council for Child Welfare. She played a leading role in the working of the Tuberculosis Association of India, the National Association for the Prevention of Blindness and the Hind Kushta Nivaran Sangh (Indian Society for the Prevention of Leprosy). She launched the All India institute of Medical Sciences, New Delhi. Her interest in sports continued throughout her life time. She was the Founder President of the National Sports Club of India and the National Institute of Sports.

Rajkumari passed away on 2 February 1964.

75

Rani Avantibai (Ramgarh)

Rani Avantibai, queen of Ramgarh State in central India, is remembered for her valiant fight against the British during the 1857 War of Independence, when she made the supreme sacrifice of her life for the freedom of motherland. The blatant annexations of estates by British officials had antagonised the local rulers and as the events of the Revolt of 1857 unfolded, they became the most dangerous opponents of the British.

Avantibai was the queen of King Vikramaditya Singh of Ramgarh. When Vikramaditya Singh became incapable of handling the affairs of the State due to ill health, Avantibai rose to the occasion and took charge of the administration.

When King Vikramaditya Singh died leaving behind his wife Avantibai and no heir to the throne, the British put the state under court administration. Avantibai felt humiliated and vowed to win back her land from the British

When the Revolt of 1857 broke out, Rani Avantibai raised an army of four thousand and led it herself. In the first encounter which took place in a village named Kheri, she routed the British troops. Stung by the defeat the British came back with vengeance and launched an attack on Ramgarh. A fierce battle ensued. Avantibai fought most valiantly but her courage and fighting spirit was not enough to match the superior strength of the British army. The Rani was forced to leave Ramgarh and move to the dense forests on the hill of Devharigarh. Surrounded and faced with the prospect of defeat Avantibai thought it better to sacrifice her life rather than to surrender. She killed herself with her own sword and became a martyr on 20th March 1858.

Rani Durgawati (1527-1564)

Durgawati was the only child of her father Kirat Rai, the Chandela king of Mahoba. The Chandelas were at one time a great power but, by the time of Kirat Rai, their influence had declined, mainly because of the expansionist policy of contemporary Muslim rulers. Durgabai had imbibed from her father the qualities of bravery and foresight and at a very young age, she developed into a crack-shot. Hunting was her pastime.

Durgawati was married to Raja Dalpat Shah of Garh Mandala (Gondwana). There are two versions of this marriage. According to one version, her father, a Rajput, in his days of adversity married away Durgawati in lower caste than his–the Gond. Another version is that the beautiful Chandela princess so maneuvered that handsom prince of the big State of Gondwana carried her away.

Durgawati and Raja Dalpat Shah had a son, Vir Narayan. Shortly after the birth of Vir Narayan, Dalpat Shah died, leaving behind a large kingdom, a widow and an infant son. Durgawati did not lose heart in this calamity. She took over the role of Regent to Vir Narayan and the administration of the kingdom. She ruled for 16 years from 1548 to 1564. In this she was assisted by Prime

Minister Adhar Singh. Rani Durgawati conducted various reforms and welfare activities. She excavated many tanks and built temples. She maintained the integrity of the kingdom under difficult circumstances. The designs of the kings of Malwa and Bengal failed to frighten her. Several times she defeated Baj Bahadur, the king of Malwa.

But, in 1564, under orders of Emperor Akbar, Moghul army invaded Gondwana. Rani Durgawati, accompanied by Vir Narayan, fought a pitched battle against the invading troops. Vir Narayan was wounded and had to be taken out of the battle field by a contingent of troops. This weakened her fighting force. Mounting on an elephant, Rani Durgawati fought with great skill and bravery. Durgawati too was wounded. and died fighting. There are two versions of her death. One, both mother and son were killed in the battle. Two, when her defeat became imminent, she plunged her dagger into herself choosing death to dishonour.

77

Rani Gaidinliu (1915-1993)

A veteran Naga freedom fighter, Rani Gaidinliu was born on 26 January 1915 in a poor family of Nangkao village of Manipur. She did not receive any formal education but knew 12 languages. She joined in the Indian freedom struggle of the 1920's at the age of 13 with her cousin Haripau Jadonang, the political and spiritual leader of the Nagas (Nagaland) who had initiated a movement to drive away the British from Manipur. The British announced prizes on her head. Within 3 years she became one of the military and tactical leaders of the movement. When Jadonang was hanged by the British, Gaidinliu took over the leadershipof the freedom movement in Manipur and challenged the Britishers. She headed well-trained and well-organised band of guerillas and led them to rebel against British rule. She was hunted in every corner of the three hill States. Government used a whole contingent of Assam Rifles to fight Gaidinliu's band of freedom fighters. She was captured in 1932 and sentenced to life imprisonment. She was only 17 at that time. She spent 15 years in jail.

In 1937, Pandit Jawaharlal Nehru, Congress leader, visited Assam and met Gaidinliu in Shillong jail. At a press conference later, referring to Gaidinliu's undaunting courage and fierce fight against the British rule, he called her the "Rani of Nagas" and since then the title has become part of her name.

Gaidinliu was released after India gained independence. In 1974, Prime Minister Indira Gandhi gave Rani Gaidinliu a *Tamrapatra* in appreciation of her sacrifices for the freedom of the country. Rani Gaidinliu worked ceaselessly for the uplift of the poor and the downtrodden. She was the patron of Akhil Bhartiya Vikas Parishad since 1974. She started a new religion called "Keraka" meaning "pure". She was honoured with Padma Bhushan award.

Rani Gaidinliu passed away on February 17, 1993.

78

Rani Lakshmibai of Jhansi (1830-1858)

Lakshmibai was born in Varanasi (Benares) to Bhagirathibai and Moropant Tambe around 1830. There is some confusion over her birthdate. She was named Manikarnika, nick-named Manu. Her mother died during her infancy and her father shifted to Bihur. There she grew up in the political atmosphere of the Peshwa's household and came in contact with Nana Sahib, Rao Sahib and Tatya Tope. As a young woman, she learned to read, write and debate. She also learned to ride horses and use weapons while playing with her adopted brothers. She was beautiful, highly intelligent and courageous. When she was about 14 years old, she married Gangadhar Rao, the Maharajah of Jhansi and became the Rani (short for Maharani) of Jhansi. Gangadhar Rao was between forty and fifty years of age at the time of their wedding. With her marriage, Manikarnika's name was changed to Lakshmibai. Lakshmibai was Gangadhar Rao's second wife, the first having died, and without bearing a child.

Lakshmibai had a son in 1851 but he died after 3 months. They adopted the 5 year old Damodar Rao, a member of Gangadhar's extended family and made him the heir to the throne. In 1853, Gangadhar Rao also died.

By efficient administration, she endeared herself to her people. The British Governor General Dalhousie announced that since Gangadhar Rao left no heir, the state of Jhansi would be annexed by the British Government. The British rejected the claim that Damodar Rao was the legal heir. Rani Laxmibai refused to part with Jhansi. Lord Dalhousie annexed Jhansi despite Rani Lakshmibai's protests. She had to quit the palace and retire on a small pension of Rs. 6000. Rani appealed her case to London, but that appeal was turned down. The refusal of the British to acknowledge the legitimacy of Raja's adopted son caused a serious consternation in the local population. This drove the Rani to rebellion in 1857. Lakshmibai assembled a volunteer army of 14,000 and challenged the British troops. Jhansi was attacked by the British in March 1858. Rani fought undauntedly leading her forces from the front and showed great courage and skill. Shelling of Jhansi was fierce and the British were determined not to allow any rebels to escape while Rani was determined not to surrender. The British noted that the Indian soldiers fighting them showed more vigor than they ever had while following British orders. Women were also seen working the batteries and carrying ammunition, food and water to the soldiers. Rani, herself, was seen constantly active in the defense of the city. Jhansi, however, fell to the British forces after a two week's siege. It is said that four to five thousand troops of Rani Lakshmibai died in battle,

With her son tied on her back, the Rani managed to escape on horseback under the cover of darkness and within twenty-four hours rode over one hundred miles to the fortress of Kalpi. Several other Indian rulers joined her force there. It is believed that the Rani was successful in convincing the others to go on the offensive and seize the fortress of Gwalior. This maneuver was successful and helped rally the rebel forces together. The joint force went on the offensive and seized the fortress of Gwalior. The

British forces launched attacks to win Gwalior back. In the fierce battle that followed, Rani Laxmibai fought determinedly to the finish, swords in both hands and reins of horse in the mouth. Rani Lakshmibai lost her life on the second day of fighting on 18 June 1858. The British won back Gwalior. Sir Hugh Rose, the commander of the British force, wrote later, "The Ranee was remarkable for her bravery, cleverness and perseverance; her generosity to her Subordinates was unbounded. These qualities, combined with her rank, rendered her the most dangerous of all the rebel leaders."

As a result of the actions of the British, Rani Laxmibai was catapulted from a 'housewife' to the leader of an army and the most important leader of the India's first war of Independence (1857) in the space of less than a year. Rani Lakshmibai's courage, deeds of valour and heroic battle against the British have become the theme of many a folklore and ballad. She was more than a martial leader. In her brief time she cast aside many conventions to unite people of all castes and religions in her cause. She put aside *purdah*, which she only observed with respect to the British, encouraged other women to do the same and trained them to fight and support the main army. She cut across the social norms of the time, refusing to accept her fate 'as a woman'.

A popular Indian ballad speaks of her valour as such:

"Bundeli har boli mein suni yehi kahani thi...
Khoob ladi mardaani woh toh Jhansi Wali Rani thi...."

How valiantly like a man fought she,
The Rani of Jhansi
On every parapet a gun she set
Raining fire of hell,
How well like a man fought the Rani of Jhansi
How valiantly and well!

79

Rani Rashmoni (1793-1861)

Rani Rashmoni was born of a poor agriculturist family of village Kona, 24 Parganas (North), West Bengal on 26th September, 1793. At the tender age of 11, she was married to Babu Rajchandra Das of Jan Bazar, a wealthy zamindar family of Calcutta. Her husband passed away leaving her all alone The onus of managing the zamindari and business after her husband's death brought out her leadership qualities and inherent managerial skills.

With the help of her son-in-law Mathur babu, who was married to her third and youngest daughter, Karunamoyi, she not only expanded the business but also became a champion for the people. Even as the prestige of the zamindari grew, Rani Rashmoni, being very pious from child hood, continued to lead an extremely religious and austere life. A divine revelation led her to found the famous temple complex on the banks of the Ganges at Dakshineswar in 24 Parganas (North). The patronage she gave to Gadadhar encouraged his spiritual awakening to become Sri Ramakrishna in later life and inspire the Great Indian Renaissance movement.

The Rani was a nationalist in her outlook and stood by what she considered fair and just. Her heroic deeds and confrontations with the British in India had become household stories in her time. By ingeniously blocking the trade and commerce on a part of Ganges, she compelled the British to abolish the tax imposed on fishing in the river which threatened the sole livelihood of poor fishermen. When the Puja processions were stopped by the British on the plea that they disturbed the peace, the Rani came forward in open defiance of the orders and the British had to withdraw the penalty imposed on her in the face of a public upsurge in her support.

Rani Rashmoni had to her credit numerous charitable works and other contributions to society. The construction of a road from Subarnarekha river to Puri for pilgrims, the building of Babughat (named after her late husband), Ahirtola Ghat and Nimtola Ghat for the daily bathers in the Ganges, and the substantial contributions to the then imperial Libnrary (now National Library) and Hindu College (now Presidency College) are a few instance of her benevolence. Her outstanding social work and philanthropic nature were notable aspects behind a great soul for which people started calling her Rani or the queen.

Rani Rashmoni passed away on 19th February, 1861. A commemorative stamp was brought out by Government of India on the occasion of bicentenary of Rani Roshmani.

80

Raziya Sultana (1205-1240)

Daughter of Sultan Iltutmush of Mumluq (slave) dynasty, Razia Sultana was the first female Muslim ruler to adorn the throne of Delhi. As the most capable son of Sultan Iltutmush died during his own life, and the rest were incompetent to govern, Iltutmush nominated his daughter, Razia Sultana, as his successor on the throne of Delhi. Progressive in outlook and dynamic in action, Razia was opposed to conservative and orthodox traditions of her times. Whenever Iltutmush had to leave his capital, he used to leave Razia in charge of the affairs in Delhi. But when Iltutmush died, Rukn-ud-din Firuz, one of his sons, occupied the throne. Rukn-ud-din left all the hard work of governing to his scheming mother Shah Turkaan and whiled away his time with nautch girls. When not smoking opium, he could be found riding an elephant on the streets of Delhi, scattering gold coins to all and sundry. Unfortunately for him Shah Turkaan used her position to avenge all real and supposed insults handed to her in the days when she was a handmaid (before Iltutmash married her). Razia Sultana rose in revolt and, with the support of the people of Delhi, secured the throne of Delhi after defeating her brother in 1236. Rukn-ud-din had lasted precisely six months and seven days.

Razia Sultana was a talented, wise, just and generous woman. She was a great administrator and was well versed in governmental affairs. She was not only a good leader in the battlefield but herself was also an excellent fighter. She was a very shrewd ruler, and for all her feminine beauty, an autocrat who kept the nobility in their place. The army and the people of Delhi were solidly behind her. She established complete law and order in her country. To rule the country, she abandoned her femininity and adopted a masculine getup. She used to dress as a man when appearing in public, be it in court or on the battlefield, wearing trousers and a turban and kept a sword. She refused to wear the veil. She was known as a great 'swordsman' in battle. One such battle was where she led an expedition against Ranthambore to control the Rajputs. She successfully established law and order in the entire length and breadth of her kingdom. A learned leader, Raziya spent much of her four-year rule bringing social reforms. She built schools and libraries, pursued foreign trade and had coins minted in her name with the following inscriptions 'Pillar of women, Queen of the times'.

The Turkish nobles resented having a woman as their ruler, especially when she started challenging their power. Razia had made an Abyssinian slave named Jalal-ud-din Yaqut her personal advisor and started trusting him the most. She raised him to the high office of Amirul-Umarara. This further eroded the monopoly of power claimed by the Turkish nobles and was yet another reason for the Turkish nobles to turn against her. Her relationship with Yakut was no secret in the Delhi court. The thought of a woman of pure Turkish descent consorting with an Abyssinian slave was not acceptable to Turkish Maliks.

Due to constant opposition from nobles and threats from her brothers, the Sultanate was left in a disarray.

They began conspiring against her. In 1239, the Turkish governor of Lahore rebelled against Razia Sultana. However, when she marched against him, he first fled and then apologized. Then the governor of Bhatinda Malik Altunia revolted. When Razia Sultana was trying to suppress the rebellion by Bhatinda, her own Turkish officers deposed her from the throne of Delhi and made her brother Bahram the Sultan. Meantime Malik Altunia's forces succeeded in slaying Yakut and taking Razia Sultana a prisoner. To save heself, Raziya Sultana decided to marry Malik Altunia, governor of Bhatinda. While all of this was happening, Raziya's brother Bahram had been named Sultan in Delhi. Raziya marched with her husband towards Delhi to reoccupy the Delhi throne but to no avail. On October 13, 1240, she was defeated by Bahram and the unfortunate couple was killed near Kaithal (Haryana). Razia lies buried in Bulblikhana in Delhi.

81

Romila Thapar Prof. (1931-)

A recognized authority on Indian history, Prof. Romila Thapar was born in India in 1931 in a Punjabi family. Her father was a medical officer in the Indian army and because of his frequesnt transfers Romila spent her early years in various parts of India. During her school days she was greatly influenced by the freedom movement. While in Pune, she frequently went to attend Gandhiji's prayer meetings. She studied in Wadia College, Pune, and Miranda House, Delhi, and went over to Simla to complete her B.A.(Hons) from Punjab University. She went to London for higher studies and took her doctorate from London University. There she also did a diploma course in Chinese art and archaeology. On return from London, she joined the newly set-up Kurukashetra University. She was appointed to a Readership at Delhi University and subsequently to the Chair in Ancient Indian History at the Jawaharlal Nehru University, New Delhi where she is now Emeritus Professor in History. Romila Thapar is an Honorary Fellow of Lady Margaret Hall, Oxford, and of the School of Oriental and African Studies (SOAS), University of London. She has been a Visiting Professor at Cornell University and the University of Pennsylvania as well as the College de France in Paris.

Romila Thapur is the recepient of numerous honours and awards. She has honorary doctorates from University of Chicago, Institut National des Langues et Civilisations Orientales in Paris, University of Oxford, University of Calcutta and Peradeniya University, Sri Lanka. In 1983 she was elected General President of the Indian History Congress and in 1999 a Corresponding Fellow of the British Academy. Romila Thapar has been named as First Holder of the Kluge Chair in Countries and Cultures of the South at Library of Congress. In 1997, she was awarded Fukoka Cultural Prize.

Ranging from her contribution to the Penguin History of India, which has been continuously in print since 1966, to her latest work, Early India: From the Origins to AD 1300 (Penguin India, 2003), she is the author of numerous academic tomes, including Ancient Indian Social History (Orient Longman, 1979), Interpreting Early India (Oxford University Press, 1994), Asoka and the Decline of the Mauryas (Oxford University Press, 1998), and Cultural Pasts: Essays in Early Indian History (Oxford University Press, 2003). That does not include numerous articles and academic papers in which she has pioneered both the study of early Indian texts and the integration of archaeology with written sources.

Some of Romila Thapar's works have been subject of controversy with a section of her countrymen. The controversy appears to be more political than academic.

Romila Thapar was awarded Padma Bhushan–the second highest State honour-in 2005 which she declined.

In 1992 too, she had refused to accept Padma Bhushan. Explaining the reasons she said: "I only accept awards from academic institutions or those associated with my professional work, and not accept State awards."

82

Rukmini Devi Arundale (1904-1986)

Rukmini Devi Arundale, a highly respected authority on dance, music and culture, was born on February 29, 1904, to Neelakanta Sastri and Seshammal. Rukmini Devi grew up in the sprawling Adyar campus of the Theosophical Society of which her father, a retired Engineer, was an important functionary. At the age of 16, she married an Englishman, Dr George Arundale, many years her senior, against the wishes of the relatives and the community. The public protest was so severe that the couple had to go to Mumbai to solemnize marriage.

In her twenties, Rukmini Devi took to training for dance under a renowned *guru,* Meenakshisundaram Pillai. She was introduced to Bharatnatyam by E. Krishna Iyer, founder-secretary of the Madras Music Academy. Rukmini Devi grew into an accomplished dancer and gave her first dance performance in 1935. Given her upper-class Brahmin background, Rukmini Devi's entry into Bharatnatyam diluted the social ostracism of the community of dancers. She did sanitise it by virtually eliminating the sringara (erotic) element and enveloping it in *bhakti.* Seeing her dancing performances, Dr Arundale realized that it was more of a spiritual experience like meditation. It was then that they decided to set up a dance academy, which they called Kalakshetra, as an international academy of arts. Kalakshetra grew to become a pioneering institution. Renowned artistes from all over the country taught there. At a time when the teaching-learning process was still anchored in the *guru-shishya* system, the Kalakshetra provided an institutional setting for the students of music and dance. It has since been recognized as a 'Deemed University'.

Rukmini Devi was a multi-faceted personality and her interests and concerns were as many as they were benign and cultured. She was interested in providing the right kind of education to children. In 1934, she became a member of the Theosophical Educational Trust of which her husband, Dr Arundale, was the President. In the same year she helped her husband and her brotherset up the Besant Memorial High School. After meeting Madame Montessorie in Holland in 1938, she founded the Montessorie Children School in 1939. After passing away of her husband in 1945, Rukmini Arundale became the President of Tgeosophical Education Trust.

Even as a child, Rukmini Devi loved animals. She was instrumental in the passing of the law for the prevention of cruelty to animals (1960) and the establishment of Animal Welfare Board (1962) of which she was appointed Chairman. In 1968, Animal Welfare entitled her "Prani Mitra". She received the Queen Victoria silver medal of the Royal Society for her efforts to prevent cruelty to animals Her landmark achievement was making sure that Act 51 (G) of the Constitution of India was included under Part IV, making it the fundamental duty of every citizen to show kindness and compassion to all living beings. She also started a powerful national vegetarian society in India. She was twice nominated to Rajya Sabha-in 1952 and 1958.

In 1977, the then prime minister Morarji Desai offered to sponsor her name for the office of the President of India but Rukmini Devi Arundale politely declined. Her powerful personality, her contribution to the renaissance of Bharatanatyam and her creation of Kalakshetra, the world-renowned temple of arts in Chennai, has earned for her great admiration.

In February, 1986, when Rukmini Devi was admitted to the Vijaya Hospital in Chennai for treatment, it is said that she refused to use allopathic medicines or injections as she was against testing of medicines on animals. On February 23, 1986, she breathed her last. She was 82.

83

Rukmini Laxmipathi (1891-1951)

Rukmini Laxmipathi was born at Madras in 1891. She was the daughter of H Srinivas Rao, a landlord and a member of the Provincial Government Service and grand-daughter of T Rama Rao, Dewan of Rravancore. Her family was a family of social reformers deeply interested in women's education. Thanks to her father's progressive views, she received both traditional and western education, a privilege not available to many girls then. She learnt Latin and French at home from a Roman Catholic teacher. She later learnt by herself Hindi and Urdu. She did her Intermediate from Women's Christian College and did graduation from Presidency College, Madras.

Hers was an inter-sect marriage. She, a Vaishnavite Brahman, married Dr. Achinta Laxmipathi, a Shaivite Neogi Brahman, in 1910. Her husband was a staunch nationalist and got her interested in politics. Before entering politics, Rukmini was engaged in social work and social reforms. She was Secretary of the Bharata Stri Mahamandal, Madras and was an active member of Women's Indian Association since its inception. She was President of the Youth League in Madras. Alongwith other social activists, she worked for the passing of legislation raising the age of marriage and age of consent.

In 1926, she attended the 10th International Women Suffrage Alliance Congress at Paris. She was seriously concerned about the rapid growth of population and believed in family planning. She worked for the establishment of Malthusian League in Madras in 1931.

Her social activities and the influence of her husband brought her close to Congress. She became a Congress member in 1928. In politics, she was greatly influenced by Gandhiji, Sarojini Naidu and C Rajagoplachari.Her activities spread over the whole of Madras province. A great patriot and an ardent Congress worker, she served the Congress as an active worker until her death in 1951. She gave up her jewellery for the Harijan Welfare Fund of Gandhiji. She participated in the Salt Satyagraha in 1931 and was sentenced to one year's imprisonment. The political prisoners' section in Vellore jail was inaugurated by her. She was arrested in Civil Disobedience Movement in 1932 and was sentenced to six months' imprisonment.

In 1935, she was elected to Madras Legislative Council. Same year, she was made Secretary, Tamil Nadu Provincial Congress Committee and Secretary, All-India Swadeshi Exhibition. In 1935-36, she was the Vice-President, Tamil Nadu Congress Committee. In 1936, she presided over the Tamil Nadu Provincial Conference held at Kraikudi. In 1937, she was elected to Madras Legislative Assembly and became its Deputy Speaker. She was member of the Working Committee of the Indian National Congress.

In 1940, she took part in the individual satyagraha movement and was sentenced to one year's imprisonment. After Second World War, in 1946, she was elected again to Madras Legislative Assembly and made Minister of Health in T. Prakasam's cabinet. After Independence, she continued to be an M.L.A. till her death in 1951. Rukmini Laxmipathi served on several local bodies like Madras

Corporation and Chingleput District Board. She served as Honorary Presidency Magistrate. She defied caste rules and encouraged inter-dining between different communities. She was member of the Senates of the Madras and Annamali universities. She was an accomplished musician and a forceful speaker.

One of the great leaders, Rukmini Laxmipathi had sacrified her whole life in the service of the nation and the society.

84

Sarojini Naidu (1879-1949)

A dynamic freedom fighter, a brilliant orator and a great poetess, Sarojini Naidu was born in Hyderabad On Feb 13, 1879. She was the eldest of the eight children of scientist-philosopher Aghorenath Chattopadhyay and the gentle poetess mother Baradasundari. Her father, the founder of the Nizam College in 1878, was a crusader, a linguist and original thinker. Learning more at home than in school, Sarojini matured very early, wrote poems and passed her matriculation at the age of 12 standing first in the Madras Presidency. She studied (1895-98) at the King's college, London and Girton College, Cambridge. During this period her creative urge found expression in poems. In course of time she became a poet of merit and her proems received rave reviews in the English press. She also happened to be a good singer. She came to be known as the 'Nightingale of India'. In 1898 she married Dr. Govindarajulu Naidu and they had 4 children: Jayasurya, Padmaja, Randheera, and Leilamani. She spoke Urdu, Telgu, English, Persian and Bengali.

During 1903-17 Sarojini came into contact with all the key personalities of India-Gokhale, Tagore, Jinnah, Annie Besant, C.P. Rama Swami Iyer, Gandhi and Nehru.

She began her political career in 1906 when she met Gokhale after Indian National Congress meeting in Calcutta. In 1907, she took active part in a Calcutta meeting against the partition of Bengal. In 1908 she made a great contribution to the women's movement at a Conference on widow re-marriage in Madras. In Hyderabad, she was awarded Kaiser-I-Hind Gold Medal (which later in life she returned) for work during plague epidemic. Her meeting with Mohammad Ali Jinnah made her his admirer for his work for the youth and the London Students Association founded by him. In March 1013, she addressed a huge gathering of Muslims at the historic session of Muslim League where she moved a resolution on self-government and paid high tributes to Jinnah. She joined the Home Rule movement launched by Annie Besant. On the call of Gopal Krishna Gokhale, she joined the Indian National Congress in 1915. She propounded the idea of Swarajya in her powerful speech at the Lucknow Conference in 1916. From 1915 to 1918, alongwith Annie Besant and C P Ramaswami Aiyyar, she lectured all over India on welfare of youth, dignity of labour, women's emancipation and nationalism. Sarojini met Jawaharlal Nehru for the first time at the Congress session in Lucknow in 1916 when she gave a stirring speech supporting the resolution on self-government. After meeting Jawaharlal Nehru, she took up the cause of the indigo workers of Champaran. From 1917-19, Sarojini was involved in campaign on Montague-Chelmsford reforms, Khilafat issue and Rowlatt act, Sabarmati Pact and the Satyagraha pledge. In 1919 she emerged as a political leader in her own right. She was Gandhiji's most ardent aide when he launched the Civil Disobedience Movement in 1919. With great courage she sold proscribed literature on Independence movement and addressed meetings on Jallianwala Bagh and martial law in Amritsar. Sarojini sailed for England in 1919 as a member of All-India Home

Rule deputation and led a powerful agitation in England against sex-discrimination. In 1921 she participated in the Non-Cooperation movement launched by Mahatma Gandhi. With the trial of Gandhiji in 1922, she gave up her luxurious silks in favour of *Khadi*. From 1922-26 she espoused the cause of Indians in South Africa.

In 1925 she was elected the Congress President at Kanpur Session. She was the first Indian woman to become the President of the Indian National Congress. In 1928, she went to USA and had a triumphant tour as Gandhiji's representative. In 1929, she presided over the East African Indian Congress in Mombassa, crossed swords with General Smuts and gave lectures all over South East Africa. Sarojini was part of the delegation consisting of Motilal Nehru, Jinnah, Gandhiji and Patel which met Lord Irwin, Viceroy of India, to discuss the demand for full Dominion Status.

When Mahatma Gandhi started his Civil disobedience movement in 1930, Sarojini Naidu became his principal assistant. She was arrested along with Gandhiji and other leaders. She took part in the Salt Satyagraha. She accompanied Gandhiji to London for the inconclusive second session of the Round Table Conference (1931). She campaigned for participation of women and youth in the public life. She organised a National Week in 1940 and organized rallies against the Cripps Mission to India. She was jailed in 1930 and 1932 for participating in political agitations. In 1942, Sarojini Naidu joined the "Quit India" movement launched by Gandhiji and again was victim of the wrath of the British government and jailed.

She published several books of poetry, all in English, and was elected to the Royal Society of Literature.

In 1947, after Independence, she became the Governor of United Provinces (now Uttar Pradesh). She was the first woman Governor. Her last great role was the inspiring Presidentship of Asian Relations Conference in 1947. She died in office at Lucknow on 2 March 1949. She was seventy-two.

Sarojini Naidu was a woman of extraordinary character, loving, human and wise. She was short, with luminous eyes. She loved rich colours, silks and jewels, flowers and children, She was a connoisseur of good food and herself cooked good dishes. Sarojini was always a woman, supremely womanly and always a patriot. She brought beauty, grace and dignity to public life.

85

Savitribai Phule (1831-1897)

The first lady teacher in India, Savitribai Phule was the daughter of Khandoji and Laxmibai Nevse and was born on 3rd January 1831 in Satara district in Maharashtra. She had studied up to third standard after which she got married to social reformer Jyotirao Phule in 1840. Mahatma Phule found able and unflinching support for his crusade in her.

Savitribai laid the foundation of woman education in the country. Under her husband's guidance, on 1 January 1848, she started the first school for girls in Maharwada, where she was appointed as the Head Mistress. She taught at the school amidst great hardships. She was abused and treated badly by the Brahmins for taking up the cause of educating the lower casrte. She also taught at the adult school at Usmansheikh's Wada where the the lower caste women were imparted education. In November 1852, Phule family was honoured by British government for their work in the field of education and Savtribai was declared as the best teacher.

With the active support of her husband Mahatma Jotirao Phule, Savitribai Phule took up all the challenges that came in her pioneering work. She campaigned for the cause of women empowerment and waged a crusade against social inequalities and evils of sati and child marriage. Throughout her life she remained actively involved in liberating women from the cultural patterns of the male dominated society, widow remarriages, and removal of untouchability. In 1868 she exhorted the lower castes to take water from her well. She did not get affected by the fact that her father-in-law asked them to leave their house if they wished to continue with the same mission. She started an orphanage along with her husband to provide shelter to orphans and pregnant widows. Savitribai provided emotional support to the destitute widows and gave a direction to their life. She practised what she preached. In 1873 she adopted a son of a Brahmin widow and called him Yashwant.

Savitri Phule started an infanticide prohibition home on 28 January 1853. A night school for agriculturist and labourers was started in 1855 and an orphanage in 1863. During 1876-77, she involved herself in relief works in famine and started 52 free food hostels in Maharashatr. She was Chairperson of Satya Shodhak Samaj Conference at Saswad in 1893.

She has to her credit "Kavya Phule"-a collection of poems-which was published in 1854. Yet another book "Lectures of Jyotiba" was published in 1856. She chaired the conference of the Satya Shodhak Samaj in the year 1893. She also took up work during the plague epidemic of 1897 and died due to the same cause on 10th March 1897. Thus till her death she was involved in the cause of the upliftment of the lower caste Hindus.

Savitribai Phule was among the forerunners of the crusaders fighting against the atrocities committed by the upper caste Hindus on the lower castes. Savitribai lent strong support to her husband Jyotirao in his mission of educating the masses, especially the downtrodden and the oppressed, and together they brought enlightenment to the people living in darkness and misery.

Hers was a life of struggle against the evils of society. On her death anniversary in 1998, Government of India issued a commemorative postage stamp in her honour.

86

Shabana Azmi (1950-)

One of India's most respected actresses, Shabana Azmi was born on 18 September, 1950, in Delhi to noted Urdu progressive poet and lyricist Kaifi Azmi and well-known theatre actress Shaukat Azmi. After completing her degree in Psychology at St. Xavier's College, Mumbai, she took a Diploma in Acting at the Film and Television Institute in Pune, India in 1972. As a little girl she accompanied her mother on tours, appearing in group sequences in costumes made especially for her. Her father took her to trade union meetings and instilled in her respect and sympathy for working people. Her early years were significantly influenced by the idealism of her parents who brought her up in a liberal atmosphere of intellectual growth. She remembers her home as constantly throbbing with activity and people. Childhood was not about materialism, but about human values. Success was measured in commitment, passion and courage, as much as rewards and accolades. She maintains close family ties, and the ideals of her childhood continue to dominate the choices she has made in later life.

She made her film debut as Lakshmi in Shyam Benegals 'Ankur' (1974), for which she received the

National Award as Best Actress. Shabana has acted in films by virtually all of India's most famous arthouse directors, including Shyam Benegal, Satyajit Ray, Mrinal Sen, Aparna Sen, and others, as well as in commercial and middle-of-the-road Hindi films. She has acted in new wave films as well as in commercial films with equal success. She has acted in Hollywood productions such as John Schlesinger's "Madame Sousatzka" and Roland Joffe's "City of Joy." She has given talks at Wellesley College and the University of California at Berkeley. She is noted for her naturalness and intensity on screen. Shabana is one of the few Indian actors who has the range and talent to sensitively portray her character and leave audiences momentarily speechless. Shabana Azmi is not only a fine actress, but also a trained classical singer.

It's in real life, not the movies, where Shabana Azmi plays her biggest part—as a crusader against injustice. She is a social and political activist. As an activist, she is associated with the Nivara Hakk Samrakshan Samiti, fighting the cause of Mumbai's slum and pavement dwellers and battling against communal forces. Azmi does not just fight for her co-religionists. In fact, her greatest battle has been against fundamentalist Islamic leaders. She is a leading advocate of AIDS awareness in India. Her husband Javed Akhtar, acclaimed lyricist, poet and writer shares her values, provides enormous intellectual stimulation and gives her both the support and the space to grow and develop.

Shabana has also acted on stage. In "Tumhari Amrita", Shabana proved her mettle in live performances. The play ran five long years to packed audiences and immense critical acclaim. She went on to do a month-long tour with The Singapore Repertory Company, in Ingmar Bergman's adaptation of Ibsen's Doll's House, directed by Rey Buono Shahbana Azmi was acknowledged for her powerful performances with many awards. She is the winner of five National Awards for Best Actress for the films Ankur (1974), Arth (1983), Khandhar (1984), Paar (1985), and Godmother (1999). She has also been the winner of Filmfare's Best Actress Awards for her roles in Swaami (1977), Arth (1982) and Bhaavna (1984). She has also won international awards for Best Actress at the Taormina Arte Festival in Italy for Gautam Ghose's 'Patang' (1994), Silver Hugo Award at the 32nd Chicago Film Festival for her controversial role as Radha in Deepa Mehta's Fire (1996), International Award for Best Actress for Gulzar's 'Libaas' in North Korea in 1993, Chicago Film Festival Award (1996), Outfest Los Angele Award (1997) and Jury Award for Best Actress in 'Fire'The Government of India honoured Shabana, a veteran of over hundred films, with Padam Shri award in 1988 for her contribution to film world. As a social activist, she was presented the Rajiv Gandhi Award as well as the Yash Bhartiya award by the government of the state of Uttar Pradesh. She is the first 'goodwill ambassador' of SOS Children's Village India. In 1998, she was appointed Goodwill Ambassador for the United Nations Population Fund. Shabana Azmi has been a nominated member of Rajya Sabha.

Shabana Azmi is the resurgent face of feminism of modern India. She is a multi-faceted personality with enormous depth and perspective. She has a ready wit, an unaffected charm and a natural grace. She laughs as readily as she expresses irritation and annoyance. She carries herself with remarkable poise and dignity.

87

Shahnaz Husain (1941-)

Shahnaz Husain, Chairperson and Managing Director, Shahnaz Herbals, the pioneer and the undisputed Queen of herbal care, was born on 5 November 1941 at Allahabad (U P). She belongs to a royal family. Her mother was a royal princess from Hyderabad. Her father, who originally came from Samarkhand, held prominent positions in the royal governments of Bhopal and Hyderabad, during pre-independence days. Her Oxford-educated father, Chief Justice of India N.U. Beg, put her through schooling in an Irish convent and instilled in her a love of poetry and English literature. He also imbued in her the right combination of traditional values and progressive ideas and Shahnaz learnt to love and respect the rich heritage of India. It was her extraordinary personal qualities that made her determined to emerge from a sheltered and secure life and venture into a totally different world of entrepreneurship, where she had to wage a lone battle to fulfil her dreams.

Shahnaz was engaged at 14, and married at 15, becoming a mother by the time she was 16. From 17 to 23, she studied cosmetology and cosmetic chemistry in beauty schools in London, New York, Paris, Germany and

Denmark. On return, she started her first own herbal salon for skin and hair care in 1970. Instead of following the existing salon treatment methods, she decided to adopt the principle of 'Natural Care and Cure' and to apply the Ayurvedic system and formulate custom-made products for skin and hair problems. Thus was born the legendary Shahnaz Herbal range of therapeutic products. She has devised clinical treatments for specific problems, like acne, pimples, rashes, pigmentation, skin-sensitivity, dehydration, premature aging, scars, dandruff, hair damage, hair loss, alopecia, and so on.

During the last three decades, Shahnaz Husain' products have acquired a tremendous global presence, having sold at prestigious stores, like Galeries Lafayette (Paris), Harrods and Selfridges (London), the Seibu chain in Japan, Bloomingdales (New York), La Rinascente in Milan (Italy), as well as exclusive outlets and clinics worldwide. In fact, Shahnaz was the first Asian to enter Galeries Lafayette in Paris in herbal care and the first Asian to be featured in the 18-foot shop window of the store.

Shahnaz Husain has received several National and International awards, including the renowned, "World's Greatest Woman Entrepreneur Award" (1996) from Success, the US business magazine and was the first and only woman in 107-year history of the magazine to have received the award. Other awards include the Golden America Award for Quality, Excellence at New York (1999) from Business Initiative Directions (BID) Madrid, Spain, "Woman of the Year 1999" for her outstanding accomplishments from the American Biographical Institute (ABI), U.S.A., The 2000 Millennium Medal of Honour" from the American Biographical Institute (ABI), U.S.A., "Outstanding Woman of the 20th Century from The American Biographical Institute, U.S.A., 'Venus

Award' 1988 from Dame Barbara Cartland, International Diamond Star for Quality" Award (1995) by the International Marketing Institute, Mexico, "Woman of the Year" Award (Silver Cup) (1995) by Princess Alexendera at Savoy Hotel London, International Herbal Queen award (1996) from J Ban Madrid, "Gem of Alternative Medicine" award (1996) from Indian Board of Alternative Medicines Calcutta, "Woman of the Year" Award (1997) from Patrons of the Greater London for the Blind, "Golden Peacock Woman Business Leadership Award" (2000) from Institute of

Directors, New Delhi, "Woman of the Year 1986" Udyog Rattan Award", "Silver Award" for the Best Woman Entrepreneur (1985), "Woman of the Decade" Udyog Rattan Award (1988), 'Indira Priyadarshini' Award (1989),, 'International Personality of the Year 1990, 'Rajiv Gandhi Gold Medal of Merit 1992', 'Glory of India Award' (1997) from International Economic Development Forum, "The Great Daughter of the Soil" award (1988), Rajiv Gandhi Gold Medal of Merit (1992).

Shahnaz loves poetry and Keats is her favourite. Right from childhood, she has expressed her innermost feelings in verse. She has one son and one daughter.

Shahnaz Husain has become a legend in her own lifetime.

Sahnaz runs a vocational beauty school–100% free–for the speech and hearing-impaired, called Shamute, which opened 25 years ago and has seen more than 50,000 male and female graduates troop through its halls.

88

Shakuntala Devi (1939-)

Shakuntala Devi, the human computer, was born in 1939 in a well-known family of Brahmin priests in Bangalore, Karnataka. She received her early lesson in Arithmetic from her grandfather. She displayed an extraordinary love for numbers at the age of 3 and, by the time she turned five, she was recognized as a child prodigy and an expert in complex mental arithmetic.

While she was six, Shakuntala demonstrated her talents at the University of Mysore to a large gathering of students and professors. That was followed by a never-ending stream of public displays at various universities and colleges around the world. She has out-done some of the fastest computers to the amazement of scientists.

Her abilities, defying common theories of human intelligence, have been the subject of much research. In addition to normal arithmetic such as addition, multiplication and division, she calculates square and cube roots as well as logarithms in her head. Given any date in the last century she could tell the day of the week, in a flash. In 1977 she won a standing ovation from an audience of mathematicians when she extracted the 23rd root of a

201-digit number. That means she found the number that when multiplied by itself 23 times equaled the 201-digit number she was given. She solved it in 50 seconds flat. The day's most sophisticated computer, a Univac 1108, also did the deed-in 62 seconds-but only after days of programming, 13 thousand instructions and 5,000 data locations. No one has a plausible theory as to how she could have arrived at the answer, for the feat far exceeds the supposed limits of human intelligence. For her feats Shakuntala Devi has been honoured with numerous medals and awards around the world. Shakuntala Devi attributes her mathematical wizardry to her friendship with Lord Ganesha, developed in her early childhood.

In 1980, she multiplied two randomly chosen 13-digit numbers and gave the correct answer in 28 seconds and earned an undisputed place in the Guinness Book of Records.

In recent years Shakuntala Devi has focused her dazzling mind on to a more esoteric field-Astrology. One can imagine the speed and more importantly the precision with which this 'human computer' can resolve complex astrological problems of those who call on her. Earlier on her astrological predictions were available only for the royalty, the statesmen, stars and celebrities. Now she has made her services available to the common man.

Shakuntala Devi is known by many names-'Human Computer', Maths Wizard, Human Calculator, Living Wonder... because of her extraordinary talents in solving complex mathematical problems without any mechanical aid.

A multi-talented personality, Shakuntala has written many books on numbers and mathematical puzzles. She is the author of a novel and many short stories for children. She has also written books on human behaviour, astrology, and cookery. Spurred by huge demand, Shakuntala has formulated a unique herbal tablet that boosts one's memory and mental power. While not traveling the world, Shakuntala divides her time between her home in Bangalore and London.

89

Shashi Deshpande (1938-)

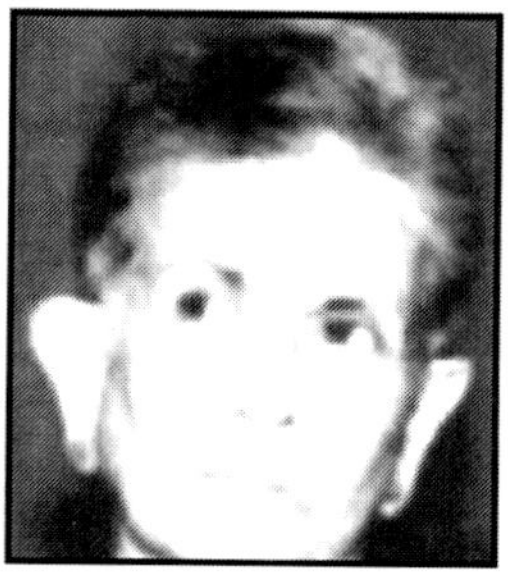

Shashi Deshpande, the daughter of the renowned Kannada writer and Sanskrit scholar, Shriranga, was born in Dharwar, Karnataka, in 1938. At the age of fifteen she went to Mumbai, graduated in economics, then moved to Bangalore, where she did a degree in law. She later received Master's degree in English Literature and did a diploma in Journalism. She is married to a doctor and has two children. Her writing career began in earnest only in 1970, initially with short stories. Since then, several volumes of her short stories have been published.

Shashi Deshpande's first novel 'The Dark Holds No Terror' was published in 1980. She received the Sahatya Akademi Award for 'That Long Silence', published by Virago Press, London. Her novels 'The Binding Vine' (1933), 'A Matter of Time (1996), and 'Small Remedies' (2000) have received high acclaim in literary circles. Her most recent novel 'Moving On' has been published in 2004.

Shashi Deshpande is also the author of four children's novels and of 'Writing From The Margin', a collection of her non-fiction writings dealing with issues of language and writing in English in India, gender, translation-in fact the whole business of writing. A prolific and committed writer, her works have been translated into a number of Indian and foreign languages. She is now translating, with her husband, the writings of her father.

Shashi Deshpande is well-known in literary circles for depicting the quotidian life of average Indian. Unlike most other writers, she refuses to embellish and package her writing to portray India as an exotic land, full of magic and mysticism. All within her fragile frame, she is a profusion of creativity. She is known for amorphous thoughts and thought-provoking issues, a treasure of simple but powerful words with which she strings an effortless prose. She is feminist in personal life but not a feminist writer. She likes to be called a novelist and a short-story writer and not a feminine writer.

90

Sheila Dikshit (1938-)

Hailing from a Punjabi Khatri family, Sheila Dixit was born on March 31, 1938 in the Kapurthala district of Punjab. She was educated at Convent of Jesus and Mary School, New Delhi, and at Miranda House, Delhi University from where she obtained her Masters degree in Arts. She married an IAS officer Vinod Dikshit in the family of noted freedom fighter and a former Governor and Union Minister Umashankar Dikshit. She has two children, one son and one daughter.

Sheila Dikshit has been the Chief Minister of Delhi since 1998, the present term being her second term. She is the second woman to hold this office. During 1984-89, Sheila Dikshit represented Kannauj Parliamentary Constituency of Uttar Pradesh in Lok Sabha. She served as a Minister in the Union Government during 1986-89, first as the Minister of State for Parliamentary Affairs and later as a Minister of State in the Prime Minister's office. As a member of Parliament, she served on the Estimates Committee of Lok Sabha. She contested the 1998 Lok Sabha election from East Delhi Parliamentary Constituency in which she lost. She was President of the Delhi Pradesh Congress Committee in 1998.

Sheila Dikshit has championed the cause of women and has played a leading part in the movement for granting of equal rights to women. She represented India on the U.N. Commission on Status of Women for five years (1984-89). In Uttar Pradesh, she along with her 82 colleagues courted arrest in August 1990 while leading a people's movement against atrocities on women. In early 1970's, she was chairperson of the Young Women's Association and was instrumental in the setting up two successful hostels for working women in Delhi. She chaired the Implementation Committee for Commemoration of Forty Years of India's Independence and Jawaharlal Nehru centenary. She is Secretary of the Indira Gandhi Memorial Trust.

Sheila Dixit has been intrested in the promotion of handicrafts and rural artisans all over the country. Promotion of the folk theatre has been one of her commitments over the years. Between 1978 to 1984, in her capacity as the executive secretary of the Garment Exporter's Association, she played a leading role in promoting garments exports. She has the reputation of being a forward looking Chief Minister and has the reputation of being accessible and helpful.

91

Shiny Abraham Wilson (1965-)

A veteran of four Olympics and three Asian Games in track events, Shiny Abraham (Wilson), the daughter of a policeman, was born at Thodupuzha village in Idukki district of Kerala on 8 May 1965. Her parents encouraged her to take interest in sports at a young age. Shiny started to run in her school days at Thodupuzha and later studied in the sports school in Kottayam. She broke the national record in the U-16 category while she was in class-IX. She was trained at G.V. Raja Sports School in Trivandrum before she moved to Alphonsa College in Palai.

Shiny emerged national champion in the 800 metres a year before the Asian Games in Delhi (1982). After that and till she announced her retirement, she won the event every time she competed on the national scene. In the 1984 Los Angeles Olympic Games, Shiny became the first Indian woman to reach the semi-final of an Olympic event in the 800m, which was also her first of four Olympic appearances. She also reached the final of 4 × 400 metres relay. In 1982 Asian Games [New Delhi], Shiny got the fifth place in the 800 metres. In1986 Asian Games in Seoul, Shiny was unfortunate to have unwittingly cut into the inner lane and was disqualified in that event while very much in front of the field. She was part of the relay squad

(4 × 400 metres) which won Gold and set the Asian record there (Seoul) and which improved upon that mark during the World Championship in Rome in 1987. At the same place, however, she won Silver in the 400 metres. In 1994 Asian Games at Hiroshima, she won Bronze in the 800 metres and Silver in the 4 × 400 metres relay.

Shiny married fellow Olympian Wilson Cherian, a champion swimmer and an Arjuna award winner, in 1988. In the Asian Track & Field Meet at Delhi in 1989, despite being in the family way, she ran the 800 metres to come second. Her husband was the inspiration behind her golden come-back Her first child was born in October 1990 and within eight months she was back on track and took part in the National Championship in Delhi to win the 400m Gold. One of her greatest achievements was that she was running even faster after the birth of her child. In an international meet soon after, she stood third. The next year in the Asian Track and Field Championship in Kuala Lumpur, she won a Silver in the 800m and a Gold in the 400m (the only individual gold medal for India in the meet) aside from a Gold in the relay. The London International Meet, 1993, and the 1995 SAF Games provided her more moments in the limelight till the Atlanta Olympics in 1996 after which she quit international competitions.

National Champion in 800 metres for 14 years, Shiny Wilson appeared in four Olympics-1984 Los Angeles, 1988 Seoul, 1992 Barcelona and 1996 Atlanta. At the 1992 Barcelona Olympics, she was named captain of the women's contingent and given the honour of being the flag bearer. Shiny represented the country more than 75 times in international meets. She was the only Indian and Asian to compete in four World Cup Athletics. She is perhaps the only athlete to have taken part in six Asian Track & Field Meets in a row beginning 1985 in Jakarta. During this period she secured seven Gold, five Silver and two Bronze medals. She represented India in seven of the eight

SAF Games and Won 18 Gold and two Silver medals. In 1991, Shiny was voted India's Best Sportswoman of the Year. She was judged the best athlete at the SAF Games held at Chennai in 1995.

Shiny was awarded the Arjuna Award in 1985, Birla Award in 1996 and Padma Shri in 1998. she is also the recipient of Chinese Journalists Award 1991 for being one of the Top Ten Athletes of Asia. She is working as Deputy Manager (Sports) with Food corporation of India. Shiny,who shifted to Chennai in 1991, has two daughters and a son.

Shiny is the golden girl of Indian athletics. No other woman has represented the country more than 75 times.

92

Sister Alphonsa (1910-1946)

Blessed Alphonsa Muttathupadathu (later known as Sister Alphonsa) was born on August 19, 1910 in Kudamaloor near Kottayam (Kerala) to Joseph and Mary Muttathupadathu. Her pet name was Annakutty. She was baptized on August 27, 1910 at Saint Mary's Church in Kudamaloor under the patronage of Saint Anna. Her mother died when she was very young; so her maternal aunt raised her. Anna was educated by her great-uncle Father Joseph Muttathupadathu. In 1917, while studying in Government Primary School Thonnankuzhy, Arpookara, Annakutty received the first communion. She was seven then. In 1923 she was badly burned on her feet when she fell into a pit of burning chaff. This accident left her permanently disabled. In 1927, she came to the Poor Clares Convent at Bharananganam near Kottayam and received Postulant's Veil on 2 August 1928, taking the name Alphonsa. In May 1929 she entered the Malayalam High School at Vazhappally. Her foster-mother died in 1930.

On May 19 1930 she received her religious habit at Bharananganam. On May 22 1930 she resumed her studies at Changanacherry, while working as a temporary teacher at the school at Vakakkad, 15 k.m. east of Bharananganam. In 1931 Sister Alphonsa joined the Noviciate for the newly professed nuns and in August 1936 she took her perpetual vows. She taught in elementary school. Her students loved her for her gentleness and her light-hearted attitude. Sister Alphonsa became seriously ill and had a miraculous cure through the intercession of St Little Theresa of Lisieux and Blessed Kuriakose Elias Chavara. She decided to dedicate her life to God and service of mankind. Her work brought great spiritual solace to the people around her in the community.

In June 1939 she was struck by a severe attack of double-pneumonia, which left here weak. In October 1940, a thief stumbled into her room in the middle of the night. She lost her memory temporarily as a result of the shock. On 30, Sep.1941, she regained her memory, as she herself had prophesied, on the Feast of St. Little Theresa. Her health continued to deteriorate over a period of time. She received extreme unction on September 29, 1941. The next day she regained her memory, though not complete health. Her health improved over the next few years, until in July 1945 she developed a serious stomach problem. She died on July 28, 1946 after a painful illness. She is buried at Bharananganam, South India in the Diocese of Palai.

On 2 December 1953, the Diocesan Tribunal was set up and Sister Alphonsa was declared Servant of God. In July.1980, the Apostolic process for the beatification of Blessed Alphonsa started. In 1985, Pope John Paul II formally approved a miracle attributed to her intercession and, on July 9, 1985 she received the title Venerable Sister Alphonsa. On February 8, 1986, during his apostolic visit to India, the Pope beatified Sister Alphonsa posthumously at Kottayam and she became the first woman in India to be raised to this honour. Bharananganam, the place where she passed away, has become a centre of pilgrimage.

93

Sister Nivedita (1867–1911)

Sister Nivedita, alias Margaret Elizabeth Noble, was born in Ireland, on 28 October 1867. to Samuel Richmond and Mary Isabel of Scottish descent. In a family where politics and religion were inextricably intermingled, Margaret's inherent qualities were nurtured and blossomed forth. She was nurtured in the intellectual climate of the European culture of the nineteenth century. This later paved the way for her study of India and Indian society. She graduated as a teacher and actively participated in literary pursuits, art, journalism and lectures. But neither her profession nor her social and political friendships could satiate the spiritual abyss within her.

Since childhood Christian religious doctrines were instilled into her. But search for 'Truth' led her in 1895-96 to Swami Vivekananda when he was in London. The transformation of Margaret's personality, character and ideals occured after her meeting with *Swami Vivekananda* in London in 1895 and became his disciple and decided to consecrate her life to service in India. Swami Vivekanand's bold utterances of all that was noblest and best in mankind, spoken with a sense of conviction born out of realisation impressed her, although the matter was intellectually new and difficult to comprehend.

Fearlessness, sacrifice and dedication were the inspiring words of Swami Vivekananda, her Guru, to Sister Nivedita, whose life personified selfless service of the highest order. In *Swami Vivekananda's* plans for the future of India, Nivedita's role was for the upliftment and education of Indian women. She came to Calcutta on 28 January 1898, was initiated into Brahmacharya and was given the name 'Nivedita' by Swami Vivekananda. She took up her residence in the narrow winding by-lanes of Bagbazar, where she started a school under the auspices of Holy mother, *Saradamoni devi*. Nivedita did not hold back anything for herself. Her entire thought and consciousness, her dreams, her intelligence, indeed her entire being was immersed in only one object-India and India alone. During the outbreak of plague in 1899, Nivedita actively participated in cleaning the rotting garbage dumps, nursing the sick and dying and consoling and comforting the bereaved.

After Swami Vivekanand's death, she resigned from the purely spiritual Ramakrishna Order and involved herself actively in the Freedom Movement. She went on lecture tours throughout India from September 1902 to 1904 to rouse the national consciousness of the people. In 1905-06 she was actively associated with all public affairs in Bengal. The strain of relief work in the flood and famine-stricken areas of East Bengal in 1906 broke her health.

The supreme goal towards which Nivedita worked was to see India emerge as a strong and powerful nation. From 1902 onwards she spoke and wrote against the British policy in India. She attacked Lord Curzon for the Universities Act of 1904, for his insulting the Indians by calling them untruthful in his Convocation Address in 1905, and for the Partition of Bengal in 1905. She attended the Benares Congress in 1905 and whole-heartedly supported the Swadeshi Movement both in principle and in practice. She maintained close association with Sri Arobindo, Rabindranath Tagore, Gokhole and J.C. Bose and her writings and speeches attracted notice.

Tall and fair, with deep blue eyes and brown hair, Nivedita was an image of purity and austerity in her simple white gown and with a rosary of *rudraksha* round her neck. She was a woman of immense dignity and great quality. She was described as 'a real lioness' by Vivekananda, 'Lokmata' (the mother of the people) by Rabindranath Tagore, and 'Agnisikha' (the flame of fire) by Aurobindo Ghose. Commenting on her dedication, Rabindranath Tagore had observed: "The life which Sister Nivedita gave for us was a great life...Every moment of every day, she gave what was noblest." Her supreme dedication made her a luminous spirit, who could dispel darkness and show others the right path to follow." In England she was known as 'The Champion for India'. Above all she was a 'Sister' to the Indian people whom she loved.

Sister Nivedita was a genius. She occupies an important place among the builders of modern India. Her love for India is reflected in her writings. "I love India as the birth place of the highest and best of all religions. I will look to India, India may look to the West if she wishes" she wrote.

She died in 1911.

94

Sonal Mansingh (1943-)

A leading exponent of Odissi, an ancient classical dance form of Orissa, Sonal Mansingh was born on 1st May 1943. Her mother Poornima Pakvasa was very artistic minded, and her unconventional grandfather Mangal-das Pakvasa, was a freedom fighter, who believed in the equality of women. Her training in Odissi took place when Odissi was being reconstructed, and her guru taught her most of the numbers, now in the Odissi repertoire. She extended the horizons of this form; studying various strands of Oriyan culture and allied performing arts traditions like Chhau from Guru Anant Charansai and Pala Sangeet. She furthered her education under the late Shri Jiwan Pani. Sonal has also received training in Hindustani classical vocal music from Prof. K.G. Ginge, Bombay and Carnatic classical vocal music from Sri Venkataraman, New Delhi. She has undergone special training in Abhinaya from Late Mylapore Gouriammal and special training in Kuchipudi under Guru Vempati Chinna Satyam in the late 1960's at Madras. Sonal learnt Bharatanatyam from Prof. U S Krishna Rao and Chandrabhaga Devi at Bangalore besides taking lessons from other gurus and teachers belonging to the Pandanallur school. She performed her *arangetram*

at Mumbai where her grandfather was Governor. She took to dance professionally from 1962 onwards.

She has been called a philosopher among dancers for her opinions and interpretations. She is a multi-faceted personality. Apart from being a classical dancer par excellence-leading exponent of Odissi, Sonal Mansingh is a social activist, thinker, researcher, orator, choreographer and teacher. She has been on stage since 1964. In 1977, she founded the Centre for Indian Classical Dances (CICD) in Delhi which has produced many talented artists. Herrenowned choreographic works based on Indian Mythology as well as contemporary issues include 'Indradhanush', Manavatta', 'Sabras', 'Devi Durga', 'Aatmayan', 'Mera Bharat', 'Draupati'. Sonal Mansingh has danced in most countries of the world, as also extensively within India in all major festivals. In her opinion dance is a part of the environment and dance forms should reflect issues of the society and she firmly believes that art has the power to bring even countries closer. Some of her choreographic works reflects issues concerning women and environment. She participates actively in environment related seminars and conduct lectures sharing her perceptions.

Sonal is proficient in Sanskrit (having acquired Degrees "Praveen" and "Kovid" in Sanskrit from Bharatiya Vidya Bhavan) and German literature. She has been a Member of the Executive Board and General Council of National Cultural Fund, Ministry of Culture. She was chairperson of Sangeet Natak Akademi from December 2003 to June 2005. She is a Trustee of the Indira Gandhi National Center for the Arts (IGNCA).

Sonal Mansingh had received several honours and awrds. She was awarded Padma Bhushan by the President of India in 1992 in recognition of her contribution to Indian classical dance. She has received Medal of Friendship from the Council of State of Cuba (1995), Indira Priyadarshini Award (1994), Rajiv Gandhi Excellence Award (1991), Bhai Veer Singh International Award (1990), National Award from Sangeet Natak Akademi, State Award from Sahitya Kala Parishad, Natya Kala Ratna from National Cultural Organisation, Sanatam Nritya Samman (1995) and 'Singar Mani' from Haridas Sangeet Sammelan.

95

Sonia Gandhi (1946-)

Sonia Gandhi, the President of the Indian National Congress, was born on December 9, 1946, to Stefano and Paola Maino in Ovassanjo (Orbassano) a small village 80 km from Turin, Italy. Originally named Antonia Maino, She spent her adolescence in Orbassano being raised in a conservative Roman Catholic family and attending a Catholic school. Her father, a building contractor, died in 1983. In 1964 she went to Cambridge to study English at a language school. There she met her future husband, Rajiv Gandhi, who was studying engineering at the university. The couple married on 25 February 1968. The marriage ceremony-simple and non-denominational-was held on Vasant Panchami day in February, the same day when Indira Gandhi married Feroze decades earlier, in the garden of 1, Safdarjang Road, New Delhi. Sonia wore a pink sari made from cotton which Jawaharlal Nehru had spun while in prison. It was the same sari which Indira Gandhi had worn for her wedding, says biographer Nicholas Nugent in his book 'Rajiv Gandhi—son of a dynasty'. After marriage, she moved into the house of her mother-in-law, the then Prime Minister, Indira Gandhi. She adopted Indian citizenship in 1983. The couple had two children, Rahul (1970) and Priyanka (1972).

Sonia Gandhi did not enter politics until after her husband's assassination on May 21, 1991. Strange as it may sound, Sonia had, in fact, shown aversion to politics for long. She is stated to have opposed her husband Rajiv entering it. After his younger brother Sanjay's death in 1980, Rajiv Gandhi resigned from Indian Airlines, where he was a pilot, to join politics. It was reported to be a joint decision arrived at after long talks with Sonia. Following Rajiv Gandhi's death, Sonia had led a life of near recluse for six years except for her appearances at a few official functions. Ultimately she was persuaded to enter politics and to lead the Congress Party. In 1998. she formally assumed the helm of the Congress Party. Sonia Gandhi became the fifth person from the Nehru family to take over the Congress reins, the other four being Motilal Nehru, Jawaharlal Nehru, Indira Gandhi and Rajiv Gandhi. She revitalized the party in a remarkably short time. She was elected to 13th Lok Sabha in general elections held in 1999 and became Leader of the Opposition. Not only was she herself re-elected to the 14th Lok Sabha in 2004 general elections, she also led the Congress Party back to power after eight years. She was unanimously elected as Chairperson of Congress Parliamentary Party (2004). Being the leader of the single largest party in Lok Sabha, she was unanimously chosen to head an alliance called the United Progressive Alliance and, and in her capacity as Chairperson of the United Progressive Alliance, she was invited to form the coalition government. But she declined to be the Prime Minister. In her capacity as Chairperson of Congress Parliamentary Party, she nominated Dr Manmohan Singh to head the coalition government. Sonia Gandhi took office as Chairperson of the newly formed National Advisory Council with the status of a Cabinet Minister.

In 2000 she asked a court to grant clemency to Nalini who had played a part in the bomb attack which killed her husband. Nalini had appealed for mercy on the grounds that her seven-year-old daughter would be orphaned if she was hanged. The court commuted Nalini's death sentence.

Sonia Gandhi was named the third most powerful woman in the world by *Forbes* magazine, next to Condoleezza Rice and Wu Yi. Sonia Gandhi has authored two books: 'Rajiv' and 'Rajiv's World'. She has also edited 'Freedom's Daughter' and 'Two Alone, Two Together' (two volumes of letters exchanged between Jawaharlal Nehru and Indira Gandhi from 1922 to 1964).

Sonia Gandhi is Chairperson of (i) Rajiv Gandhi Foundation; (ii) Indira Gandhi Memorial Trust; (iii) Jawaharlal Nehru Memorial Fund; (iv) Nehru Trust for Cambridge University; (v) Kamala Nehru Memorial Society and Hospital; (vi) Nehru Memorial Museum and Library; (vii) Indian Council for Child Welfare Trust; (viii) Swaraj Bhawan Trust; Patron, Round Square (International Group of Schools), United Kingdom.

96

Subhadra Kumari Chauhan
(1904-1948)

A luminary of Hindi literature, Subhadra Kumari Chauhan was born in 1904 in a village called Nihalpur in Allahabad. Her father Thakur Ram Nath Singh was a strict vegetarian. She had three sisters and two brothers. The elder brothe, a police Sub-Inspector, resigned his job during non-cooperation movement. The second brother was a Sessions Judge in Ajaigarh State and later an Advocate at Banda (UP).

Subhadra Kumari belonged to a middle class Rajput family and was brought up in an orthodox atmosphere where untouchability was practiced and *purdah* was observed. She had early education in the Crosthwaite Girls School, Allahabad. She passed the Middle examination in 1919 at the age of 15, securing a scholarship, when she was married to Thakur Lakshman Singh Chauhan of Khandwa. Her husband later settled and practiced law at Jubbalpur. After her marriage, Subhadra Kumari joined the Theosophical School, Benares, but could not continue her studies. She was a devoted wife and mother.

Inspired by non-co-operation movement in 1921, she had left school and rushed to be beside her husband who was busy organizing a big *hartal.* From then onwards, this husband-wife team of freedom fighters was always in the forefront of freedom struggle. The first test of her political career came in March 1923 when she was hardly 19. The Congress workers hoisted the National flag on the Jubblepur municipality building which was pulled down and trampled upon by the police. This ignited an indignant country-wide agitation. The center of agitation shifted to Nagpur. Subhadra Kumari and her husband led a large batch of *Satyagrahis* from Jubblepur. She was the first woman Satyagrahi to court arrest in Nagpur.

As one of the forefront leaders of the Congress in Mahakoshal region, Subhadra Kumari threw herself heart and soul in the freedom struggle. In 1930's, she presided over the women's section of Mahakoshal Congress Committee. She was not allowed to court arrest in the Civil Disobedience Movement because she had small children. But she went to jail in 1940 and again in 1942 with a babe in her arms. She went to jail a number of times in the course of freedom movement. Subhadra Kumari was elected to the C P and Berar Legislative Assembly in 1938 and again in 1946, the second time unopposed.

Subhadra Kumari was a born poetess and short story writer. Her first poem was published in 1913. She found a place in 'Kavita Kaumdi', a collection of eminent poets. Her most famous collection of poems is 'Mukul' (1930) for which she was awarded the Seksaria Prize by Hindi Sahitya Sammelan. She received Seksariya Prize second time in 1933 for 'Bikhre Moti', a collection of short stories. She was a great Hindi poetess who combined in her personality the patriotism of Joan of Arc and the lyricism of Meera. She wrote highly inspiring patriotic poems like 'Senani Ka Swagat;' Veeronka Kaise ho Vasant'. Her 'Jhansi ki Rani' was one of the most stirring and most recited and sung poems in Hindi literature. Subhadra Kumari was assistant editor of 'Karmavira' magazine for many years. She was awarded 'Kesariya' award for her works.

Subhadra Kumari was an extremely simple and unassuming person. Till 1930, she was moving about bare-footed. She was compassionate towards Dalits and downtrodden and many of her poems highlighted their miserable lot. She was deadly against the dowry system. She was a believer in inter-caste marriages and had married her own children outside her caste. Faith in Gandhian non-cooperation and secularism were the main planks of her political philosophy. During the worst phase of Hindu-Muslim riots in Jabblepur in 1946-47, she spent a fortnight in a Muslim locality to ensure their safety.

She died in a car accident in 1948.

97

Sucheta Kripalani (1908–1974)

Wife of the towering Gandhian, Acharya J B Kripalani, Sucheta Kripalani was born at Ambala (Haryana) on 25 June 1908 in an upper-midle class Bengali family. Her father, Dr S N Mazumdar, was a medical officer in the Punjab Medical Service. He belonged to the Brahmo sect and had very liberal and progressive views. He was also a staunch nationalist. He wore *khadi* at home and his house was an open house for freedom fighters, despite Government's displeasure. Sucheta grew up in her father's traditions. Becaue of frequent transfers of her father, Sucheta studied in ten different places including Loreto Convent at Simla, Queen Mary's School from where she matriculated. She graduated from Government Women's College, Lahore and did her M.A. in History and Political Science at St Stephens College, Delhi.

Sucheta started her life as a teacher and, among other schools, taught at Sir Gangaram High School, Lahore. She taught in Benaras Hindu University till 1939. While teaching at Benaras, she came into contact in 1929 with her future husband, Acharya J B Kripalani, who had established Gandhi Ashram at Benaras. They married in 1936. It was a happy marriage with close understanding between husband and wife. In the post-Independence period, however, they differed in political views and party affiliation. But this did not affect their personal relations.

Having come from Brahmo background, Sucheta was opposed to castism and was the proponent of equality of sexes, widow re-marriage and other social reforms. She was very fond of Bhagvad Gita which she used to read out to her husband regularly.

In her early life, Sucheta was greatly influenced by Russian Revolution and radical political thought in India. But after 1935, she came under the influence of Gandhiji and became a Gandhian. In 1939, she left Benaras and came to Allahabad where she started working in Congress office. She started a women's section of which she was made the Secretary. She was also in-charge of the Foreign Department of Congress Party as Secretary. In 1940, she participated in Individual Satyagrah Movement at Faizabad and was sentenced to two years' imprisonment. She became an all-India leader in the 1942 'Quit India' movement. When the senior Congress leadership was put in jail in 1942, she alongwith Aruna Asaf Ali, Achyut Patwardhan and Ram Manohar Lohia and others took charge of the movement, went underground and organized resistence in Bombay, Calcutta and Delhi to bring the government to a standstill. She was arrested in 1944 and kept in solitary cell for more than a year.After her release in 1945, She was appointed Secretary of Kasturba Trust. During Noakhli riots, she went there with Gandhiji to work for peace.

In 1946, She was elected to Constituent Assembly of India. On August 14, 1947, just before the dawn of Independence, Sucheta Kripalani sang in the Constituent Assembly the first verses of three patriotic songs-*"Vande Mataram"*, *"Sare Jahan Se Achcha"* and *"Jana Gana Mana"*. She was nominated to Congress Working

Committee. She retained that position even after the resignation of her husband, Acharya Kripalani, from Presidentship of Congress. She was General Secretary of Indian National Congress from 1958 to 1960.

In 1962, She joined the UP cabinet as a Minister and in 1963, she became the Chief Minister of UP. She was India's first woman Chief Minister in the State of Uttar Pradesh.After Chinese action in Tibet, she worked for the establishment of Tibetan Relief Committee. Later she set up Lok Kalyan Samiti for social work among women, children and Dalits. Sucheta was a member of Indian Delegation to United nations in 1949. She attended Peace Conference in Germany in 1952 and was a member of Cultural Delegation which visited Russia.

Sucheta Kripalani was elected to Lok Sabha from Delhi in 1952 and 1957. In 1967 she won the Lok Sabha election from Gonda. She passed away in 1974. Sucheta Kripalani was in the words of Shrimati Indira Gandhi, "a person of rare courage and character who brought credit to Indian womanhood."

98

Surinder Kaur

Groomed by the pioneering film composer Master Ghulam Haider in the early 1940s, Surinder Kaur has been the most accomplished ambassador of Punjabi folk music for over 60 years. Decades ago when she took to singing, foray into music had meant defying tradition. It was a taboo. But her brothers stood by her. An audition in 1943 marked the making of a singing legend who would go on to epitomise the best of Punjabi culture.

Her long career as a singer began with a Hindi song. Her husband, Joginder Singh Sidhu, introduced her to lyrical compositions of Punjabi literary giants, Amrita Pritam, Nandlal Noorpuri, Shiv Kumar Batalvi, Mohan Singh and others. She sang them all with gusto and purity. For decades she has reigned supreme as the foremost Punjabi folk singer. Now nearing 75, and having become great-grandmother, Surinder Kaur confesses to be leading a retired life. But she is not reclusive. Queen of Punjabi folk music, as she has been called, she has not lost her sense of humour. On being hailed as the nightingale of Punjab, she, in a lighter vein said : "It was a befitting epithet for my dark complexion." Her tryst with music continues unbroken. Hours are spent in isolation with harmonium honing the dulcet voice that reigned popularity charts. Music, she says, is her soul mate. Her advice to young singers has been 'don't forget your culture'.

Surinder Kaur has done playback singing for about 20 odds films. She has sung over thousands of Punjabi songs which have become household themes and assumed an eternal quality. Her *'lathe di chaddar'* and her personal favourite *'kinah jammeyan kinha le jaaneyan,'* resonate with evergreen verve till today. While many folk compositions were dug from rural areas, some like *"maavaan te dhiyaan ral baitheyan ne"* were picked up by her from her mother. With her sister Prakash, her duet partner, she shared a special bond. Her daughter Dolly Guleria has now taken over the baton from her and is on the way to become equally popular.

Surinder has received numerous honours for her contribution to Punjabi music. Even at 75, she hasn't called it a day. She is busy preparing an album on Bulle Shah's Kaafi. Besides she nurses a desire to set up an academy so that she can bequeath the rich legacy she carries within.

Today she lives in the USA. Though not very active, she still manages to enthral audiences with her concerts alongside singer-daughter Dolly.

Surinder Kaur has achieved the status of a living legend in her life time. Her depth and intensity, the poise of her stage performances still hold audiences spellbound. That stirring feel and tingle is simply unique.

99

Sushila Nayar, Dr. (1914–2001)

Born on 26th December 1914, in Kunjah (Gujarat), now in Pakistan, Dr Sushila Nayar was brought up in a rural middle class family. Soon after her graduation from Lady Hardinge Medical College, her brother Pyarelal brought her to Mahatma Gandhi at Sevagram. In 1939. Dr BC Roy asked her to look after Mahatma Gandhi, who had a high blood pressure and needed medical attention. While young Sushila treated Mahatma Gandhi for blood pressure, the Mahatma honed her skills in modern English usage. In the eighteen months that she stayed in Mahatma Gandhi's *Ashram*, Dr Sushila Nayar learned many things from her mentor: Like her master, she was a champion of austerity and abnegation. She devoted herself to his causes, denying herself all personal comforts of life.

During her stay in Sevagram, cholera broke out in the nearby villages. Mahatma Gandhi asked her to deal with the problem with "village as the hospital and the houses as the wards". With her bare hands and with no medical personnel to help or guide her, it was a challenge to the young inexperienced doctor which she met successfully.

Dr Sushila nayar obtained her MD in Medicine and came back to Sevagram in 1942. This was the most tumultuous year in the freedom struggle movement: At Mahatma Gandhi's call, thousands of Indians staged Satyagraha and were sent to prison. Young Sushila Nayar was arrested with Kasturba Gandhi and was packed off to the prison in Aga Khan Palace, Pune, where she continued to look after Mahatma Gandhi. In 1944, she started a small dispensary in Sevagram. When the dispensary became popular, at Mahatma Gandhi's advice, it was shifted to the guesthouse built by Birlas where a small hospital with 15 beds started functioning in 1945 and was named the Kasturba Hospital. From there, under Mahatma Gandhi's instructions, Dr Nayar moved to Noakhali, Punjab and Kashmir to look after the victims of pre-partition riots.

After Mahatma Gandhi's death in 1948, she obtained M.P.H. and Dr PH from Johns Hopkins University, USA in 1950. Back in India, she worked for the refugees, and started a tuberculosis sanatorium in Faridabad. As chief of The Gandhi Memorial Leprosy Foundation, she showed firm commitment to eradicate leprosy. Dr Sushila Nayar then entered the political field. She was elected to the Delhi state assembly in 1952 and served as Health Minister from 1952 to 1955. She was the speaker of Delhi *Vidhan Sabha* from 1955 to 1956. In 1957, she was elected to the *Lok Sabha* and was its member from 1957 to 1971 and again from 1977 to 1979. She served as the Union Health Minister from 1962 to 1967.

During her tenure as Health Minister, under Prime Minister Lal Bahadur Shastri's instructions Dr Nayar developed the Kasturba Hospital at Sevagram into Mahatma Gandhi Institute of Medical Sciences to train and motivate doctors to work in villages of which she was the Director. She was President, Indian Council of Medical Research, 1962-67; Chairman, Indian Red Cross Society,

1964-67; President, PGIMER, Chandigarh, 1978-79. She was awarded Doctrate in Medicine and Public Health and President's Award for Literature in 1962.

Dr Sushila Nayar possessed a charming personality. Her natural charm and wit coupled with a radiant smile and a majestic voice used to enthrall the audiences. She was a social reformer. For over three decades, she was the chairperson of Prohibition Committee and worked with missionary zeal against the evil of alcoholism. Dr Nayar was the Chairperson of Kasturba National Memorial Trust and worked for the uplift of women. Community health interested her, as did eradication of illiteracy particularly in women. She was a staunch vegetarian. Dr Sushila Nayar was a gifted writer, and a voracious reader. Her book, "The story of Bapu's imprisonment" gives a succinct account of life and time of Mahatma Gandhi. She completed several volumes of the unfinished biography of Mahatma Gandhi by Pyarelal, her brother. Though a stickler for discipline, she was kind and affectionate.

In 1995, Dr Sushila Nayar suffered a heart attack. Heart ailment and osteo-arthritis severely handicapped her. Dr Sushila Nayar however was made of tougher stuff. Her spirit defied age and illness. At the age of 86, she became Chancellor of The Gujarat Vidyapeeth.

Dr Sushila Nayar passed away on 3 January 2001 in Sevagram.

100

Sushila Gopalan (1929–2001)

Sushila Gopalan, born on 29 December 1929, was the youngest daughter of Thrissur Pazhavil Kannolil Veettil Velukkutty Thandar and Muhamma Chirappanchirayil Madhaviyamma. She received education in Kayamkulam Boys High School and S.D. High School, Alleppey, St Mary's College, Trichur, Women's College, Trivandrum and S.D. College, Alleppey. She was attracted to communist movement in her school days when she met A K Gopalan, a Communist underground worker who later in life became a legendary communist leader. They married on 10 September 1952. She became a member of the Communist Party at the age of 18. She went to jail several times in the course of her political work.

She was a member of Fourth, Seventh and Tenth Lok from 1967 to 1970, 1980 to 1984 and 1991 to 1996 representing Ambalapuzha, Alleppey and Chirayinkil Parliamentary Constituencies of Kerala. An outstanding parliamentarian, Sushila Gopalan played a leading role in pushing through important reforms in laws concerning women. She was a member of the Joint Committee of the Houses of Parliament to examine the working of the Dowry Prohibition Act, 1961 during 1981-82 and played a leading role in the amendment of anti-dowry law. Sushila Gopalan was elected to Kerala Legislative Assembly in 1965 and 1996 and served as Minister for Industries and Social Welfare in the Kerala State Government. She was an active political and social worker and a reputed trade unionist and occupied important positions in various trade unions and social organisations. Sushila Gopalan was founding General Secretary of the All India Democratic Women's Association in 1981 and later its All India President. She was the All India President of CITU, the President of Kerala Coir workers Centre, the Chairperson of NFPTE Co-ordination Committee.

Sushila Gopalan translated the book "The Golden Flower" from English to Malayalam.

After a grim battle against Cancer, Sushila Gopalan passed away on 19th December, 2001 at Thiruvananthapuram, Kerala at the age of 72. At the time of her death she was a patron of All India Democratic Women's Association, vice president of the CITU and a member of the Central Committee of the CPI(M).

101

Sushma Swaraj (1952-)

Sushma Swaraj was born at Ambala Cantt. (Haryana) on 14 February 1952 to Shri Hardev Sharma and Shrimati Laxmi Devi. She did her graduation from S D College, Ambala Cantt and took her Law degree from Chandigarh University. While doing law she met her future husband, Swaraj Kaushal, a lawyer, whom she married on 13 July 1975. (Swaraj Kaushal later became the Governor of Mizoram.) They have one daughter. She was advocate by profession. Sushma Swaraj, together with her husband, campaigned for the release of MISA prisoners during Emergency and participated in J P movement. In Baroda dynamite case, they successfully defended George Fernandez which brought Sushma in political limelight. Sushma swaraj won numerous awards during her early career: Best student of S.D. College, Ambala Cantt. 1970; Best cadet of N.C.C. of S.D. College, Ambala Cantt. for 3 years consecutively; Best speaker in Hindi of Haryana State for 3 years consecutively in a competition held at the State level by the Language Department of Haryana; Best speaker in Hindi of Punjab University in A.C. Bali Memorial declamation contest; and University colour. She was President of Hindi Sahitya Sammelan of Haryana State for 4 years. Sushma Swaraj began her political career through Janata Party of which she was the State Unit President for 4 years. She was active in Haryana State politics from 1977 to 1990. She has been member of the National Executive of Janata Party for 4 years, General Secretary of Bhartiya Janata Party and the official spokesperson of B.J.P. She wasMember of Haryana Legislative Assembly from 1977-82 and 1987-90. She was Cabinet Minister during both terms. She was elected to the Rajya Sabha in 1990, and served on the Panel of Vice-Chairmen of the Rajya Sabha, 1991-98. She was Chief Minister of Delhi, 1998. She was elected to Lok Sabha in 1996 and re-elected in 1998. She has been Union Minister of Information and Broadcasting, Health and Family Welfare and Parliamentary Affairs for various spells during 1996-2004. From 2004, she is a Member of Rajya Sabha and Deputy Leader of BJP in Rajya Sabha.

Sushma Swaraj and her husband Swaraj Kaushal were adjudged as "Distinguished couple" in the Limca Book of Records.Suave and articulate, Sushma inspires appreciation for her uprightness, dedication and oratorical skill.

102

Uma Bharati (1959-)

A *sanyasin* turned politician, Uma Bharati was born in a Lodha family in Dunda village, District Tikamgarh, Madhya Pradesh, on 3 May 1959. She was an avid reader as a child, particularly of religious, philosophical and scientific books. She was formally educated only upto Class 6. At an early age, she had started giving religious discourses. By 16, she had attained fame for discourses on the Ramayan. She became *sadhvi* at a young age.

Uma Bharati is known for her fiery speeches and passionate discussions. She has an immense following among the youth. She entered politics in 1980 when she came into contact with Vijaya Raje Scindia and other RSS and VHP leaders. She was appointed President of the Bharatiya Janata Yuv Manch. Soon, she became the Vice-President of BJP in Madhya Pradesh. She was President of the Bhartiya Yuv Manch. Soon she became Vice-President of BJP in Madhya Pradesh. In 1984, at the age of 25, she first ran for a Lok Sabha seat but lost. In 1989, she fought the election again and won. She was re-elected to Lok Sabha in next four general elections in 1991,1996, 1998, and 1999. During her tenure in the Lok Sabha, she served as Union Minister of State for HRD (1998-99) and

Tourism (1999-2000). She was Cabinet Minister for Youth Affair and Sports (2000-2002) and Coal and Mines (2002-2003). In November 2003 she was elected to the Madhya Pradesh Legislative Assembly and became the first woman Chief Minister of the State. In May 2004 she resigned from the office of Chief Minister and returned to active politics. She has been Vice-President, BJP, Madhya Pradesh. She is Member, Ram Janam Bhoomi Trust. She has written three books titled (1) Swami Vivekananda (2) Peace of Mind (3) Manav Ek Bhakti ka Naata.

Uma Bharti loves traveling and driving was stated to be a passion with her. Occasionally she plays Badminton. She loves adventures and challenges. Though she did not go beyond 6th class in school, she has a good command of and fluency in English and Hindi which is evident in her speeches.

103

Vasundhara Raje (1953-)

Vasundhara Raje was born on March 8, 1953 in Mumbai. She was the fourth child of the then Ruler of Gwalior His Highness Jivaji Rao Scindia and his wife Rajmata Vijaya Raje and sister of late Madhavrao Scindhia She completed her schooling from Presentation Convent, Kodaikanal and graduated in Economic and Political Science (Hons.) from Sophia College, Mumbai. In 1972 she married Hemant Singh, the 7th Maharaja of Dholpur, Rajasthan. The marriage did not last long. They separated after two years. But she continued to live in Dholpur and opened her palace to the public, listening to their problems.

Brought up on Jan Sangh and BJP philosophy from her childhood, Vasundhara Raje used to accompany her mother to remote and backward areas to see the real India. She has been working for social causes since an early age. Her political involvement started with her induction in the National working Committee of Bhartiya Janta Party in the year 1984. She was the Vice President of the State BJP Yuva Morcha in 1980's. She was Member of National Executive Committee of BJP and Vice-President of BJP 1987 onwards. She represented Dholpur as MLA in the State Assembly of Rajasthan from 1985-1989. She was the Vice-President of the State Unit of BJP from 1987 to 1989. She was elected to Lok Sabha from Jhalawar for the first time in 1989 and thereafter re-elected to Lok Sabha in 1991, 1996, 1998, and 1999. In 1997, she was appointed Joint Secretary, BJP Parliamentary Committee.

Vasundhara Raje was appointed Union Minister of State for External Affairs in 1998 in the Council of Ministers headed by Atal Bihari Vajpayee and later made Union Minister of State (Independent Charge) for Small Scale Industries and Agro & Rural Industries. She also assisted the Prime Minister as Minister of State in managing the affairs of Department of Personnel, Public Grievances & Pensions, Department of Space and Department of Atomic Energy.

Vasundhara Raje was appointed President of the Rajasthan Unit of BJP in September 2002. In the general election held in 2003, Vasundhara Raje led the BJP party and was elected to the State Assembly of Rajasthan. She was elected unanimously as the leader of the BJP Legislature Party and became the Chief Minister of Rajasthan on December 8, 2003, the first woman to hold the office.

104

Vijay Laxmi Pandit (1900-1990)

Born in Allahabad on 18 August 1900, Vijaya Lakshmi Pandit was the daughter of Motilal Nehru and the sister of Jawaharlal Nehru, the first Prime Minister of free India. Vijayalaxmi did not have any formal education but was trained at home by an English governess. she did her higher studies at the University of Allahabad and abroad. Her marriage to Ranjit Sitaram Pandit in 1921 helped her espouse the cause of Indian freedom movement with those living abroad. She was arrested by British when she returned to India. She was deeply involved in India's fight for freedom. As with the rest of her family, she was a staunch follower of Gandhiji and was imprisoned several times in the 1930s and 1940s along with her husband, father-in-law, and other members of her family.

Vijaya Laxmi Pandit was elected to Uttar Pradesh Assembly in 1936 and in 1946. She was appointed Minister of Local Self-government and Public Health. She held the office until 1939 and again from 1946-47. She had served on the Allahabad Municipal Board, where she was elected Chairman of the Education Committee. She was Vice-President of Women's International League for Peace and

Freedom. From 1940 to 1942 she was President of the All Indian Women's Conference.

After independence, she was appointed India's ambassador to the Soviet Union from 1947-49, and to the US and Mexico from 1949-51. She headed the Indian delegation to the United Nations from 1946-49 and in 1952. In 1953 she was elected President of the UN General Assembly, the first women to serve in that position. She also served as Indian High Commissioner to Great Britain and ambassador to Ireland (1955-61) and to Spain (1958-61). In 1961 Vijaya Laxmi Pandit returned to India, and was Governor of Maharashtra from 1962-64. She was Member of Lok Sabha 1952-53 and 1964-67.

Vijaya Lakshmi Pandit was deeply opposed to the Emergency promulgated by Prime Minister Indira Gandhi. She left the Indira-dominated Congress and joined the Janata party and campaigned against Indira Gandhi in the elections that followed the lifting of Emergency in 1977 in which Indira Gandhi and her party were defeated. In 1979 she was appointed Indian representative to the UN Human Rights Commission, after which she retired from public life.

Vijaya Lakshmi Pandit attended Pacific Relations Conference, USA, as Leader of Indian Delegation. She was also present in San Fransisco during first meeting od UNO and challenged the right of British appointed Indian Delegation to represent India.

Her writings include The Evolution of India (1958) and The Scope of Happiness: A Personal Memoir (1979). Vijaya Lakshmi Pandit died in 1990

105

Vijaya Raje Scindia (1919-2001)

Vijaya Raje Scindia was born Lekha Divyeshwari on 12 October 1919 at Sagar, Madhya Pradesh. She was from a branch of the Nepali royal family which had been banished to Sagar in India in the late 1880s. Her mother died in childbirth, and her father, Thakur Mahendra Singh, a Deputy Collector, had another wife and family to look after. She was brought up largely by her maternal grandfather who was a Rana from Nepal in exile. After school in Sagar, she studied at the Dr. Annie Besant Theosophical College, Benares and the Isabel Thorborne College, Lucknow. Moved by patriotic fervour, she gave up her pretty pearls and clothes and became a vegetarian. In 1941, wearing a Swadeshi cotton sari, she married Maharaja Jivajirao Scindia of Gwalior 21 February 1941 and took the name Vijayaraje. They had one son and four daughters. The Maharaja died in 1960.

She entered politics in 1957, running as a Congress party candidate from Gwalior in Madhya Pradesh. She was elected to the Lok Sabha in 1957, 1962, 1971, 1989, 1991, 1996 and 1998. She was Member of Madhya Pradesh Legislative Assembly (1967-71) and was elected to Rajya Sabha, 1978. Till 1967, she was with Congress party.

Reacting to the Congress government's handling of student agitation and the death of maharaja of Bastar, she resigned from Congress in 1967 and turned to Jan Sangh/BJP on principle and ideology. After her husband's death, she got actively involved with Jan Sangh/BJP's activities. In 1975, during Emergency, she was imprisoned in Tihar Jail as a political prisoner. During this time, a rift started between her and her son, Madhavrao, when he contested election as an independent candidate with Congress support. She rose into a leadership role in 1980 when she became one of the BJP vice-presidents. She left politics in 1998 for health reasons.

Vijaya Raje Scindia was President, All India Women's Conference (Gwalior Branch) for 40 years and Madhav Institute of Technology and Science Board of Governors, Gwalior. She was Pro-Chancellor of Sagar University and Trustee of Viswa Hindu Parishad. She was conferred Hony Doctorate of Vikram University, Ujjain, and Sagar Unversity, Sagar (M P). She was Founder President of Shishu Mandir; and Scindia Kanya Vidhyalaya, Gwalior.

She wrote two books—an autobiography with Manohar Malgonkar called *The Last Maharani of Gwalior*, and *Lok Path se Raj Path*, in Hindi.

Vijaya Raje Scindia died in 2001.

106

V. S. Rama Devi (1934-)

Governor of Himachal Pradesh and Governor of Karnataka (1997-99) V S Rama Devi was born 15th January 1934 at Chebrolu in Andhra pradesh to V.V.Subbhiah and V. Venkata Ratnamma. She was educated at Eluru and Hyderabad. She is married to V.S.Ramavatar and has a son and two daughters. After doing her M.A. and LLM, she enrolled herself as Advocate in the High Court of Andhra Pradesh. She Joined the Central Government Service as an officer belonging to Group-A Service and after working in various capacities as a Member of the Indian Legal Service in the Legislative Department served as Special Secretary in the Legislative Department, Member-Secretary of the Law Commission; and Secretary to the Government of India. V S Rama Devi became Chief Election Commissioner for a short period and served as Honorary Advisor to the National Commission for Women. She was Secretary-General, Rajya Sabha from 1st July 1993 to 25th July 1997. She served as Judicial Member of the Customs, Excise and Gold Control Appellate Tribunal in the first batch under the Ministry of Finance (Department of Revenue).

V S Rama Devi has written on legal topics like Women and law, children and law, handicapped and law, defection law and certain other Constitutional aspects. She was co-author of the "Rajya Sabha at Work". She has written novels, short stories, essays and plays in Telugu and also wrote middles in dailies in Telugu.

107

Yamini Krishnamurthy (1940-)

Yamini Krishnamurthy, accomplished Bharatanatyam and Kuchipudi dancer, was born in 1940, in Madanapalli, Andhra Pradesh. in an eminent family.Yamini's father, M. Krishnamurthy, was a Sanskrit scholar and grandfather was an expert in Urdu poetry. Yamini's initial training in Bharata Natyam took place at Rukmini Devi Arundale's Kalakshetra, at that time India's premier institution for training in this art. After acquiring an impeccable structural base at Kalakshetra, she went on to higher studies under renowned masters such as Kanchipuram Ellappa Pillai, Thanjavur Kittapa Pillai, Dhandayudhapani Pillai and Mylapore Gouri Amma. She also trained in Kuchipudi under illustrious gurus such as Vedantam Lakshmi Narayana Shastri, Chinta Krishnamurthi and Pasumarthy Venugopal Krishna Sharma. This was a period when scholars were looking with renewed interest at the classical arts, and Yamini played a significant role in popularizing Kuchipudi which was then emerging as a solo dance form of Andhra Pradesh in southern India. In addition to classical dances, She was trained in Carnatic vocal music by M.D. Ramanathan and learnt the Veena from Kalpakam Swaminathan.

Yamini gave her debut in 1957 in Chennai, when she was only seventeen and instantly enthralled people with her charisma and stage performance. From then on she took her chosen dance styles of Bharata Natyam and Kuchipudi to all corners of India and the world. By 1960, she became one of the most admired dancer in the country. Her performances brought about national and international recognition to the classical styles of Bharat Natyam and Kuchipudi. Yamini Krishnamurthy has been for decades a symbol of sheer power and radiance of Indian classical dance. For her inimitable technique and style, she has earned the respect and adulation of people from all walks of life and has been regarded as cultural ambassador of India on her tours abroad, with the world bowing in recognition of her art.

A multi-faceted artist, Yamini recieved 'Padmashree' in 1968 at the age of 28 and 'Sangeet Natak Academy Award' in 1977. The title of 'Asthana Narthaki' was bestowed upon her by the Tirumala Tirupathi Devasthanam, one of the most sacrosanct temples of India. Along with stage performances, Yamini made a 13-part serial for Doordarshan on dance. In 1990, she started 'Yamini school of Dance' in Delhi. She wrote a book 'A Passion For Dance', which was well-received by the critics.

108

Zohra Sehgal (1912-)

Zohra Sehgal was born in 1912 in a land-owning family of Rohilla Pathans settled around Rampur. Her full name on birth was Sahibzadi Zohra Begum Mumtaz-ullah Khan. She was one of the seven children. She was brought up in Sunni Muslim traditions—five prayers a day and fasting during Ramadan. Zohra was a rebel against tradition. As a girl she was a tomboy fond of climbing trees and playing games. As she attained puberty, she was forced to wear a *burqa* which she did not like to wear but had to wear. With her uncle who was closer to her than her father, she travelled all the way across India, West Asia and Europe by car with the tacit understanding of marrying his son, then an undergraduate at Oxford. To escape the eventuality, she dropped off at Dresden and learnt dance for two years. On her return she was once again put in a *burqa* and sent to Queen Mary's Girls College, Lahore, meant for daughters of aristocratic families. No sooner did Zohra pass out of Queen Mary's, she shed her *burqa*—this time for ever. She started her professional career in 1935 as a leading dancer with the Uday Shankar Ballet Company and travelled the world from the North Cape to the Nile, from San Fransisco to Penang. During this period that she met fellow-dancer

Kameshwar Sehgal, a Hindu belonging to the Radha Soami sect, and fell in love with him. He was eight years younger than her. Initially there was opposition from her parents but they came round. Although Kameshwar was willing to convert to Islam to marry Zohra, neither she nor her parents insisted on it. The two had a civil marriage in August 1942. They had two children who had the choice of being Hindu or Muslim. For a while they accepted both, then discarded them.

After some time, she stopped working with Uday Shankar and, alongwith her husband, migrated to Lahore and set up their own Zoresh Dance Institute. The growing communal tension preceding the Partition of India made them feel unwelcome there. They migrated to Bombay. In 1945, she joined Prithviraj Kapoor's Prithvi Theatre as an actress on a salary of Rs. 400 a month. From a dancer, she turned into a stage actress. For 14 years she toured every corner of India in the most successful example of a travelling repertory in modern theatre. The experience made her sister Uzra Butt and her national stars. Zohra was so excited on the approaching Independence that on the eve of Independence she went around dancing barefoot along the streets of Bombay while Raj Kapoor played the drums, an event her Hindu husband could not reconcile with.

After her husband's death, Zohra first moved to Delhi and then went to London in 1962 on a drama scholarship. She stayed on in London to educate her two children. Jobless and broke, she eked out a living as a dresser in London's greenrooms and tailoring establishments for 10 years. But from the late 1970s onwards, British TV and films rediscovered her in a big way. A star was reborn in Arthur Rank and Merchant Ivory productions' serials such as The Raj Quartet, Jewel in the Crown, Tandoori Nights, My Beautiful Laundrettee and dozens of others.

Back in Delhi, her plan was to live a quiet retired life near her family. But this being Zohra Sehgal's life, she has more offers of work and money today than at any other stage of her life. She has played the leading role in Sadia Dahlvi's TV serial *Amma & Family*. Her age has not deterred her from featuring in films like "Saaya" and "Kal Ho Naa Ho". She has also featured in a string of Hollywood films including "Bend it like Beckham". Though in her nineties and wrinkled, she remains as animated and saucy as ever. Her daughter, Kiran, summed her up in a few words, "Energy, Sun, Sparkling, Shaking and Crazy."

Zohra Sehgal is unquestionably one of India's greatest living stage actresses. She has a truly computerised memory and a vast range of poets whose works she knows by heart. Hearing her recite poetry is an experience of a life-time.

She has put her life's story in her memoirs titled Stages: The Art & Adventures of Zohra Sehgal. She was awarded "Ratna" fellowship for 2004 by the Sangeet Natak Akademi.